WOMEN, POVERTY
and
RESOURCES

The views expressed are those of the author and do not necessarily reflect the policies or the views of UNICEF.

WOMEN, POVERTY
and
RESOURCES

Ponna Wignaraja

SAGE Publications
New Delhi/Newbury Park/London

First published in 1990 by

Sage Publications India Pvt Ltd
32 M–Block Market, Greater Kailash I
New Delhi 110048

Sage Publications Inc
2111 West Hillcrest Drive
Newbury Park, California 91320

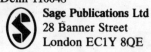

Sage Publications Ltd
28 Banner Street
London EC1Y 8QE

Published by Tejeshwar Singh for Sage Publications India Pvt Ltd, phototypeset by Mudra Typesetters, Pondicherry and printed at Chaman Offset Printers, New Delhi.

Library of Congress Cataloging-in-Publication Data

Wignaraja, Ponna.
    Women, poverty, and resources / Ponna Wignaraja.
        p.   cm.
    Includes bibliographical references.
    1. Women in rural development—Developing countries.   2. Poor women—Developing countries—Economic conditions.   3. Rural development projects—Developing countries.   I. Title.
HQ1240.5.D44W54   307.72'082—dc20   1989   89–39055

ISBN 0–8039–9624–1 (US–hbk)   81–7036–167–2 (India–hbk)
       0–8039–9625–x (US–pbk)   81–7036–168–0 (India–pbk)

To
Ganeshan, Gowrie and Rohan
for their continuing commitment
to development with social justice.

Contents

Q: In what sense do you think outside help is useful?

A: We need outside help for analyzing and for a better understanding of our situation and experience, but not for telling us what we should do.

An outsider who comes with ready-made solutions and advice is worse than useless. He must first understand from us what our questions are and help us articulate the questions better, and then help us find solutions. Outsiders also have to change. He alone is a friend who helps us to think about our problems on our own.

From a dialogue with activists of the Bhoomi Sena Movement in India, 1977.

(Reproduced from *Towards a Theory of Rural Development* by de Silva, Haque, Mehta, Rahman, and Wignaraja, Progressive Publications, Lahore, 1988).

Foreword

Poverty alleviation initially became a matter of major concern in the seventies. A large number of alternative development approaches were explored and promoted but with the major exceptions of Primary Health Care and Basic Services, most were isolated experiments. Even these were overshadowed in development theory and practice by issues of structural adjustments in the 1980s. A rising concern amongst an increasing number of development economists with the effects of adjustment policies on the poor, brought again to the fore the problem of alleviation of poverty.

Ponna Wignaraja was one of the five members of a South Asian team that in the early 1970s produced the pioneer study, truly ground breaking at that time, titled 'Towards a Theory of Rural Development'. The methodology they identified has informed much of the innovative experiments in poverty alleviation. Since then, working with United Nations, in his writings, as editor of 'Development' and also as Secretary-General of the Society for International Development, he has continued to pursue the same conceptual path and to refine the methodology of participatory development.

In 1987, UNICEF with IFAD asked Ponna Wignaraja to review his experiences on these issues in a number of countries of Asia, Africa and Latin America. The result is this book. The starting point of Wignaraja's analysis is that 'the poor are left out because the conceptual framework and the institutional framework within which the problem is looked at is inadequate.' In this book, he specifically addresses the issue of alleviation of women's poverty, a new dimension which was not highlighted nor developed in the earlier writings of the team.

The issues of gender and equity point to the double burden women have to bear: that of being poor and being a woman. For Ponna Wignaraja, the solutions to women's poverty can only come from actions by women's groups and by their better organization.

Individuals cannot address the problem of their powerlessness; this can only be done through collective action. The organization of women around issues of common concern is a prerequisite for effective and sustainable economic and social development. Ponna Wignaraja further states that 'provision of credit in the absence of this organization is not developmental, but further erodes self-respect, dignity and collective action and leads to depletion of even the resources and assets already available to poor women'.

A corollary is that the provision of credit alone has little impact on the economic status of poor women. A holistic approach incorporating awareness creation and group organization, struggle for the fair implementation of various legislations in their support, support in marketing, availability of various materials, skill training, legal aid, health and child care, maternity and social security, and getting out of debt are some of the key elements that need to go hand in hand with the availability of credit.

To make this happen, political space has to be found and the programmes themselves will help to further widen that space. Where the process does not take place spontaneously, sensitized animators can help to catalyze the process.

These are some of the elements that Ponna Wignaraja considers crucial to enable poor women to move out of poverty into sustainable development.

Numerous case studies have been published on income generating activities for women. These are usually small projects which are never extended nationwide because they are not incorporated into the mainstream of economic development. Other studies have highlighted the failures of targeted credit programmes for the poor and for poor women through conventional government or credit institutions. A number of case studies have been published on the better known successful programmes with credit components for women, such as, the Grameen Bank or the BRAC, some occasionally written by those who conceived the projects. There are fewer publications available analyzing the conceptual issues underlying the access of poor women to credit, and the possibilities of organization, awareness creation and credit and asset creation together, to strengthen their capacity to survive, to improve their economic and social conditions and that of their children, to go to scale and to sustain this process over time.

Ponna Wignaraja's book belongs to the latter category. The conditions for the sustainment of such programmes in a variety of socio-economic and cultural settings is an especially important theme.

The experience of providing micro-loans is not new to UNICEF. The process of developing and extending such systems and sustaining them within the community-level constraints and within the constraints and pressures of national and international bureaucracies (including their financial rules and regulations) is of great interest to UNICEF.

We hope this book will help to stimulate reflection and discussion and lead to a renewed analysis of the problems and opportunities faced in improving the design of projects and evaluation of programmes for and with poor women.

UNICEF
New York

RICHARD JOLLY
Deputy Executive Director,
Programmes

Preface

THIS book, which covers poor women in both rural and urban areas, is based on a study for UNICEF (within the framework of IFAD/UNICEF collaboration) on credit for poor women. The study was primarily intended to reinforce the implementation strategy for UNICEF's policy on women in development. It was to contain a summary of the lessons drawn from the experiences from selected South Asian cases and their relevance for women's programmes in Africa and Latin America. Upon completion of the study, it was found that the case profiles as also the concepts and the methodology of participatory development that emerged were of wider interest to all those concerned with the issues of gender and equity.

This book goes beyond the current debate on the efficacy of conventional development strategies and the aid relationship in reaching the real poor, the majority of whom are poor women. The issues in the current debate and a great deal of factual information—which highlights the concern over the permanence of the poverty crisis which is mainly being perpetuated by these very conventional strategies, donor procedures, and the way the global system works—are recorded in a plethora of recent studies that have been published. These studies also confirm that the formal economic growth process has bypassed the majority of the people, namely, the poor. All this information and analysis will not be repeated here except when essential to the main arguments. The more recent of these studies include UNICEF's 'Adjustment with a Human Face'; the ODI's 'Foreign Aid Reconsidered'; the Report of the World Commission on Environment and Development 'Our Common Future'; *Shramshakti: Report of the National Commission on Self Employed Women and Women in the Informal Sector*; and 'Women in Development: AID's Experience, 1979–85.' The latter two sharply point to the need for an alternative approach, not only for poverty alleviation but also for a new approach to design programmes for meeting the double burden poor women face.

The perspective of this book has grown from the search for development alternatives initiated as early as the 1970s by the UN Asian Institute's trilogy of studies: 'Towards a Theory of Rural Development'; 'Micro-level Development: Design and Evaluation of Rural Development Projects'; and 'Bhoomi Sena—Struggle for People's Power', by G.V.S. de Silva, Wahidul Haque, Niranjan Mehta, Anisur Rahman, and Ponna Wignaraja. The Dag Hammarskjold Foundation in 'What Now'; the ILO World Employment Conference Report on 'A Basic Needs Strategy'; and, more recently, writings of persons like Robert Chambers (*Rural Development: Putting the Last First*); Manfred Max Neef ('The Human Scale'); Bernard Lecomte (*Project AID: Limitations and Alternatives*); Keith Griffin ('Alternative Strategies for Economic Development') and many other contributions in the Third World confirm the need for an alternative to conventional thinking. The search for development alternatives is steadily expanding with greater clarity regarding the concepts and methodologies to be followed.

From this perspective, several committed Third World scholars and development activists, through in-depth experimentation, have also evolved in an interaction with the poor, the methodology of 'Participatory Action Research'. This action-research methodology and the peoples' praxis permits the poor, as subjects in the process, to bring about a change in their economic and social conditions, using primarily their own creative energies, local resources, and local knowledge. Where there is a sensitive support system involving a Government Agency, an NGO and/or a donor, these experiments have grown in scale and become sustainable. This is very different from situations where various groups of poor are merely treated as the objects of a process which, in the main, delivers inputs to them from the outside, whether as charity or paternalism. Both the concept and the methodology of participatory action are further reinforced by the cases studied here which respond to the total concerns of poor women. There is, thus, no longer any need for *a priori* theorizing.

Given the time limitation for the original study, it was possible to survey only a selected number of experiences in detail. The groups studied were able to assist poor women to move out of poverty into sustainable development in Bangladesh, Nepal, India and Pakistan. We also examined selected processes which were beginning to emerge in Africa and Latin America. In most of the cases analyzed, sensitive donors had related to or actively supported the initiation, expansion, or multiplication of these innovative approaches which enabled poor women to move out of their poverty. As the study proceeded, more generalized guidelines emerged for other donors attempting to design programmes in support of poor women.

From the selective survey in South Asia, it was evident that the innovative approaches for poverty alleviation adopted by poor women appeared to have gone beyond experimentation. It was possible to identify the essential elements in the total process of going beyond credit, which contribute to sustainable economic and social development. In this sense this book, though on gender and equity, is equally about poverty alleviation. If the problems of poor women who constitute more than half the poor can be solved, it would mean winning more than half the war on poverty.

These elements provide an alternative approach (to the conventional 'delivery of inputs' approaches) for rural and urban poverty alleviation involving poor women, and a methodology which can be used with appropriate adaptation for initiating, expanding or multiplying similar processes in Africa and Latin America and under different socio-political conditions. It is now clear that the process can be multiplied. It is not, however, a question of simple replicability. The process must start with the poor women themselves articulating their needs with a collective consciousness and organization, and having a support system from governments, NGOs and donors.

The original study (as also this book) would not have been possible without the active collaboration of several development activists, national level facilitators in the innovative programmes visited in South Asia, Africa and Latin America, and the assistance of the UNICEF country offices in Bangladesh, India, Nepal, Pakistan, Sri Lanka, Kenya, Tanzania, Colombia and Mexico, the UNICEF regional offices in South Asia, Eastern and Southern Africa, and Latin America, and several staff members of UNICEF's headquarters. I also wish to express my appreciation to IFAD staff members with whom I interacted and to Madeleine Salem who painstakingly typed and corrected the drafts of the original manuscript with precision. Swasti Mitter and Gowrie Ponniah read the manuscript of the book at various stages and made useful comments for which I am grateful. Naleer Lantra typed the final manuscript.

A particular word of thanks is due to my colleagues in the United Nations University South Asian Perspectives Project (SAPP) network and at the Participatory Institute for Development Alternatives (PIDA) in Sri Lanka whose commitment and untiring efforts over the past ten years at refining the methodology of Participatory Action-Research (PAR) in the field has also helped to increase our overall understanding of the methodology and the emerging new process for poverty.alleviation.

PONNA WIGNARAJA

The Context

Du:ring the past decade, women's movements in South Asia and some of the studies conducted during the UN Decade for Women have helped to focus unambiguously on the issues of gender and equity. This marks a radical departure from previous feminist concerns with gender conflicts in general and women's rights in particular. This new focus, however, is not only the result of a greater awareness among scholars that issues of gender and equity are closely interlinked. It has also followed from a better understanding of the social experiments conducted on the ground by activists and action researchers which have enabled poor women to move out of poverty into sustainable development. Taken together, these experiments constitute a response by poor women to the multiple crises in their lives. Moreover, problems encountered in daily life are viewed by poor women in their totality and not in a fragmented manner.

There are three interrelated aspects to issues of gender and equity in South Asian development. The first aspect goes beyond gender conflicts in general and highlights the fact that a section of the population who are both women and poor face a double burden. The second aspect relates to the important role poor women play in development, and to the various factors which have prevented them from benefiting from the kind of economic and growth-oriented development processes that have hitherto been dominant. The third aspect focuses on the continued adverse effects on poor women of the conventional reformist solutions implemented through the 'delivery' of inputs, particularly credit. The way in which inputs are delivered has further marginalized poor women and even eroded their capacity to survive, let alone develop.

GENDER CONFLICTS AND THE DOUBLE BURDEN

Over the last fifteen years the South Asian region has seen the slow but steady growth of women's struggles, not only for a legitimate share in the development process, but also as the most trenchant challenge to the encoded patriarchy of modern development. Until this period, the strategies and programmes for development had largely overlooked the questions of gender and equity. Where poverty alleviation was a fundamental objective in national policy, the rural poor and other oppressed minorities were viewed as the recipients of the benefits of development. In each of these categories only the male population was considered significant to the process. The contributions of women, who formed more than half of the total numbers, particularly those of poor women, were all but ignored as was the deeper impact of the 'development' process on the latter. But as the women's movement evolved, the whole problem of social change itself began to be viewed in an entirely different context.

To this awareness—that women, both in the traditional and modern social structures, have always been the victims of the greatest exploitation[1]—was added the corollary that poor women face a double burden: i.e., not only as a result of being women but also by virtue of being poor. It is now well established that poor women have the least access to basic needs, such as, food, health and education, both within the family and without. Their work remains primarily invisible permitting little social recognition. They are often the first to be thrown out of jobs, particularly when an employment squeeze occurs. The displacement is more acute if the labour force is restructured as a consequence of newer, more productive technologies which can support a higher rate of return to labour. In fact, the only sectors of the economy in which women remain a dominant section of the labour force are those which demand low skills and repetitive functions, and which generate low returns. As such, poor women function mainly in the informal sectors and have hitherto not been organized. Even when belonging to trade unions, they are marginalized and invisible. Alongside exploitation and invisibility in the economic sphere, women face an atmosphere of violence within and outside the family. Wife-beating, rape, bride-burning—which are all familiar forms of social oppression—demonstrate the hazardous and insecure nature of the lives of women in most Third World societies. For poor women, who are at the bottom of every hierarchy, these oppressions are further magnified as they toil under the double burden of gender and economic deprivation.

The women's movement in South Asia, which first began to take shape in India in the 1970s, developed into an articulate force in the 1980s, and has since challenged the traditional concept of social change. It has, in fact, deepened the understanding of social relations and has addressed all aspects of the relationship between exploitation and authority. The women's movement sees social change not as a cataclysmic event but as a slow and sure process, given the day-to-day struggles of the oppressed. It is, thus, not surprising that women have been the backbone of the Chipko Movement in India since it is they, much more than the men, who are affected by the food, fuel, fodder and water crisis resulting from deforestation. Women have also been in the forefront of the efforts to combat communalism. They have also fought religious fundamentalism in Pakistan. Women have understood the implications of the codified and rigid religious tenets, which have defined their social and moral edifice by placing further restrictions on the mobility of women.

While a clearer understanding of the double burden is emerging, there are still a number of contradictions that exist within the women's movement which need to be resolved before clearer answers can be found. For instance, on the one hand the drive towards modernization is largely responsible for bringing the sub-surface questions about the status of women to the fore. But it is considerations of equality for all, the utopia promised by modern democracy, that permitted the question of the status of women to become a central referent in politics. In this debate, while the reasons behind the past and current oppression of women are obvious, what is still not properly understood is the combination of strategies to overcome this structural bias and the double burden on poor women.

Women have been oppressed in all social formations through all stages of history so much so that the oppressions have almost become internalized in the norms of behaviour observed by and towards men and women. Surprisingly, a reworking of these balances often leads to resistance from women themselves. Moreover, women belong to different classes and castes and hence often have different and contradictory interests. To take an example, a woman domestic worker and her employer do not share the same perspective. Poor women in the informal sector constitute yet another category. Issues of age and function also come into play when considering the status of women. Older women—particularly as mothers, mothers-in-law and grandmothers—invariably enjoy a higher status than younger women.

Again, in a society where men dominate over women, organizations which take up issues common to both are likely to undermine those that relate more specifically to women, even within the framework of that organization. The tensions between men and women are rarely addressed here. This is due to the vested interests of men, including those who participate in movements for social change. This issue came sharply to the fore in the textile workers' union in Gujarat and led to the formation of the Self-Employed Women's Association (SEWA). These vested interests which have been handed down through the ages, have gained social sanction, thereby becoming difficult to identify and harder to give up.

The necessity to organize women separately, even within a broader movement, has been felt in all organizations like trade unions and workers' and peasants' movements. It would be incorrect to treat such separate organizations of women as alternatives for they are really complementary and supplementary efforts. In fact, there are bound to be contradictions between such organizations in the short run. However, all this is inherent in the process of struggle and cannot be given as a rationale for negating the women's movement, or any other group for that matter. Women's existence is complex, so are their lives, their problems and, hence, their struggles.

For a better understanding of these contradictions, more research is necessary into the cultural dimensions of the problem. However, an increasing number of studies show that, at different stages in the region's history, women and particularly poor women in South Asia have periodically asserted their rights.[2] These studies also show that while the process of struggling against institutionalized male domination has more recently led to an anti-male stance (following the tone and terms set by the women's movements in the West), another tradition exists in South Asian Hindu society of a 'complementarity' between men and women. This concept has its roots in the image of god as *ardhanarishwara* (half man half woman). Such cultural symbols not only epitomize the commonality of interest on issues of equity between men and women, but also reinforce the notion that conjugality and love can be kept alive while women struggle uncompromisingly against male chauvinism and gender oppression.

THE IMPACT OF THE CONVENTIONAL
DEVELOPMENT STRATEGIES

The conventional development strategies of the post-war period—and the models that informed them—have not directly addressed the issue of poverty, let alone issues relating to the double burden poor women face. In fact, these conventional strategies neither recognize the role poor women play in development nor the factors which prevent them from benefiting from the development processes which have hitherto been dominant.

From the time of the fifth Five Year Plan in India, it became very clear that Indian planning had not given sufficient attention to the problems of poverty.[3] What is true for India is also true for other countries in the sub-continent. The population of Pakistan is predominantly rural with approximately 75 million persons living in about 45,000 villages. It is only recently being recognized that past development programmes had not benefited the most needy, of whom poor women constitute a significant section.[4]

The present agricultural sector is the lynchpin of the economics of South Asia. In this sector poor women play an important part.

TABLE 1

The Size and Contribution of Agriculture to Development in South Asia

Country	Size		Contribution	
	Rural Population (percentage of total)		*Agricultural Labour, 1980 (percentage of total labour force)*	*Agricultural Output, 1984 (percentage of GDP)*
	1960	*1985*		
India	82.0	74.5	70	35
Pakistan	77.9	70.9	55	24
Bangladesh	94.9	88.1	75	48
Sri Lanka	82.1	78.1	53	28
Nepal	96.9	94.2	n.a.	56
Average for South Asia	**86.8**	**81.2**	**63.2**	**38.2**

Sources: *World Resources 1987*, A Report by the International Institute for Environment and Development and the World Resources Institute, Basic Books, New York, 1987; and World Bank, *World Development Report 1986*, Washington D.C., 1986.

A glance at Table 1 shows that in 1985 a majority of the people in South Asia lived in rural areas. Nepal has the highest percentage of rural population and is followed by Bangladesh, Sri Lanka, India and Pakistan. Despite migration to urban centres, the proportions have not changed significantly since 1960. Moreover, the rural sector accounts for a high proportion of output and employment in South Asia. If activities in the non-monetized sectors are added the proportions would be even higher. In all the economies of the region this sector contributed to approximately a third of the total output in 1984 and over half of the total employment in 1980. Because of the nature of the informal sector—its non-monetized part of the economy and the bias in statistics— agriculture's real importance to development gets overshadowed in the statistics for this sector. The agricultural sector also provides a large part of household food supplies, a market for local produce and goods, services from the rest of the economy and, above all, a locally generated surplus for investment.[5] However, the role of women, and particularly poor women, in this sector is yet to be fully appreciated.

Despite agriculture's significant contribution to development, the benefits of progress have not spread in an equitable manner. The majority of South Asia's poor are concentrated in the rural sector. Studies conducted using a common poverty line during the mid 1970s found that South Asia had a severe problem of absolute poverty in this sector and that the poverty syndrome was perpetuating itself.[6] It had now become a permanent poverty crisis. One estimate for 1975 suggested that the proportions of the population in absolute poverty were: Bangladesh sixty-four per cent, India forty-six per cent, and Pakistan forty-three per cent.[7] Sri Lanka with fourteen per cent was the exception, though this situation has worsened since.

The figures for Bangladesh, India and Pakistan make evident that their poor were among the poorest of the developing countries during this period. Evidence also suggests that the incidence of landlessness has been rising in South Asia and that a growing percentage of the rural labour force is engaged in insecure, part time employment in agriculture. Estimates prepared for the early 1970s showed that landlessness affected seventy-seven per cent of Sri Lanka's rural population and seventy-five per cent and fifty-three per cent of Bangladesh and India's rural population respectively.[8] More recent studies show that in all countries the problems of poverty and malnutrition are increasing with poor women being affected the most. Levels of primary education and primary health care in Pakistan is one of the lowest despite a high economic growth rate.

It is evident that poor women have a critical role in the rural economy of South Asia. But limited information is available quantifying the contribution of poor women to agricultural production, distribution and exports. There are, however, a few studies which point to the significant role played by women in all these activities.[9] Many surveys have been conducted on rural poverty in South Asia in the 1970s and 1980s, but few address specifically the questions of gender and equity. Empirical evidence suggests that South Asian women in the rural sector are more adversely affected by poverty than men.[10] While the subject merits further research at the micro-level, there is, however, an observable reality that cannot be ignored. It is also clear that unless there is a dramatic change in the development strategies and processes, poor rural women will be further marginalized in the future. The Second World Conference for Women, held in Nairobi (Kenya) in 1985 reported that:

> ... the significant contribution of women to agricultural development had been more recognised during the period but that there were certain indications that poverty among rural women would increase significantly by the year 2000. It was thus found of utmost importance for governments to rapidly embark on multi-sectoral programmes to promote the capacity of rural women in food and animal production and to help in creating off-farm employment opportunities, to reduce the work load of women and, among a number of things, assist in the improvement of their access to services.[11]

South Asia is no exception to this global trend. This is remarkable given that many of the countries of this region have experienced growth in gross domestic product and agricultural output per head. The causes of the paradox—of rising poverty among women together with increasing agricultural output per head—are complex, encompassing both the general reasons behind poverty and a number of factors peculiar to gender.[12] But, a greater part of the explanation lies in the approach to rural development adopted over the last thirty-five years in South Asia.

During the last three decades, three broad approaches to rural development may be distinguished in South Asia: first, dual economy models of the 1950s; second, redistributive land reforms of the 1960s and 1970s; and third, the green revolution of the 1970s and 1980s. The most influential of the dual economy models has been the Lewis Model, first elaborated in an article published in 1953.[13] The Lewis Model was based on a classical economic framework composed of two sectors: a modern industrial sector and the traditional subsistence based agricultural sector. The industrial sector was characterized by the use of wage labour, production for profit and the use of modern imported technology. By contrast, the traditional sector was characterized by self or family employment and a marginal product of labour approximately equal to zero. Lewis assumed that workers in the traditional sector received an income equal to the average product of labour, and wages in the industrial sector were set by income levels in the traditional sector and a premium to cover the costs of migration. At any given time, the supply of labour to the industrial sector was further assumed to be fixed, owing to the low marginal productivity of labour in the traditional sector.

In the Lewis Model, the engine of economic expansion moves on the use made of the profit from the industrial sector, which is assumed to be reinvested in this sector to create new capacity. The expansion of the industrial sector stimulates further labour migration into industry, the margin of profit increases, there is a further reinvestment of profit and so on. In this way, over time, the modern industrial sector expands and the traditional agricultural sector contracts; 'development' is achieved when dualism finally disappears through rapid industrialization. The dual economy models depicted the rural sector as a homogeneous, faceless entity consisting of unorganized subsistence farms. The approach failed to take into account the rural power structure, land ownership and the gender differentiation.

A second approach which emerged in the 1950s and 1960s and continued into the 1970s focused on the structural questions and advocated institutional change in the form of redistributive land reform for rural development in South Asia. Some of the earliest studies pointed to the existence of different patterns of land tenure.

ranging from owner occupation, commercial ownership, to feudal tenant-landlord systems in the countries of the region.[14] Other studies focused on land systems in which large estates dominated.

In South Asia, large estate systems included plantation estates (owned by a company with foreign capital and management employing very intensive methods of cultivation), share cropping,[15] as well as share contract, wherein the large estate is leased in small units to tenant cultivators on the basis of such a contract.

The case for redistributive land reforms in South Asia was partly based on the notion that in developing countries, peasant agriculture (consisting of small family farms) used capital more efficiently than industry. This was reinforced by the existence of the inverse relationship between size of holding and output per acre. That is to say, the productivity of small farms (created by land reforms) is the same as that of existing farms of equal size. Hence, breaking up large farms into smaller units would achieve both greater productivity and equity.[16]

Another strand of thought focused on *equity* rather than on efficiency as the principal reason for redistributive land reforms in South Asia. These writers pointed to inequality in land ownership as the major cause for rural income differentials; and to the fact that neither the land reforms to date nor the green revolution had had a substantial impact on the incomes of the poorest farmers, the landless labourers or poor women. Instead, they argued for redistributive land reforms as part of a wider development strategy based on satisfying basic needs to alleviate the worst forms of poverty in rural South Asia.[17]

The third approach to rural development in South Asia was the 'green revolution'—a package of modern agricultural technologies introduced into rural areas. Hybrid seed varieties was the central element of the package which also included high and regular amounts of fertilizers, irrigation, pesticides and careful management. The new seeds—high yielding dwarf varieties of rice and wheat—constituted a scientific breakthrough in the late 1960s for two international research centers (IRRI in the Philippines and CIMMYT in Mexico) set up a few years earlier to develop agricultural technologies. The green revolution has since spread to all the countries in South Asia except, possibly, Nepal.

The rapid spread of the green revolution was due to its being: land saving, thereby leading to a large increase in production without bringing further land under cultivation; scale neutral, thereby allowing the gains in output to accrue to small and large farmers alike; and labour absorbing, thereby generating new full and part time employment in agriculture. The proponents of the new technologies argued that they had the ability to completely transform South Asian agriculture. The scientific features of the hybrid seeds implied that they could increase the growth of agricultural production by doubling output per acre of rice and wheat. In narrow economic terms, this meant more self-sufficiency in staple food, less dependence on food aid and imports, an increase in exports of rice and wheat, and a greater agricultural surplus (of production over consumption) to facilitate financial investments. Rapid growth of agricultural production coupled with the above macro-economic effects also implied more rapid GDP growth rates.[18] Proponents of the new technologies further argued that the green revolution could be a vital mechanism for social change. The land saving and scale neutral features of the new seeds would enable small and medium farmers to directly participate in the process of agricultural modernization. Similarly, the increased production was argued to create more full time and part time employment on the small and medium farms for a substantial landless population, and to lead to lower prices for staple foods thereby enabling the poor to benefit as well.[19]

With the benefit of hindsight, it is becoming increasingly clear that all three approaches to rural development have not reduced the levels of absolute poverty in South Asia in the past forty years. Also, poor women and other vulnerable social groups, e.g., the landless poor have been further impoverished.

A major evaluation of these broad approaches by a group of South Asian Scholars in the 1970s concluded that for South Asia:[20]

In practice, the model failed for two basic reasons:
1. External aid, both in terms of resources and of adequate transfer of technology, failed to materialize at the necessary rate; instead the 'gap' kept on widening, leading to increasing dependence on foreign sources and the inevitable loss of autonomy. Repayment of past debts alone threatened to choke off future development. What was given as aid was withdrawn through adverse terms of trade. Multinational corporations, which were the main conduits for the transfer

of technology, extracted an exorbitant price for their know-how and machines while obstructing the means of repayment by restrictive export clauses. The highly capital-intensive, import-substituting technology which was implanted had little relation to real factor endowment, particularly availability of labour.

2. Internal resources for development had to come mainly from rural areas where, having alienated and exploited the peasants, the possibility of transferring surplus labour into realized savings was greatly diminished. Moreover, the regimes were unable to use coercive methods of capital accumulation, which countries with stronger administrative systems and commitment have successfully employed even while agricultural production has stagnated.

The model not only failed on its own terms, but also caused fundamental damage to the possibility of these nations mobilizing their own resources and shaping their own destinies. By borrowing foreign technology, the growth of appropriate local technology was smothered; as a result, the developing nations neglected to foster their own research capabilities and innovativeness, perpetuating a dependent relationship. The top–down method of centralized planning succeeded in alienating the people while failing to construct an administrative machinery capable of implementing programmes.

The choice between dependence and greater self-reliance had to be faced. Given the character of the regimes, the soft option of external assistance remained the preference and the combination of moderate internal savings and limited foreign aid produced some growth. The very character of development, however, ensured a grossly unequal distribution of the benefits and the disparity grew enormously. Even in the rural areas, when profitable technology finally arrived in the sixties, the primary beneficiaries were the richer farmers who had pre-emptive access to the inputs and the necessary credit. The 'Green Revolution,' introduced into an existing iniquitous rural social structure, further exacerbated the problems of inequality. While overall production showed an increase in some areas, the polarization in the rural society grew even more.

The magnitude of the problem had finally become too large
to be ignored—both internally and internationally.

The above conclusions were further reinforced by two major
groups of scholars.

It is now clear that more than a decade of rapid growth in
underdeveloped countries has been of little or no benefit to
perhaps a third of their population. Although the average per
capita income of the Third World has increased by 50 per cent
since 1960, this growth has been very unequally distributed
among countries, regions within countries and socio-economic
groups.[21]

. . . The crisis of development lies in the poverty of the mass
of the Third World, as well as that of others, whose needs, even
the most basic—food, habitat, health, education—are not met;
it lies, in a large part of the world, in the alienation whether in
misery or in affluence, of the masses, deprived of the means to
understand and master their social and political environment. . . [22]

TARGETED CREDIT PROGRAMMES
ARE NOT THE ANSWER

While these evaluations brought out a new concern for poverty
alleviation none focused specifically on gender conflicts and the
special role of poor women in development. It was only as the
women's movements around the world raised awareness in the mid
1970s, first on the gender issue and then on the issues of gender
and equity, that an attempt was made to incorporate the questions
of gender and equity into the development debate.

The emerging literature confirms that the response of dominant
processes to this new awareness, even when well-intentioned,
resulted in marginal tinkering in relation to the problems of poor
women. Since the strategies neither addressed the fundamental
gender conflicts nor the equity issue squarely, the designs of the
resulting programmes and projects were also inadequate to tackle
the double burden poor women faced. The attempted solutions
have tended to reinforce various forms of exploitation and
environmental degradation, which further marginalizes poor
women and threatens their very survival.

Strategies for the upliftment of poor women takes the form of income and employment generation projects. These suffer from being narrow in scope, scattered and peripheral to the main thrust of the development and planning processes. Different national and international development agencies continue to finance a number of such fragmented activities without a concern for a more comprehensive design including those social aspects which are essential if the double burden is to be tackled. Only recently the financial viability of these conventional income generating projects, with their delivered inputs, their ability to grow, multiply and be sustainable, is being seriously questioned.

A number of studies have confirmed the failure of the fragmented 'targeted' credit programmes for poor men and women—such as, the conventional government or credit institutions and 'delivery' of inputs approaches—to achieve the desired results in development.[23] Even in their own terms, the record of these 'targeted' and 'delivered' credit programmes in reaching poor women is disappointing in that the poor women are not reached. Repayment rates for this kind of 'delivered' credit are, in any case, low. A few of these studies have also outlined an alternate approach.[24]

In India, during the transition from the sixth Five Year Plan to the seventh, the implementation of the anti-poverty programmes—i.e., those programmes which attempted a direct attack on poverty for poor men and women through 'delivery' of credit and other inputs, such as, the Integrated Rural Development Programme (IRDP) and the National Rural Employment Programme (RLEGP)—was reviewed by the Planning Commission, the National Bank for Agricultural and Rural Development and the Institute of Financial Management and Research. They identified two major failings in the programmes:

1. The wrong identification of beneficiaries, and

2. The selection of activities undertaken without consideration of the abilities of the beneficiaries, the infrastructural support or the forward or backward linkages.

In a penetrating analysis of these and other reports and studies on the anti-poverty projects, Sundeep Bagchee has concluded that these programmes suffer from a lack of conceptual clarity and an inadequate understanding of the complex nature of the environment in which they have to be implemented. It is thus the programme design which needs to be reviewed.[25]

A recent study by the Asian Development Bank in six countries (Bangladesh, India, Indonesia, the Philippines, the Republic of Korea and Thailand) confirmed that despite the existence of several targeted government programmes poor women continued to rely on informal credit markets for their economic and social needs, because of easy access, flexibility of re-scheduling and non-requirement of collateral. These advantages far outweighed even the exhorbitant rate of interest they had to pay to the traditional money lender, traders, and others who were part of the informal credit system. Reliance on these informal credit markets further increased their dependence and permitted continuation of their exploitation in various forms.

There are several other constraints in the existing formal credit systems which poor women find difficult to overcome, despite the rhetoric of policy pronouncements.[26] The formal system requires certification of identity, ownership of assets, etc., which are not required of the poor women by the informal sector. The formal system works on the assumption that credit is the 'missing' element and does not address the other social requirements and survival needs of the poor women. There are also several legal restrictions on women's access to credit, e.g., the husband is required to co-sign a loan since a woman's rights to property are often restricted. The formal system does not recognize the importance of personal savings, the use of credit for poor women, and their modest but absorptive capacity for loans. The formal system has yet to formulate an interest rate policy that encourages savings among the poor women, and relates the use of these savings both to economic and non-economic needs, as well as, to the use of credit to supplement their savings. Formal co-operative credit systems also have a bias against poor women. A woman cannot become a member if a male member of her family is already a shareholder and the limits on lending are fixed to a proportion of the share capital. This latter constraint is over and above those, where most co-operative institutions established to benefit the poor have been captured by the rich, irrespective of the gender issue.

Another aspect of the problems of formal targeted credit for the poor is described in a report to IFAD on 'Credit to the Poorest':[27]

> Management costs are often prohibitively high because trans-
> actions usually involve small amounts, and financial regulations
> or bureaucratic habit and procedures demand as much paper
> work for small as for large loans. Overheads are also high
> because a large staff is needed to serve a widely dispersed
> clientele. When credit is offered at subsidised interest rates for
> the poor, the lending institutions' costs may not be covered and,
> moreover, well-off borrowers may be particularly attracted and
> will benefit from the loans, with the result that income distri-
> bution may actually worsen rather than improve. This is
> especially likely when the eligibility for credit requires assets
> and thus eliminates the poor who are most in need and who
> have none. Too often credit conditions are not responsive to
> local needs; too often credit is too little or too late. The poor
> generally lack banking experience; they are ignorant or sus-
> picious of formal 'outside' institutions with complicated regu-
> lations. They may also feel little responsibility to repay an
> 'anonymous' lender, one of the reasons why high default rates
> are common—although it is frequently the rich, experienced
> borrowers who fail to repay.

The analysis is clear. But this kind of reasoning, based on conventional economic thinking and market analysis, then dis-misses the poor in terms of high management costs, inability to get interest rates sorted out and the right prices. Credit programmes designed with these latter considerations in mind end up benefiting the rich or the richer. The poor are left out because the conceptual framework and the institutional framework within which the problem is perceived is inadequate. Credit programmes for the poor and the existing institutions, designed with this perspective and approach, only marginally facilitates the mainstream credit system and fails, even on their own terms, let alone providing an alternative approach benefiting the poorest.

In a recent article Everett and Savara have described some further problems which affect official targeted credit pro-grammes.[28] In describing a major programme in India and the Differential Interest Rate (DRI) credit programmes for the weaker sections of society, they touched on two additional problems:

People who seek careers in banking generally have neither the motivation nor the training to work effectively with the poor. When they join the bank, the lower level staff who are now charged with extending DRI credit, expect that they would be sitting behind a desk in a proper office dealing with substantial businessmen and shopkeepers. They do not expect to have to walk through hot, dusty tenements seeking out clients whose social and economic backgrounds are so different from their own—who have nothing to offer as collateral and who may not be educated. Given this staffing, or one might even say, ideological constraint on the nationalised banks, there has been a tendency for local power brokers of various types (sometimes styling themselves as 'social workers') to step into the very real and potentially profitable gap between the banks (with their reluctant, poorly trained staff and large disbursement targets) and their poor clients.

As Everett and Savara state:

> The patron-client relationship establishes vertical ties that the social worker can use to his advantage, but no horizontal ties through which borrowers can fight for collective goals. Under these conditions the lending programmes merely provide new channels through which ties of dependence and exploitation are established.

This is in addition to the inability of the trained bank staff to be sensitive to the problems of poor women.

The issues highlighted by Everett and Savara bring to the surface the questions relating to the depth of our understanding of the real problems, motivational issues and the question of commitment and identity with the poor. The concerns raised in the article also reveal the need for major training and reorientation of the staff of both conventional financial institutions and NGOs, before they can intervene for the benefit of the poor, let alone poor women.

THE POSITIVE SIDE

Despite this bleak picture of the conventional response to the problems of poor women and the marginally reformist options, there is a positive side. These past ten years have also demonstrated that when poor women are organized and actively participate in development as subjects rather than as passive objects of the process, they are able to move from a condition of dehumanization and survival to income generating activities which not only enhance their economic and social condition, but also result in health and nutrition for children and a capacity for building personal savings and using credit for capital accumulation, asset creation, and sustainable development efforts. A second important lesson that emerged from the new experiments for poverty alleviation is that poor women do not view their lives in a fragmented manner separating the economic from non-economic aspects of their lives. They do not focus on economic inputs or credit in isolation but view these elements as part of a total process. When credit has been sensitively made available at the right time, with due preparation and organization of recipients, it has played a significant part along with several other factors of a social or organizational nature. The experiments which have matured in the past ten years have also shown that a sensitive and flexible government, banking system, and NGO or donor support, without imposition of their ideologies and fragmented rigid procedures, can reinforce these processes and permit small experiments to be carefully nurtured, multiplied and grow in scale.

In many of the successful experiments with the total process starting with the poor, which have now grown in scale in South Asia, donor organizations have played a significant and critical catalytic role, with small well placed and timely interventions. In Africa and Latin America there are, so far, not too many such total processes—where the poor women are the subjects and not merely the objects of a delivery of economic and social inputs process from above—which start with poor women and leads them to sustainable development. Clearly, there are some 'entry points' for a total process to be built on, or fragile on-going processes which could be deepened and expanded in these regions. Some of these are described in the following chapters.

As mentioned earlier, a few sensitive government agencies, banks, NGOs and donors have related to or actively supported the initiation, expansion or multiplication of most of these innovative processes in South Asia. The two following chapters will attempt to briefly discuss some of these innovative approaches, analyze the concepts and methodology of project designs and evaluations used, the process as it evolved, and identify the lessons learnt. In the last four chapters, recommendations are made on how these innovative processes could be initiated and multiplied with new kinds of support systems, intermediaries and sensitive donor supports (under different economic, social and political conditions) so that additional lessons could be learnt for sustaining micro-processes and the growth in scale where possible. A basic premise underlying the book is that the more experiments that are initiated and sustained with the methodology that has emerged, the greater the demonstrative effect and basis for further experiential learning by all concerned in the very complex process of poverty alleviation.

NOTES

1. See *Shramashakti—Report of the N tional Commission on Self Employed Women and Women in the Informal Sector*, New Delhi, June 1988.
2. See Gowrie Ponniah, 'Ideology and the Status of Women in Hindu Society,' in P. Wignaraja and A. Hussain (eds.), *The Challenge in South Asia: Development, Democracy and Regional Co-operation*, Sage Publications, New Delhi, 1989.
3. Sukhamoy Chakravarty, *Development Planning: The Indian Experience*, Clarendon Press, Oxford, 1987.
4. Shoib Sultan Khan, *Rural Development in Pakistan*, Vikas, New Delhi, 1980.
5. The contribution of agriculture to economic development is more fully explained in B.F. Johnson and J.W. Mellor, 'The Role of Agriculture in Economic Development,' *American Economic Review*, September 1961. See also S. Chakravarty, *Development Planning: The Indian Experience*, Clarendon Press, Oxford, 1987, pp. 59–69.
6. See P. Wignaraja and Akmal Hussain (eds.), (1989).
7. These estimates of absolute poverty were based on the Kravis adjustment factors. The estimates for 1975 using official exchange rates were: Bangladesh 60 per cent, India 46 per cent, Pakistan 34 per cent and Sri Lanka 10 per cent. See M.S. Ahluwalia, N.G. Carter and H.B. Chenery, 'Growth and Poverty in Developing Countries,' *Journal of Development Economics*, Vol. 6, No. 3, 1979, Table 1. More recent estimates of rural poverty in South Asia can be obtained from A.R. Khan and E. Leel (eds.), *Poverty in Rural Asia*, ILO (ARTEP), Bangkok, 1985.
8. R.P. Sinha, 'Landlessness: is there a cure?' in FAO, *Studies in Agrarian Reform and Rural Poverty*, Rome, 1984.
9. See, for example, (1974); E. Boserup, and W. Weeks Wagliani, *The Inte-*

gration of Women in Development Projects, OECD Development Centre, Paris, 1985.

10. Consult M. Buvinic and Lycette (1982); and K. Larsson et al., *Mobilizing Rural Women: Two Tripartite Evaluation Reports on Community Action for Disadvantaged Rural Women in Sri Lanka and Kenya*, Swedish International Development Authority, Stockholm, 1987.

11. Reported in Larsson et al. (1987), p. 3.

12. See Buvinic and Lycette (1982); A.K. Sen, *Poverty and Famines: An Essay on Entitlement and Deprivation*, Oxford University Press, Oxford, 1981; and W. Haque, et al. (1977).

13. W.A. Lewis, 'Economic Development with Unlimited Supplies of Labour,' The Manchester School of Economic and Social Studies, May 1954.

14. One of the earliest studies on agrarian structure in South Asia was: United Nations, *Land Reform: Defects in Agrarian Structure as Obstacles to Economic Development*, New York, 1951.

15. See, for example, D. Warriner, 'Land Reform and Economic Development,' in C. Eicher and L. Witt (eds.), *Agriculture in Economic Development*, McGraw-Hill, New York, 1964.

16. The arguments for small farms were the key elements in the 'so-called populist case' for redistributive land reform. The following were influential in formulating this case: M. Lipton, *Why Poor Stay Poor: A Study of Urban Bias in World Development*, Temple Smith, London, 1977; and R.A. Berry and W.R. Cline, *Agrarian Structure and Productivity in Developing Countries*, Johns Hopkins University Press, Baltimore, 1979.

17. See ILO, *Poverty and Landlessness in Rural Asia*, Geneva, 1977.

18. For a detailed account of the positive *economic* impact of the green revolution see Johnson and Mellor (1961); B.F. Johnson and J. Cownie 'The Seed Fertilizer Revolution and Labour Force Absorption,' *American Economic Review*, 1969; and Y. Hayami and V.W. Ruttan, *Agricultural Development: An International Perspective*, Johns Hopkins University Press, Baltimore, 1971.

19. The role of the green revolution in social and political transformation in rural South Asia is discussed in: Johnson and Cownie (1969); and J. Mellor, *The New Economics of Growth: A Strategy for India and the Developing World*, Cornell University Press, Ithaca, 1976.

20. See Wahidul Haque, et al. (1977).

21. 'What Now: Another Development,' *Development Dialogue*, Dag Hammarskjold Foundation, No. 1/2, 1975, p. 5.

22. H. Chenery, et al., *Redistribution with Growth*, Oxford University Press, Oxford, 1972, pp. xiii.

23. See Keith Griffin (1988); Bernard Le Compte (1986); and Robert Chambers (1983).

24. Ibid.; also G.V.S. de Silva, Wahidul Haque, Niranjan Mehta, M.D. Anisur Rahman, Ponna Wignaraja, *Towards a Theory of Rural Development*, Progressive Publishers, Lahore, 1988.

25. Sundeep Bagchee, 'Poverty Alleviation Programme in Seventh Plan: an Appraisal,' *Economic and Political Weekly*, Vol. XIII, No. 4, Jan. 1987.

26. See Usha Jumani (1985).
27. 'Credit to the Poorest—the Grameen Bank and the Small Farmer Development Programme,' IFAD, Rome, March 1987 (unpublished).
28. Jana Everett and Mira Savara, 'Bank Credit to Women in the Informal Sector,' Shreemathi Nathibhai Damodar Thakersey Women's University, Research Unit of Women's Studies, Bombay, 1983.

Innovative Approaches in South Asia

THE innovative approaches for poverty alleviation—such as, savings, credit, and asset creation for poor women which have evolved in South Asia, and which have led to poor women strengthening their capacity to survive, meeting their social needs, entering into income generating activities, increasing their savings, utilizing these savings along with available credit, both for further improving their socio-economic conditions and that of their families, and sustaining the process—can be discussed in relation to how these experiments came into being, who initiated them and how.

First, there are those experiments that were initiated by a women's organization/NGO like the Self-Employed Women's Association (SEWA) in Ahmedabad, or the Working Women's Forum (WWF) in Madras. From these efforts at organizing poor women, alternative banks were created such as the SEWA Bank and the WWF Credit Society. The Grameen Bank in Bangladesh started as a grassroots credit organization for the landless poor and then transformed itself into an alternative development bank with government support. Poor women are now the major participants in the Grameen Bank. In Pakistan, the Home School for Poor Women was initiated by the faculty and students of the Department of Social Welfare, University of Karachi, and the process was institutionalized through the creation of an NGO named BUSTI.

Another set of experiments was initiated by the different governments, e.g., the Production Credit for Rural Women (PCRW) in Nepal . The Fund for Poor Women in the Informal Sector in India is another such initiative, which is yet to become operational. This was intended as an umbrella support organization for forty to fifty small banks and credit societies established by poor women from their own savings.

Finally, there were experiments initiated through a sensitive banking intermediary which opened a special window for reaching poor (men and women). Although these projects used somewhat similar methods of organization of the poor as in the parent models, they, however, implemented new lending norms. For example, the Small Farmer Development Programme (SFDP) of the Agricultural Development Bank in Nepal. The PCRW in Nepal was based on this experience.

The approaches and experiments mentioned above have several country specific or topical aspects but they also have in common basic characteristics which need to be noted right from the outset. In all cases the poor women first form their own homogeneous organizations. The women are participatory in the real sense, i.e., participation not merely superimposed on the purely 'targeted' or 'delivery' approach and technical package, but where the poor women are the subjects and not the mere objects of the process. These organizations of women have emerged spontaneously or have been catalyzed by a sensitive facilitator or change agent. The innovative experiments have greatly reduced and almost eliminated the problems which formal credit institutions often run into. The following sections of this chapter will describe in greater detail the process by which the women organizations were initiated, expanded and are leading to sustainable development.

BANGLADESH

Two innovative experiments which have grown in scale in Bangladesh, and the process by which poor women are moving out of poverty are analyzed in this section. One such experiment is the Grameen Bank, which started as a small village credit society for the poor and is now an example of an alternative national banking system for the poor, primarily women. It has become a public sector organization functioning with new norms, financial discipline and sound management at all levels. This bank has been able to overcome the constraints which restricted the conventional banks in reaching poor women and has made an impact on the local capital accumulation and the economic and social conditions of its members. The other is an NGO, the Bangladesh Rural Advancement Committee (BRAC), which places an even stronger emphasis on awareness creation and empowerment of poor women and in this process responds both to their social and economic priorities and their survival needs.

Grameen Bank

The Setting

The Grameen Bank came into being in the aftermath of the independence struggle of 1971. It started in 1976 in a single village and now covers 7,502 villages providing loans to over 339,000 persons, 81 per cent of whom are poor women. The ethos underlying the bank cannot be understood without some reference to the nature of the independence struggle itself and the subsequent release of creative energy in the poor.

The struggle represented a divorce from centuries of administrative, social and cultural norms. In a country where over 80 per cent of its rural population, of close to a 100 million, live below the absolute poverty line, with more than half being landless, the poor were mobilized, (and often mobilized themselves) during and after the struggle to organize economic and social activities which no one had ever thought could be undertaken by the poor people. The poor suffered and worked together in difficult environments without privileges and hierarchical or elitist divisions; they innovated individually and socially; and they set up institutions which reflected the people's initiative, administration, vigilance and accountability. People from different walks of life—academics, administrators, politicians, students, specialists and professionals—identified with the cause of the poor and reinforced the process of their development. This was an entirely new experience and released many of those involved, from deep-rooted prejudices and inhibitions that had held them back from creative efforts and collective endurance. While, for a variety of reasons, the overall rural scene in Bangladesh has considerably worsened since independence, these impulses of alternative development generated during the independence struggle have not totally died out. Other experiments, to name a few, are BRAC, Nigera Kori and Proshika.

The Grameen Bank represents one of the attempts to mobilize the poor and move them forward primarily through local capital accumulation and asset creation. Its five major objectives are:

1. To extend banking facilities to the poorest men and women in the community,
2. To eliminate exploitation by money lenders,

3. To create opportunities for self-employment for the un-
employed and underemployed,

4. To provide an organizational structure which the poor can
understand and in which they can participate fully, thereby
increasing their economic, social and political strength
through mutual support,

5. To reverse the age-old vicious circle of 'low income, low
savings, low investment, low income' to an expanding cycle
of 'low income, credit, investment, more income, more investment, more income.'

The Process

The Grameen Bank is not a conventional organization like other
banks or credit institutions which extend rural credit, though it too
is a legal entity under the Banking and Co-operative Acts.

The Grameen Bank has evolved over a period of time to perform a
series of interrelated economic and social functions in accordance
with the objectives stated above. By starting with the poor, these
functions have evolved in response to their needs, and the organization has become a socio-economic formation that is continuously
adapting itself and functioning rigorously with new norms. There
is nothing soft or 'charitable' about it. Those who use the bank are
not 'clients' but members. The success of the bank is attributable
to the attitudes and behaviour of all the participants: the members,
the bank workers, the managers and the various government support agencies. The new kind of communication processes and
dialogues among these participants, set in motion by the bank,
breaks down the fragmentation of knowledge and action and unites
them for undertaking a series of development activities.

All the activities start with groups of poor and their centers.
People organize themselves in homogeneous groups of five, and
an average of six such groups join to make up a center of 30
persons. There is no ambiguity about the identification of the poor
and no attempt is made to involve the whole village. The center
becomes the focal point of all socio-economic investigations, dialogues and decisions. Each center has a regular weekly meeting
which coincides with the weekly repayment of instalments. During
the meeting all issues of interest to the group—survival, social and
economic—are discussed. This results in a better understanding of
their reality by the poor, and the knowledge for overcoming their

problems, as far as possible, by their own efforts. There are currently 14,390 centers functioning, of which 11,848 or 82 per cent are for women. The total population reached by the Grameen Bank is over 2,000,000 poor men, women and children. Trained bank workers help the bank in reaching out to the poor. This has required a major organizational effort with painstaking attention to detail.

A visual representation of the interrelated functions is set out for facilitating an understanding of the process involved.[1]

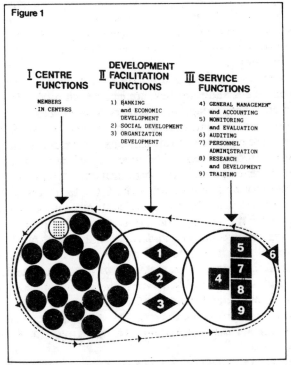

Figure 1

I CENTRE FUNCTIONS	**DEVELOPMENT II FACILITATION FUNCTIONS**	**III SERVICE FUNCTIONS**
MEMBERS IN CENTRES	1) BANKING and ECONOMIC DEVELOPMENT 2) SOCIAL DEVELOPMENT 3) ORGANIZATION DEVELOPMENT	4) GENERAL MANAGEMENT and ACCOUNTING 5) MONITORING and EVALUATION 6) AUDITING 7) PERSONNEL ADMINISTRATION 8) RESEARCH and DEVELOPMENT 9) TRAINING

Grameen Bank's operation is characterised by many types of interacting functions. In our description we follow this figure step-by-step.

Source: Andreas Fugelsang and Dale Chandler eds., *Participation as Process — What we Can Learn from the Grameen Bank*, Norway: NORAD, 1986.

A trained bank worker assists in group formation and then acts as an intermediary between the group, the center and the bank, monitoring the use of credit, repayments and other follow-up activities. The bank worker meets with each group once a week at the center. All members are obliged to attend these meetings and are made fully aware of the simple rules governing the activities of the group. The complete set of rules applying to groups and centers are specified in the Grameen Bank's bye-laws, 'Bidimala'. The group makes decisions on all banking matters and guarantees repayment so that there is mutual accountability. This social responsibility replaces material collateral. All bank business is conducted openly in front of the members. The willingness of the members to subject themselves voluntarily to a combination of self-discipline and communal discipline is an important part in the raising of consciousness and awareness of the people. The process starts with trust.

The economic and social development activities, in response to communal needs and priorities, are carried out by the groups and the centers. The groups and centers also develop the instrumentalities and organizational arrangements necessary for the effective implementation of this participatory development process. The bank worker facilitates the processes of banking, economic and social development, and organization. Continuous participatory monitoring and evaluation of all three processes are built into the total development process, and internal monitoring and evaluation by the group members is an integral part of it. The monitoring and evaluation is undertaken not only by outsiders, but also internally by the groups and the centers themselves. The Grameen Bank gathers a great deal of socio-economic data in the process and is able not only to assess the impact of its operations but also to anticipate difficulties, find answers and take corrective actions through group discussions. The discussions generate new ideas for further implementation. All this is part of the participatory process.

The bank staff performs a number of service functions for the groups, apart from its own detailed duties of general management and accounting. All these functions are performed by qualified individuals, who also identify with and are committed to the poor. The system is based on trust rather than distrust. The training function for these bank staff and catalysts is the lifeblood of the Grameen Bank. Eighty per cent of the training for all categories of persons is undertaken in the field so that everyone, whether a bank worker or a branch manager, has an understanding of the total process. Training takes approximately 6 months in real life situations. It involves not only mastering forms and simple accounting procedures but also learning to listen and learning from each other, undertaking socio-economic investigations of the reality through the action-research methodology and learning co-operative values. A change in attitude is continuously occurring as a greater awareness is created among the poor that it is possible for them to alleviate their poverty by their own creativity and through the use of local resources and local knowledge. The activities are initiated by the groups. The bank staff operates as a sensitive support system for the missing elements, whenever needed. In the process, problems of all kinds are prevented or solved while they are still small and manageable. Attention to detail may appear to be time consuming, but the pay-off is high. The whole approach is one of building self-reliance. The process of extension of credit and interest rate structure is designed towards that end.

The loan pattern of the bank covers four broad fields: livestock and fisheries; processing and manufacture; trading; and house loans. Within these broad fields there are about 400 purposes for which loans are granted. By focusing on those who have been considered the greatest credit risks, the bank has established the fact that the poor are credit-worthy and that poor women are able to repay their loans if organized in the above manner. In this way, the bank addresses the double burden of gender and equity which poor women face.

The granting of credit is closely linked to savings. The bank is concerned with the poor building on their survival capacity and moving on to sustainable development. Hence, savings' funds are started simultaneously with credit operations. There is the group fund, the emergency fund, children's welfare fund, as well as the individual saving deposits. Personal savings also protects the poor from resorting to money lenders in case of an emergency, or for their immediate survival needs. But more importantly, this expansion in the savings habit helps them to cater for the totality of their needs, not only for the purely economic and income generating activities. In the longer run, increased savings is also required for asset creation, capital formation and sustaining the self-reliant development process.

The Grameen Bank adopts the interest rate structure set in the official money market, charging 16 per cent per annum for its loans and 8.5 per cent on deposits. These differential rates provide a margin for the bank to cover its overheads. The loans are repaid in fifty-two weekly instalments, thus each instalment is small enough not to create hardship on the borrower. The rate of interest is significantly less than the minimum 10 per cent per month (which is often much higher) or 120 per cent per year as charged by the money lenders. The default rate is very low—less than 3 per cent. This record compares favourably with other credit programmes where 40 to 60 per cent default rates are common. One hundred per cent of the women had no overdue repayments compared to the 98 per cent of men.

The high loan repayment rate can be explained by the fact that the real necessity for the loan is identified through the participatory process—the initial screening and training of group members which creates a sense of responsibility and awareness. Repayment of loans is reinforced by peer pressure, close supervision and dialogue with bank workers, weekly repayment schedule, and the continuous internal monitoring and participatory evaluation. The credit, which is used for a carefully assessed need resulting from group discussion gives a better control over the surplus, prevents exploitation through group awareness and assertion, and helps reinforce the process of poverty alleviation.

The question of expansion and multiplication of the bank's activities requires comment. The expansion in terms of villages and the number of loans has already been mentioned. In 1980, four years after its inception, the Grameen Bank was able to create twenty-two branches in addition to the existing three with the help of the Bangladesh Central Bank and six nationalized commercial banks. In the same year, IFAD granted a loan of US $3.4 million matched by the Bangladesh Bank in association with the government. The IFAD loan covered 50 per cent of the expenditure for further expansion to 100 branches over the next four years, covering 100,000 borrowers. In 1983, IFAD approved a second loan of US $23.6 million, co-financed by SIDA and NORAD for US $13.6 million and a Ford Foundation grant for US $1.8 million was also made. The Grameen Bank itself was to supply US $11.3 million from its own funds making a total funding package of US $50.5 million with an appropriate blend of loan and grant funds. Subsequently, the Ford Foundation has also funded a Studies, Innovation, Development and Experimentation Unit (SIDE) at the cost of US $710,000. This unit is an additional instrument for multiplication. A new direction was initiated in 1986 when the bank took over the management of the failed Ningachi Aquaculture Project with some 800 fish ponds. The bank treated the operation as a joint enterprise owned by all its members. Within 3 months of the bank's takeover, the fish hatcheries were functioning.

This expansion in activities was also made possible essentially by continuous training/sensitization and retraining of all those associated with the participatory development process. Second, sensitive donors associated with the Grameen Bank project provided the necessary mix of loan and grant funding to initiate the expansion process expecting the internally generated savings to help sustain the process further. Finally, donors resisted the temptation to impose their own ideologies or procedures and followed the bank's leadership in evolving the programmes in response to the needs of the poor.

Until mid-1980, the Grameen Bank was mainly concerned with the extension of credit services to the landless to promote income/employment generation. UNICEF intervened at this juncture, and through a dialogue with its top management, encouraged the Grameen Bank to take a holistic view to expand its parameters beyond the purely economic concerns into social issues. A direct outcome of the dialogue between UNICEF and the bank was the organization of a trainers' training programme, in social aspects, to be implemented with the support of UNICEF.

The training programme aimed at training female bank workers and loanee group leaders to play a vital role in the strengthening of women's groups along three major dimensions: (a) train the Grameen Bank group members in organizational procedures, banking services and credit management; (b) raise the level of social awareness among village women; and (c) develop viable loanee co-operative groups to undertake activities such as primary health care, child nutrition, sanitation, literacy and family planning.

In other words, the UNICEF intervention at this juncture permitted the Grameen Bank to take a holistic approach and respond to both the social and the economic needs of poor women. The bank's village groups became the instrument for the extension of the primary health care and nutrition messages which UNICEF programmes carry. Training became an entry point and the new change agents/catalysts were able to understand both village level banking with new norms, as well as the social dimensions. The trainers were being trained to train both categories of change agents—the barefoot bankers and the community workers.[2]

Several external evaluations of the Grameen Bank have been made by donors, academics and others interested in learning from its experience.[3] These evaluations point to the fact that the Grameen Bank is a major innovation in poverty alleviation, employment and income generating activities and asset creation for poor women. Incomes for borrowers are estimated to have increased by approximately 60 per cent or higher. Alternative work and income generating activities, other than solely agricultural wage labour, have also resulted. New banking norms and organizational arrangements have been established and a number of intangible benefits have been reaped by the members, such as, group solidarity and self-reliance, not to mention enhanced self-awareness. The parallel emphasis on social aspects has had a consequential impact on improved nutrition, health and education for the poor families. Finally, the process has been sustained over a ten year period, with sensitivity, a high degree of professionalism by the leadership and, above all, continued participation of the poor women. Some attempts are being made to introduce the Grameen Bank process in other neighbouring countries, e.g., the Northwest Selangor Integrated Agricultural Development Project area of Malaysia.

Despite its success the Grameen Bank remains at the periphery of the Bangladesh banking system and donor concern. The approach adopted by the Bank is still an exception rather than the rule in poverty alleviation strategies. The question of making it the central concern with governments and donors still remains to be answered.

Bangladesh Rural Advancement Committee (BRAC)

The Setting

The Bangladesh Rural Advancement Committee (BRAC), a non-government development organization, was also born in the aftermath of the independence struggle as was the Grameen Bank.

However, unlike the Grameen Bank, it has continued as an NGO. Since its inception in 1972, BRAC has been involved in multi-pronged rural development programmes in different parts of the country. It started as a relief and rehabilitation effort in the aftermath of the war and went on to support development activities by poor men and women. BRAC is a complex organization. Participation of the poor is the key to this organization. In keeping with the vision of creating a society based on justice and opportunities for all, BRAC programmes are meant for the poorest segment of the rural community who are suffering from illiteracy, mulnutrition, diseases and economic exploitation. Within a brief period of fifteen years, BRAC has gradually but purposefully emerged as a highly flexible organization capable of undertaking innovative approaches for rural development. BRAC's target constituency are those men and women who do not own any productive assets and are forced to survive by selling their labour. The number of female members of BRAC groups is slightly more than the male. The main challenge for BRAC was to expand its activities and to engage the support of government services, since the poor also have a right to these services.

BRAC's Sulla project, Manikganj project, Rural Development Programme (RDP) and Jamalpur Women's Programme cover a wide range of activities. These include institution building (formation of village organizations, economic activity groups, organizational committees); human development (including teacher training, health workers' training, vocational training, and leadership training); and economic support for income and employment generating activities, functional education, health care and family planning. BRAC's Outreach Project also performs similar activities but with no economic support from BRAC. The above five development programmes alone cover 107,900 target households in 2,148 villages in the country.

Objectives of BRAC

1. Halting the ever-widening syndrome of pauperization and marginalization in rural areas by building power at the grass-roots level through the landless groups;
2. Bringing changes in the rural power structure through economic activities and a participation in the local power;

3. Ensuring the participation of the people in the development activities;
4. Disseminating skills to the landless groups through training and developing leadership at the grassroots level.
5. Making the target group self-reliant through income and employment generation in such a way that they do not falter when they are left alone.
6. Ensuring better health, esteem and a sustainable life to the rural poor.

The Process

In 1972—after the upheavals of the liberation war and the commencement of the return of ten million refugees from India—Bangladesh began its reconstruction efforts. Alongwith the refugees came BRAC's founder, a Bangladeshi who had been active in refugee relief work in India. He found a group of young persons ready to join his efforts. This group came with the refugees and started rehabilitation work amongst the people of the Sulla region of Bangladesh, where all the villages had been destroyed.

Initially, women fitted into this rehabilitation process only in a conventional way. Widows and women whose husbands had deserted them received vocational training. All women received health, family planning and education services. They were also helped in producing and processing food and in raising cattle and poultry.

BRAC's early experience, though conventional, provided insights on what would or would not work. BRAC's vocational training programme was discontinued. It was also clear that credit alone was not sufficient to change the situation of poor women. Credit for income generation had to be seen as part of a total package where survival and social issues were also addressed. BRAC's functional education programme proved innovative and enduring as it related directly to the knowledge people already had and the problems they were faced with. BRAC designed its own curriculum of learning materials and recruited village men and women as volunteer teachers in the programme. BRAC trained other village women to deliver low cost health and family planning services.

Thereafter, BRAC concentrated its attention on developing the social consciousness of women through functional literacy and formation of women's working groups. Small personal savings were encouraged by these working groups and small income generating activities followed from the creation of these savings' funds. Assistance to women in traditional skills helped to further increase their capacity, self-confidence and income. All this was further reinforced by the fact that the poor women belonged to a group and participated collectively in socio-economic reflections and actions. Through group discussions the women were helped out of their isolation.

The BRAC process has been characterized as one of continuous learning through a responsive inductive process. There is no pre-conceived model for development nor an ideology in a dogmatic sense or sectoral priority. The BRAC process has evolved a planning methodology which starts with people and is humanistic in approach. It allows for flexibility in timing and in content so that continuous adjustments occur even as the process responds to reality and people evaluate themselves. BRAC has now, through experience, established a more systematic approach for establishing a working relationship with the poor. The process starts with BRAC's research & evaluation division conducting a baseline survey and an income asset survey in each village.

Once the survey is completed, the BRAC staff identifies the poor and organizes them into their own village organizations. From this initial work the successive stages of the strategy begins to unfold. These are: training, functional education and conscientization, socio-economic planning by group members, and sanctioning of loans for group schemes. The schemes for which credit is given by BRAC include crop production, release of mortgaged land, irrigation, weaving, sericulture, ericulture, food processing, nakshi kantha, handicrafts, poultry, goat and cattle raising, paddy husking and pisciculture.

Income and employment generation, local resource mobilization, introduction and transfer of improved technology are given top priority in sanctioning loans. While this process of economic betterment is continuing; the social dimension is not ignored nor separated from the process.

The Credit Programme

The objectives of the credit programme include:

1. Building viable people's organizations capable of bringing desired changes in their own conditions.
2. Improving the economic and social status of the rural poor by extending credit facilities to undertake profitable income and employment generation activities.
3. Improving managerial and entrepreneurial capabilities of the poor.

Underlying these objectives is the assumption that by conscientizing the poor, developing an efficient mechanism for rural credit accompanied by necessary training and logistical support, it is possible to emancipate the rural poor from dependence on money lenders and exploitative landowners. Thus, the rural development and credit programme starts not with the giving of credit but with conscientizing and building new organizations of the poor.

Credit normally starts after the center has been in operation for one year and the consciousness of the members has been raised. The process does not start with credit giving. In this initial one year the groups function with their own small savings. At present, there are three categories of credit:

1. Short-term: Repayable within 12 months.
2. Medium-term: Repayable within 3 years.
3. Long-term: Repayable over more than 3 years.

On all loans BRAC charges a minimum of 18 per cent interest per annum. The prevailing interest rates in Bangladesh in the formal credit system range from 16 to 36 per cent per annum, while the village money lenders charge 120 per cent and over.

The following are the pre-conditions for being eligible for BRAC loans:

1. Regular attendance in meetings;
2. regular savings by the members;
3. A group bank account;
4. Completion of the functional education course;
5. Demonstration of efficiency in collective economic or social activities;
6. Capacity to manage finances and administration by the group;

7. Ability to provide at least 10 per cent of the project cost.

BRAC extends credit on the basis of some basic principles which serve as its guidelines.

A loan is granted on a self-liquidating basis. Repayment of principal and interest must derive from the use to which the loan is put. Thus, to given a loan for agricultural purposes and arrange repayment from, say, land rent income, would not satisfy that condition.

Therefore, loan is given either for consumption or for ostentatious expenditure, such as, spending for weddings and funerals beyond the poor's means. Clients of BRAC are discouraged from seeking such loans from other sources as it jeopardizes their ability to repay BRAC loans. No loan is given to a borrower to buy land from another borrower who owns less.

However, loans are given on margin. The concept of margin is that the borrowing organization is expected to contribute its own resources to the extent that all members will have a significant stake in the success of the venture. In other words, the margin is a threshold commitment figure below which it is estimated that the members of the borrowing organization will not feel a personal stake strongly enough to make the necessary effort for its success. The margin figure normally depends on the village organization's net worth. The higher the net worth, the higher is the margin figure.

The existing credit process has moved away from insistence on mortgage security. Land mortgage security as a pre-condition for credit to the poor is virtually useless. Titles are often defective and such mortgages can never be enforced, in case of default. Moreover, the target people of BRAC have virtually nothing to give as security, let alone land. Hence, a different approach had to be adopted.

Elimination of collateral raises the problem of security of the loan. Since the primary objective of BRAC is to lend to those poor people who have little or no worthwhile assets to offer as collateral, it aims to substitute collateral with a thorough investigation of the borrower's commitment and ability to repay by virtue of the proposed venture's income generating potential, prior to sanctioning a loan. Such an investigation is supplemented by continuous, intensive monitoring during the entire life of the loan both by the people themselves and the BRAC staff. These strategies require a thorough knowledge of the borrower on the part of the BRAC worker. The BRAC staff must also have a working knowledge of the production techniques, economics and profitability (including marketing prospects) of the income generating activities in the area covered by them.

Needless to say, collateral is not foregone where available. Where loan is given for purchase of income producing assets, the asset remains hypothetic until the loan is completely repaid. Loan repayment is expected and scheduled in increasing instalments to correspond with the completion of the scheme's gestation period and increasing income from the venture. Since people with limited subsistence have competing demands on their income, loan repayment must follow immediately on receipt of the income.

People living at subsistence level are invariably forced to sell their surplus output right after the harvest when prices are depressed. In already established centers, the BRAC credit programme has been providing warehousing facilities so that borrowers may store their immediate surplus and obtain a loan against it to meet their urgent obligations. They can then sell their produce when the price is more favourable. This facility not only strengthens the borrowers' survival capacity to a great extent, but also permits savings.

Loans are given for rural economic activities which have a strong development component. Loans are given preferably for activities where the return is higher than the return the borrowers have received from similar activities in the past. Thus the poor who have been growing the traditional varieties of rice will have a much better likelihood of getting a BRAC loan if they switch over to HYV. Implicit in this policy is the availability of all inputs and the immediate profit potential of the scheme. This proviso can create some problems for poor borrowers, but it appears to have worked in BRAC.

Loans are given only to the organizations of the poor and not to individuals as it is the organization which is responsible to BRAC for loan repayment. A village organization also evolves as an umbrella for several groups. The organization can re-lend to the individuals or to the group as a whole. If the loan is to an individual within a group it must receive the approval of the group before it can be given. For effective supervision of loans, a management committee of five to seven members, selected by all members, is formed for each village organization. The duties of the committee are to supervise all loans and the schemes that are being carried out with the loans. For these activities the management committee members receive 3 per cent of the loan amount as a service charge for each loan they supervise.

As BRAC gained experience with credit, it also found various constraints surrounding income generating activities. A need for BRAC to develop a technical and logistical support service became clear, particularly when the types of schemes for the poor became more diversified. The rural areas are still lacking the normal infrastructural support system required for development activity which the government should normally provide. Assistance with such services is still relatively new to BRAC and it is in the process of experimentation and development. The technical and logistical supports now being provided include the facilitating of input supplies, extension services, provision of warehousing and marketing assistance, and veterinary facilities for livestock.

BRAC has 50 RDP centers. Each covers an area of thirty villages. Each village has one male and one female group. Each center employs a manager and three Programme Organizers (POs), each of whom supervises twenty groups spread over ten villages. POs are responsible for identifying, mobilizing and organizing the village organizations; for helping to set group norms; and for financial discipline. The POs supervise the fund management of the groups and assist the groups to find and plan viable economic schemes in preparing their loan proposals. They also monitor and supervise the loans. These POs are university graduates, male, mostly young and have held no jobs before joining BRAC. There are no women POs in the Rural Development Programme (although there are successful female staff members in other women's programmes of BRAC), because the social mores in a traditionally muslim society do not permit women to travel alone day and night into the villages—a necessary requirement of the work of a PO. The POs are, however, assisted in their work by *Polli Shebok* (PS) male village workers and by *Gram Shebika* (GS) female village workers who are native to these villages. These helpers have ten years of schooling. The PS and GS assist in supervising the male and female groups respectively. They help the groups in the implementation of their economic schemes with group accounts, banking services, funds, and technical assistance. Each center has a center manager who is in charge of administration and co-ordination. Each ten centers are supervised by a regional manager based at the Dhaka head office of BRAC. An RDP programme co-ordinator heads the programme and reports to the executive director.

The financial experience of the credit programme in the 1979–1985 period indicates that the credit programme can become self-sustaining in an individual center when the annual loan volume outstanding averages about Tk.2.5–3 million. All the centers are expected to attain self-sufficiency by 1988. The assumptions under which the Tk.2.5–3 million break even point is calculated are: a) a loan repayment rate of 95 per cent; b) interest rates averaging 16 per cent, c) costs including full depreciation on facilities; full costs of logistical and technical supports; full costs of head office administrative overheads; and 50 per cent of the total costs of center managers, programme organizers and training. The other 50 per cent of the managers, POs, and training costs are chargeable to regular development activities which would take place whether or not a credit component was included. By December 1987, nearly seven million person days of jobs had been created by BRAC not including home based income generating activities such as poultry and livestock rearing.

For providing support services to its Rural Development Programme BRAC has established some complementary institutions, such as, the Research and Evaluation Division, Material Development and Publications Unit, *Gonokendra*, a publication, a rural crafts marketing institution known as 'Aarong', a Textile and Design Center and the Training and Resource Center (TARC). Some commercial projects relevant to the development of BRAC have also been started with a view to reducing dependency on foreign donors and generating funds for BRAC activities, e.g., the BRAC Printers, the Potato Cold Storage and the Ice Plant Project.

As BRAC expanded, 'ginger groups' from BRAC split off and started their own organizations, at the same time, deepening different aspects of the total process. One group, for instance, joined Nijera Kori and this group is now experimenting further with the participatory action-research methodology and conscientization processes, as they have felt that in expanding its economic and social development programmes BRAC may be diffusing the conscientizing process, an essential pre-requisite for wider social change.

BRAC has received small external assistance from a number of donors at various times. Some of them have maintained close and continuous relations with BRAC, and helped reinforce BRAC's total economic and social programme.

NEPAL

Production Credit for Rural Women (PCRW)

The PCRW is a case where, as a result of previous experience in Nepal with development for small farmers including women, a programme was initiated to enable poor women to move out of their poverty. The project was started in a ministry which did not have a narrow sectoral orientation. It is of interest that the women's development section of the Ministry of Panchayat and Local Development was able to function almost like an NGO. This department deployed a great deal of flexibility in organizing poor women and was also able to address a large variety of issues, such as, health, education, credit and economic activities, in response to the needs of the poor. This was possible because the women's development section was headed by a woman deeply committed to the cause of poor women. Also, by creating a new administrative unit and training new kinds of women catalysts it was possible to overcome many of the difficulties encountered by the more conventional bureaucracies in reaching the poor.

The Setting: Panchayat System and the SFDP

The PCRW programme in Nepal, now in its sixth year of operation, was not initiated in a vacuum but has benefited from the lessons of several predecessor experiments conducted by the Government of Nepal, involving both participatory development and poverty alleviation.

Nepal is still one of the poorest countries of the world with a per capita income of US$ 160. Here, 93 per cent of the population lives in rural areas and are subsistence farmers. Nepal is a landlocked independent Hindu Kingdom, which emerged in the 1950s, isolated from the outside world and with little communication between parts of the country. A decentralized political and development practice called the Panchayat System was experimented with and is continuing, with various modifications, as the existing form of government. A great deal of self-reliant social and economic development, generation of local savings and training of the Panchayat political and development workers characterized the early phase of this Panchayat system. Then came a phase of massive 'delivered' external assistance for infrastructure and rural development, which resulted in the usual problems and benefited the poor only marginally.

Three other experiments of note followed. The first was the 'National Development Service' where university graduates were required to spend a year working in rural villages before they graduated. This programme was discontinued after a time, but important lessons were learnt on how to use graduates in rural development. The second programme was the Small Farmer Development Programme, providing credit through the Agricultural Development Bank of Nepal (ADBN) for small farmers and the landless poor. The third project was the Intensive Banking Programme which encouraged the various branches of commercial banks to lend 7 per cent of their annual lending to the rural poor for income generating activities. The conventional approaches of the commercial banks which were followed in the IBP did not, however, result in benefiting the poor.

The combination of these four experiments created a body of positive and negative experiences in rural intervention, and the PCRW was in a position to take advantage of all these sets of lessons in its design and operations.

The Agricultural Bank's SFDP, however, provided the most direct lessons. The ADBN acted as a catalytic organization and created a special window within the Agricultural Bank for this purpose. The SFDP included women (13 per cent) among their participants, but the majority of the groups were for men (87 per cent). Five specific objectives of the SFDP are:

1. To improve living standards by drawing on the skills and labour of the small farmers themselves and making full use of available local resources;
2. To make the small farmer self-reliant, through constructive participatory group action, in planning and implementing development programmes;

3. To increase the people's ability to make effective use of available public sector agricultural and social services;
4. To promote and make accessible appropriate locally available technology;
5. To adopt and strengthen delivery mechanisms for the public, and technical and community services, to meet the needs of the rural poor.

The characteristics of the SFDP which distinguish it from the more conventional rural development programmes are:

1. A clear identification of the beneficiary group, i.e., households having a per capita income of less then US$ 60 per annum;
2. The group organizer who is instrumental in forming the groups and helping them become self-reliant;
3. The formation of small groups of between six to twelve persons which serve as the focus for both loans and development activities; the members of the group are homogeneous, i.e., separate men and women groups; members come from the same ethnic group or caste, etc.;
4. The active participation of the small farmer group members in deciding to what uses individual and group loans will be put and what group activities will best serve the group and the community;
5. The provision of credit at normal bank rates but without collateral;
6. To help create the real farmer's organizations able to undertake socio-economic activities benefiting the rural poor and the community where they live;
7. The SFDP started to work with the poor farmer's household. Initially the men in the household joined the group but later women also started to join the programme. Thus, SFDP considers the family as an entity irrespective of the sex representation. After discussion with several families with common interests a group begins to form.
8. In the SFDP, credit for income generating activities by the ADBN is also an entry point for creating an awareness and desire to undertake other community development activities. The small farmers' groups begin to save from the income generating projects. This groups' savings are used for financing

both additional income generating projects and consumption during distress. Training for providing skill and knowledge is also built in the SFDP activities.

There are 250 SFDP offices in sixty districts and approximately 6,000 groups with 60,000 small farmer members. The Agricultural Development Bank provides the credit for a range of activities such as livestock raising, crop production, farm mechanization, cottage industries and small businesses. More recently, group community activities include small gravity irrigation and power projects, shallow tubewells and bio-gas plants. Eighteen thousand illiterate women have passed through the adult literacy classes and now have a measure of formal education. Small farmers' groups completed on their own sixteen community irrigation systems irrigating approximately 2,000 hectares of land. These small farmer community constructed irrigation schemes are cost-effective as compared to the government sponsored irrigation schemes. The cost per hectare, for irrigation under the small farmer schemes, is between Rs. 4,000 to Rs. 13,000, whereas cost per hectare under the government schemes is generally above Rs. 40,000.[5] Group community forestry programmes are being implemented by twelve SFDP groups. A few groups are also beginning to harness small streams for power generation, small agro based industrial activities and rural electrification. Several evaluation reports by UNICEF, IFAD and the Asian Development Bank provide more detailed information.

Most of the SFDP loans are small and short-term, averaging about Rs. 2,700. The average rate of interest charged by the ADBN to the small farmers is 15 per cent per annum. Loans to women are smaller in number. The ADBN has a better overall loan repayment record than other rural development programmes. Women have a better loan repayment record than men.

The small farmers in their group meetings decide to undertake other community development activities, such as, running of literacy classes, planting fodder and fuelwood trees, building trails and schools. Community activities benefiting women and children are also being operated by the small farmers' groups. SFDP thus is not a credit programme but a community development programme by the rural poor.

These positive results have recently led to SFDP being recognized as an effective programme providing an alternative strategy for rural development to the more conventional approaches such as the Integrated Rural Development Programmes (IRDPs). Its expansion, to cover wider geographic areas in Nepal and larger numbers of the population, will facilitate meeting the minimum 'basic needs of the rural poor by the year 2000' strategy which has been enunciated recently by the Government of Nepal.

The PCRW Process

The idea for the PCRW programme emerged from a series of studies on the 'Status of Women in Nepal'.[6] The results of this report indicated that the rural poor women have limited access to the services introduced by the government and donor agencies for rural development. It also indicated that poor women, when given the opportunity to participate in economic activities, used a large portion of their earnings to improve the lives of their families, apart from enhancing their status and economic security. The main recommendation was for a comprehensive programme which would respond to all the needs of poor women and which was not for fragmented sectoral interventions. The sixth National Development Plan of Nepal also focused in this direction and reinforced this recommendation.

The original design of the PCRW explicitly recognized that simply 'delivering' services and technical expertise in a fragmented manner to the poor rural women was insufficient. The successful implementation of the PCRW required the 'delivery' and 'receiving' mechanisms to be re-oriented and designed innovatively towards the specific objective of poverty alleviation in a holistic fashion; incorporating the real participation of the poor women from the outset. This implied an active participation of the poor women in the process, in organized groups and not as isolated individuals. The PCRW also recognized that purely income generating activities, skills training, or credit, without other community development and social activities, such as, debt relief, health and education, were insufficient. To get to the point of being able to generate income and sustain an economic base, poor women also needed to address their immediate survival needs. In order to do so; poor women needed to view their lives in its totality and several priority needs had to be addressed simultaneously.

As already mentioned, the PCRW was initiated by a new Women's Development Section (WDS) of the Ministry of Panchayat and Local Development. The function of this section was to ensure that women's development needs were incorporated into the national programmes. This was to be done by identifying the needs particularly of poor women, finding resources and services to respond to these needs, and to use these innovatively for the benefit of poor women. The PCRW project was to address the poorest sections of women (for instance, those below the poverty line (US$ 91)) with preference given to disadvantaged ethnic and caste groups, landless and female headed households.

In formulating this programme for poor women, the WDS innovatively collaborated with the central government, the line ministries, the commercial banks, donor agencies and poor women's groups. This was a major achievement not only in a fragmented bureaucratic machinery but also in a culture where men had a dominant decision making role at the village, district and national level. The PCRW approach also addressed the economic and social aspects of the lives of the poor women, which were identified with their participation. The energy generated by the women's movement was also to be harnessed in the process.

The implementation of the PCRW began in mid 1982. UNICEF was associated with the project right from the outset. In five years of experimentation the programme was operating on a limited scale in thirty-two out of the seventy-five districts in the country. The programme, though initiated by the Ministry of Panchayat and Local Government under which the Women's Development Section operates, was, in effect, operated by the poor women's groups. The groups ensured participation and formed the basis of a new type of village level development organization, with the ministry and the WDS providing a promotional role and a support system.

PCRW's economic development and community service activities were facilitated in a district by a trained Women Development Officer. Initially, these Nepalese WDOs were assisted by international volunteers from the Netherlands or the US Peace Corps as a requirement by the donors. Gradually, as the programmes matured, Nepalese women development assistants were recruited to assist the WDOs. Sending foreign volunteers with the WDOs could be alienating to all concerned in this kind of innovative poverty alleviating programme, where the WDOs and the WDAs had to identify with the poorest women. The WDOs and WDAs are government employees and paid workers from local recruits trained for this purpose, but, in effect, function as catalysts do in an NGO. The WDOs and the WDAs perform three functions:

1. They act as catalysts and motivators in mobilizing and raising the awareness of poor women and forming them into groups for deeper understanding of their problems and income generation or community development activities at the village level. Identification of the basic needs of poor women takes place in this process;
2. They facilitate training and technical support to meet these needs, drawing from services available, from relevant line agencies, and the banks when necessary;
3. As the process gathers momentum they perform a wider role of ensuring that women's needs are taken into account at the district panchayat level and also report back to the ministry level from the field. Gradually, the WDOs have been transferring their village level responsibilities to the WDAs. From the district level they will help to multiply the process in other villages.

Training of the WDOs becomes a critical part of the process. They, in turn, also become trainers of the WDAs. Three types of training are organized for the WDOs who are university graduates:

1. Pre-service training before they assume their posts, to provide a basic orientation and develop a commitment and identity with the poor, which is followed by a team formation workshop, where all the concerned agencies participate;
2. A periodic refresher training so that they remain up to date with the latest experience of the programme and reinforce their commitment to the poor;
3. In-service training to extend special skills such as primary health care, credit, administration, agriculture, marketing, etc., so that they can deepen their role as facilitators.

Donor agencies, such as, the UNICEF (using both its own resources as well as 'noted' funds from the Government of Netherlands) supported a great deal of the initial activities, e.g., the capacity building process. Capacity building was undertaken at the ministry level for the establishment of the women's development section, as well as for all the expenses incurred in the field sites including the salaries of the WDOs (for the first year 100 per cent; second year 75 per cent and third year 50 per cent for a period of three years, after which the government took over). Where administrative capability has to be built for these newer concerns, such initial institution building investment is inescapable. The following expenditures were also included in the capacity building process:

1. Pre-service training and refresher courses for WDOs and WDAs;
2. Design and implementation of a monitoring and evaluation system.
3. Design and implementation of health surveys and health training for WDS field staff.
4. Creation of special community development funds and skills and training for rural women.
5. Purchase of office and shelter equipment.

As the process evolved, PCRW played a leading support role in poor women's development. While the social and community development activities have moved forward, constraints in credit activities have arisen because of difficulties in re-orienting the commercial banks to respond to the goals and activities of the PCRW. The intensive banking programme has undergone various revisions. It is dependent on initiatives of local bank staff who are not necessarily trained for extending credit to the poor in an innovative manner.

To overcome this constraint the PCRW programme is moving in two directions. One is to provide more training and reorientation to the commercial bank staff at all levels. The second is to find alternative sources of funding for the income generating activities. The latter is currently being considered jointly by IFAD and UNICEF. In formulating its projects for funding the deepening and gradual expansion of PCRW, IFAD and UNICEF have recognized the need for:

1. Strengthening the central co-ordinating mechanisms of WDS;
2. Intensified training for the beneficiary groups, the staff of WDS including the WDOs and WDAs, and the staff of the concerned commercial banks;
3. Provision for improved support services, including credit and technical services and training for on-line ministry staff.

For the next five years, an investment of US$ 14.8 million is envisaged. IFAD will provide 50 per cent by way of a concessional loan, and the Nepal Government, UNICEF and other donors will provide the balance as a grant. This will not only cover the expansion of the programme in the twenty-four districts already covered but will also permit a phased expansion into thirteen new districts.[7]

INDIA

For a period of nearly 30 years, prior to independence, the architects of India's liberation from colonial rule had evolved a vision of a new India and a programme for social change which included social justice and the nurturing of human potential. The expectation was that the energy of the masses could be redirected from the struggle for freedom to the task of all round development. Mahatma Gandhi had favoured attention on rural India and on 'Antodaya', i.e., starting the process, with the destitutes, of building a 'wantless' community and enabling them to move out of the condition of poverty and dependence into self-reliance and sustainable development. In this period there emerged many women activists and leaders who were committed to and pursued these development ideals. They also agitated for equality between men and women as essential to the building of a new nation, a principle which was embodied in the Indian Constitution in 1946.

After independence, while Indian planners vigorously pursued the more conventional model for development—based on modernization, industrialization and urbanization—some major programmes for rural development were also launched with the expectation that they would benefit the rural poor.

The community development programme, the co-operatives

and the panchayats of the 1950s were the first of these programmes for social upliftment of the rural poor. These programmes, though well intentioned, failed to benefit the rural poor. Party politics, excessive bureaucratization, lack of participation by the poor, social structure and unequal distribution of benefits were some of the causal factors. The solution to this failure was sought in the 'Intensive Agricultural Development Programmes' of the 1960s, later called the Green Revolution. This strategy provided growth to certain areas and increased production in certain crops, but the overall benefits accrued mainly to the large farmers who could mobilize the necessary resources for the purchase of inputs and new technology. The poorest and among these the poor women were further marginalized. Several other programmes were also initiated to speed up the 'trickle down' of benefits and make the 'delivery of inputs' more efficient. These projects included the establishment of minimum needs programmes to directly ensure a minimum quality of life for the rural poor; establishment of various specialized agencies and institutions to subsidize and support small farmers, landless labourers and poor women. These kinds of reformist approaches are still continuing, while mass poverty is perpetuating itself and poor women, with their double burden, are being further marginalized.

However, the failure of the above mentioned development strategies to ensure equity and social justice, and the disillusionment with vote-bank oriented politics resulted (in the late 1960s and 1970s) in a large number of younger men and women seeking alternative development pathways and forming poverty alleviating action groups both in urban and rural areas. In some cases—as in the Chipko movement, SEWA and the Working Women's Forum—the young men and women clustered around charismatic figures associated with the Gandhian movement. These action groups were neither homogeneous in their outlook nor in their methods and strategies.

With the birth of the women's movement in the 1970s the problem of social change in India began to be viewed in an entirely different context. Until then, though women had participated in various political and social movements in India, the male workers, the intellectuals, the rural poor in general were considered the bulwark of social change. However, women who formed over 50 per cent of the population were largely ignored. Whenever exploitation was considered, the emphasis was on the exploitation of male members of these groups and classes. The women's movement in India in the 1970s challenged this concept and centralized the concern over women. The daily struggle of the poor women for survival was highlighted at a later stage. Several innovative initiatives towards poverty alleviation were attempted in India through organizations of poor women. These initiatives gained support from the 1975 Report of the Committee on the Status of Women in India. In that Report it was recognized that the issue of women's employment and income, particularly for poor women, was not only an economic or social issue but an issue with deep-rooted political and cultural dimensions, which cannot be resolved in narrow technical terms or by addressing fragmented isolated aspects. Two other new developments of note were the appointment of a Commission for Self-Employed Women by the Prime Minister in 1987 and a separate chapter in the sixth Five Year Plan on the 'Self-Employed'. All this represented greater economic and political 'space' for enabling poor women to move out of poverty into sustainable development.

The three cases described in the earlier sections on Bangladesh and Nepal relate to the innovative approaches for enabling poor rural women in those countries to move out of their poverty with the help of a bank, an NGO and a government department. The two cases described below in India relate to urban poverty alleviation by NGOs through mobilization, conscientization and organization of poor women in the informal sectors in two urban environments. The two processes are now being deepened and expanded into rural areas, as well as multiplied by these NGOs in other states of India. Several hundreds of other urban and rural experiments are also underway. As the process of multiplication evolved in India, it became clear that there was a need in such a large country for new types of institutions and an umbrella organization to reinforce these NGO processes. Hence the proposal for the establishment of an autonomous fund for poor women is described in that section of this chapter. These three attempts at responding to the gender and equity problems in India are described in greater detail in the following sections.

The Working Women's Forum (WWF) and the
Working Women's Credit Society (WWCS)

The Setting

The Working Women's Forum (an NGO) started in Tamil Nadu in
South India initially as a response to urban poverty and the acute
malaise afflicting poor women in the informal sector. These poor
women were not only caught in a vicious circle of extreme poverty,
indebtedness and illiteracy but also had scant knowledge of basic
services related to their economic and social well-being. The poor
now spreading both to rural areas, as well as to the neighbouring
states of Andhra Pradesh and Karnataka.

In 1978, women political activists started organizing poor
women working in isolation in the urban informal sectors, both for
political action, as well as for assertion of their rights in various
services related to their economic and social well being. The poor
women were categorized under similar occupations—such as,
hawkers and vendors, providers of urban services, home based
petty traders and petty manufacturers—all exhibiting common
problems. The nature of goods they produced and services distributed could be classified under: distribution of food items,
vegetables and fruits, clothing, household necessities and orna-
ments. As the movement spread to rural areas, the organization
concentrated its activities on petty home based crafts, fish trading
and dairy farming. But for purposes of solidarity, the women were
organized by locality rather than by trade.

In all cases, urban or rural, these women coming from the
poorest households were continuously in debt to money lenders
and traders who supplied them with raw materials. In addition,
they suffered a number of social abuses at home including lack of
elementary health care, desertion, and wife beating. Furthermore,
family problems and responsibility were also shouldered by the
women, such as, care of the elderly. Any temporary relief or
charity giving approach, or a conventional project approach delivering fragmented inputs, such as, credit was clearly not enough to
help them break out of this vicious cycle. The ultimate purpose of
organization by the Working Women's Forum was to free these
poor women from the vicious circle of indebtedness and exploitation by forming their own solidarity groups. In this process they
were also ensured access to resources and its equitable distribution
among them.

Initially, credit was thought to be an instrument for initiating the liberating process, though experience showed that this was too narrow an entry point. At the beginning the WWF acted as an intermediary between the nationalized banking system, which provided credit to the WWF through its differential rate of interest scheme (4 per cent per annum), and the poor women's groups. The WWF organized women into groups, helped negotiate the loan and ensured repayment to the bank by linking loan repayment to cash sales and marketing arrangements for the activities financed. For the reasons mentioned earlier the banking system did not respond effectively.

In 1981, the WWF established its own Working Women's Credit Society under the Tamil Nadu Co-operative Act, which in effect is its own bank, and engages in both mobilizing savings from its members and providing credit to them. A token grant of US$ 25,000 was provided by the Appropriate Technology Institute in Washington. This credit society has, among other results, helped to overcome not only the problems of red tape, slow processing of loans, and biases of the conventional banking system but has also helped to better mobilize the savings potential of the forum members. The fact that poor women save for their survival needs through traditional savings institutions like the 'Chit System', helped the credit society to take off without difficulty. As the savings habit already existed among the poor women, it was possible to build on this traditional system. After the establishment of WWF credit society, commercial bank credit became a supplementary source of finance, not the primary source as was initially the case.

The WWF has in the process released the creative potential of the poorest of women by mobilizing, conscientizing and organizing them, through a participatory process, into urban (and now rural) co-operatives that are totally managed by the poor women workers themselves, who are its shareholders and directors. There is no elite intermediary. The WWF is a pioneering effort at grassroot mobilization and works through the concept of the 'multiplier leadership' where ninety-nine per cent of the organization is managed by the poor women themselves or by persons identified with them who are also living in the slums or in the villages. It combines human resource development and credit with consciousness raising, so as to bring out the untapped potential of poor women, leading to sustainable social and economic development.

The Objectives:

The objectives of the Working Women's Forum are:

1. To provide organizational support to women workers in the informal sector on trade lines for improving their living/working conditions;
2. To devise an innovative organizational structure to reach out to the women workers at the grassroots level and in large numbers;
3. To be women intensive in nature, and to address itself to struggle against caste, class and gender oppressions;
4. To adopt an effective programming strategy addressing the critical needs—both economic and social—of women workers in the informal sector;
5. To carry on an intensive health and family planning programme to strengthen women's productive roles and restrict their reproductive roles.

The Process

The success of the WWF is due to its recognition that poor women's problems cannot be tackled individually and requires organization into groups. Each person pays a membership fee of Rs. 6/– (US $0.50) towards the group fund. The Forum's smallest organizational unit is the loan group comprising of twenty to thirty poor women. The groups are organized on the basis of locality rather than trade. Each group elects its leader and functions in a participatory manner through dialogue, discussion and regular group meetings. These group meetings identify the participants' economic and social needs, and the projects and activities are designed to respond to these needs.

A continuous dialogue and communication is established right from the outset of the formation of a group, between members of the group and between the members and the Forum. The group leaders not only visit the work sites of members, but also their homes. All aspects of their lives are discussed. Loan forms are filled by the group leaders and the members are then taken to the credit society or the commercial banks, as the case may be, for identification through photographs in lieu of other forms of identification. Where necessary, the group leaders sign the guarantee forms. Interest rates on loans are between 4 and 7 per cent payable in ten monthly instalments. The monthly instalments are collected by the group leaders and paid into the bank, or in some cases the banks themselves employ loan collection workers who collect repayment at the work site, thus saving the group leader's time.

Default in loan repayment is dealt with, initially, by discussion to ascertain the cause. In case of temporary default due to illness, children's education needs, or other unforeseeable reasons like sudden death in the family, the credit society extends additional credit facilities to overcome the difficulties. Other kinds of default are rectified by peer pressure. The continuous discussion, collective awareness and consciousness raising, follow-up loans and finally peer pressure accounts for the high loan repayment rate. The working women's credit society has been able to achieve a recovery rate of 90–95 per cent while the national average of recovery of commercial banks for similar loans is only 30–40 per cent. An important achievement was that poor women learnt the use of financial institutions and financial discipline through group processes and dynamics.[8] Loan collection, however, is not the only task of the group leader.

The group leader is the link between the WWF and the loan group. She organizes the meetings, helps identify the needs and options and helps secure the credit, and ensures group guarantee of repayment. Along with credit, the group leader also ensures that other needs of the group members are also met through the delivery of available health services, technical inputs, educational programmes, etc. Group leaders are supervized by area leaders, who themselves are highly motivated group leaders. These persons are volunteers and are remunerated only to the extent of fringe benefits and expenses. Exceptionally competent area leaders become the WWF's paid organizers and link the groups and areas with the central WWF organization. Decision making within the organization is highly decentralized.

Training of group organizers and other kinds of technical training and non-formal adult education is a key part of the WWF process. The methodology is innovative and uses a 'learning' and sharing of experiences method of training/sensitization. Training becomes critical for building organizations of the poor, undertaking essential services, promotional programmes, credit and loan servicing, family planning, primary health care and leadership skills. Sensitization workshops are also organized to conscientize poor women in forms of social oppression and exploitative structures. As part of its awareness creation and damage limitation functions, the Forum also organizes protest meetings and dialogues with politicians, government officials and bank staff. This is a two way learning process and not only releases the creative energies of poor women but also encourages the poor women to assert their right to the various services and facilities provided by the government and banking system.

The Working Women's Forum assists its members in securing a number of other services as well. These include night schooling for school going children to prevent dropouts; health care; family planning; nutrition and environmental sanitation. Currently, the WWF is implementing the third phase of its health, nutrition and family welfare programme covering 90,000 families in the city slums and 27,000 landless rural families which will further expand to 450,000 and 135,000 respectively. Grassroots workers initiate action on provision of these services. Child labour centers conscientize children on workers' rights, as well as provide literacy classes at group meetings. The workers are also made aware of protective laws, minimum wages, appropriate hours of work and appropriate technology. In 1983, the WWF instituted a contributory Group Insurance Scheme to cover accidents or death. An insurance scheme for cattle has also been established, as these animals constitute one of the main assets of the poor families.

As the participatory development process unfolds, many results are observable. First, the participatory process gives poor women a new sense of dignity and confidence in their ability to overcome their problems. Group action also gives a sense of solidarity and brings them out of isolation. Second, it permits women to throw up their own leaders in a natural process of selection. These leaders are neither imposed nor elitist. These women have also demonstrated that this kind of leadership can be multiplied. Third, poor women achieve a measure of economic independence. Women who used to earn between Rs. 60 to Rs.70 per month, working for an average of eight to ten hours a day, now earn three to four times as much whereby they are able to save and, at the same time, increase the food intake of their family. The latter is a cultural trait where the observable evidence shows that when poor women get income, the children are fed first, then the husband and the woman eats last. Fourth, over a period of time women improve their living conditions and acquire some small capital assets either in the form of a savings' account or improvement in living quarters and health, or provision of education for their children. Group dynamics and self-management are two major elements which have contributed towards bringing these poor women out of their poverty and de-humanized condition. They have also been able to establish and manage their own bank—cost-effectively and with financial discipline. This total process is poverty alleviating and sustainable.

Unlike the Grameen Bank, BRAC, SFDP or PCRW the WWF has not received large external funding. It, however, maintains a continuous dialogue with some donors who provide limited external funding.

On the other hand, WWF provides some assistance to other organizations. For instance, some donors have used WWF to provide technical assistance to the Tamil Nadu Government and NGOs in the following areas:

Training
Dissemination of ideas and experiences
Developing specific programmes.

More recently, WWF has provided training to representatives from various NGOs in North and East Sri Lanka where, following the ethnic conflict, the peasant economy was completely disrupted and a large number of refugees and displaced persons had to be rehabilitated. The WWF experience demonstrated to these NGOs that the rehabilitation of refugees does not necessarily have to be looked at in a purely relief giving light, whereby following the WWF methodology refugees could move out of relief into sustainable development.

The Self-Employed Women's Association and the SEWA Bank

The Setting

To understand the SEWA Bank it is necessary to go beyond the failure of conventional credit programmes in India and the early

co-operative movement both of which benefited the richer strata of
urban and rural society. In addition, there was the failure of the
trade union movement to address the issue of the double burden of
poor women. As has been mentioned from the struggle for political
independence, the Gandhian movement continued into various
experiments in self-reliant development. The better known concept is that of 'Sarvodaya,' where development was intended for
the benefit of all, not only the rich. Equity and social justice were the
cornerstones of the Gandhian development process. However, as
already mentioned, Mahatma Gandhi also enunciated the principle of 'Antodaya,' that of starting with the poorest. SEWA is
based on this principle of 'Antodaya'.

Two other movements contributed to SEWA's emergence. One
was the trade union movement. The Self-Employed Women's
Association started in Ahmedabad (Gujarat) as a trade union in
1972. Prior to its establishment as an independent registered trade
union under the Trade Union Act, its origin was the women's
group of the Textile Labour Association (TLA). Though the TLA, a
conventional trade union, had a women's group, it did not really
protect and support the interest of the poorer and lower caste
women who worked in the textile factories on a casual piece-rate
basis. The TLA was also primarily interested in formal employer-
employee relations. The new SEWA Union went beyond conventional trade unionism. Self-employed women both in the urban
and rural areas had no formal employer to bargain with; they had
no means of production and were borrowing at high rates of
interest for their day-to-day existence. The early assumption of the
SEWA, as in the case of WWF, was also that if these poor women
were linked to the formal institutional credit system, they could, at
least, become independent of the money lenders. This assumption
was gradually changed with experience and SEWA also established
its own bank.

The other movement which contributed to SEWA's growth was
the women's movement in India itself. As the women's movement
gathered momentum it became apparent that the struggle of poor
women went beyond the gender conflicts and purely economic
issues to an inter-related set of problems including the social,
cultural and political aspects which had to be addressed if poor
women were to benefit. It also became clear that poor women
needed a more comprehensive basis for organization. Once

SEWA was organized, very quickly it set up its own bank. The trade union of poor women in the informal sector and the bank became mutually reinforcing, in both the struggle against injustice of various kinds as well as for sustainable development through the building of alternative co-operative economic and social structures.

The Process

As has been mentioned, SEWA was a response to the inability of a conventional trade union to deal with the total problems of poor women in the informal sector. Conventional trade unions have their own parameters, but have demonstrated that by organizing themselves, women workers can improve their situation. SEWA went beyond conventional trade unionism, in another sense. SEWA means 'Service' and the term 'self-employed' conveyed a sense of dignity to the participant in the organization. Thus, SEWA provided poor women a support system not only in the workplace but also in their homes and in relation to the totality of their lives.

SEWA was unambiguously an organization of the poorest women, for their struggles related to legal issues and protection within the law, for their right to employment and fair wages, their right to the law, and their right to access to normal social, economic and welfare services available through government, etc. Thus, SEWA attempted to address not only the gender issue but also the poverty and equity issue.

SEWA has approximately 21,000 members organized into small groups according to their activities. These activities can be divided into three categories where the members have similar problems arising from the fact that they are both poor and women:

1. Vendors and traders in vegetables, fruit, fish, eggs, and allied activities.
2. Homebased producers such as garments, food products and handicrafts.
3. Providers of labour and services such as agricultural labour, construction work, cleaning and laundry.

Each group elects a leader and these leaders form the association's representative board, then the executive committee is elected which manages the association. The group leaders are thrown up naturally in the participatory group formation process. This is the method for identifying the natural leaders, as the women's awareness is also increased.

As in the case of the WWF, SEWA, too, initially acted as an intermediary between the poor women's groups and the nationalized banking system. SEWA guaranteed the loans. This was a learning period for both the SEWA workers and the bank's staff. The bank granted loans at 4 per cent, but failed to understand the workings of the informal sector. Even with SEWA as an intermediary, the poor women's groups ran into numerous difficulties relating to time consuming banking procedures, needlessly complicated application forms, the banking hours and attitudes of male bank staff. In addition, it became increasingly clear that credit alone did not solve the problems of these poor women in the informal sector.

Early in SEWA's struggle for the development of poor women, it became clear that protest and advocacy alone were insufficient. It was necessary for SEWA to generate alternative forms of production and opportunities for creating new kinds of work and income generating activities. To this effect, some of the social disabilities had to be taken care of first.

In 1974, SEWA registered its own bank—the Mahila SEWA Sahakari Bank and the Women's Co-operative Bank—with deposits and share capital from its members. Poor women habituated to save for their survival needs, as in the 'Chit System,' found no difficulty in understanding and operating a simple credit society. SEWA and the SEWA Bank are accountable to both the Co-operative Act and the Banking Regulation Act. The bank started with members purchasing a Rs.10 share. The bank was launched with a total capital of US $5,500. In one year it had 9,000 depositors and a capital of US $33,000 thus permitting it to cover part of the overhead costs. The repayment rate on SEWA Bank loans is nearly 90 per cent.

The SEWA Bank has proved to be a viable financial unit. It has made poor women credit-worthy. They are now free from the exploitation of money lenders and are able to utilize the income they generate for the benefit of their families and themselves. The women overcome the constraints of the formal banking system. Photographs replaced signatures for identification purposes, a different kind of information is requested to establish credit needs, and loan appraisal is undertaken through dialogue and personal contact. Judgements on credit-worthiness and loan amounts are made with new norms and the new kinds of information. The system is based on trust rather than distrust and on personal follow-up by the bank staff. The totality of the life of the poor borrower is understood and not looked at purely in economic or credit terms. Cushions are provided in the form of repeat loans, even for immediate relief, for unforeseen calamities or needs. This implies that the bank also has the responsibility for ensuring the staying power of the borrower until the loan is repaid. This process is helped by the fact that invariably women save more. The borrowers now also have an additional cushion for unforeseen calamities from their savings, which earlier were expropriated in one way or another by the money lender, traders and others who had power over them. The rate of interest on savings is fixed by the Reserve Bank at 6 per cent for Primary Co-operative Banks and the SEWA Bank follows this rule. The Reserve Bank also fixes the upper limit on loans and advances at around 17.5 per cent (it keeps getting revised) and within this limit SEWA has a differential rate depending on the size of the loan. The lowest interest rate poor women paid to the money lender was 12 per cent per month or 120 per cent per annum and sometimes the rate went up to 300 per cent per month. SEWA does not have large borrowers to cushion the process. Their margin of profit is smaller. Profit is not the major criterion for the SEWA Bank. Its objective is to reach as many poor women as possible. The rate of interest is also not the issue in the current debate. Subsidized rates are not necessary, reasonable commercial rates can apply. The poor women are prepared to pay normal rates of interest. More importantly the issue is one of access to credit by poor women with meagre means.

The SEWA banking process, however, would not have been possible without close supervision, self-monitoring through participatory processes and building of a collective consciousness, and co-operative values among the SEWA groups. Training and technical inputs to improve the efficiency of the activities were also necessary. In 1975, SEWA established the SEWA Mahila Trust to cater to the training requirements, technical inputs, legal aid, maternity benefits, death benefits, widow benefits, health, creche, group insurance and other follow-up needs of members and borrowers. This was followed by the establishment of their own producer co-operatives so that they could purchase their own raw materials and also market the produce thus avoiding the middlemen who appropriated a large share of the surplus.

SEWA started its organization among the urban poor. Since 1977, it has extended its organization to cover poor rural women as well. The rural wing organized groups of poor rural women to demand minimum wages for agricultural workers. From this struggle they moved to a multi-pronged income generating strategy around farm labour, and home based craft and livestock improvement. With a steady flow of cash income, women's status in the community improved along with their self image, creating a chain reaction in the social conditions through improved health care practices and other means of self-improvement. This process is supported by intensive training of grassroots leadership and rural cadres.

In addition, SEWA itself continues its advocacy role on behalf of self-employed women. In 1980, it was at SEWA's insistence that the Government of Gujarat established an unorganized Labour Board to give the same protection to self-employed women as is enjoyed by industrial workers. In 1986, as a result of a resolution in the SEWA Annual Conference of the preceding year, the Prime Minister appointed a Commission for Self Employed Women with the Head of SEWA as the Chairperson. The Report of the Commission is entitled *Shramasakti*.[10]

The SEWA process evolved from stage to stage, in a way that was not with the continued preconceived, participation of poor women.[11] SEWA in collaboration with the Women's World Bank is setting up affiliates of WWB in four states—Gujarat, Rajasthan, Maharashtra and Madhya Pradesh. The SEWA experience, alongwith other similar programmes contributed in the setting up of the DWCRA programme of the Government of India. DWCRA was a response to the evaluation of the Integrated Rural Development Programmes (IRDP) under the Sixth Plan. DWCRA is, for the most part, an integrated programme of delivered services for women and children, and under it banks are required to ensure that 30 per cent of their loans should go to women (not necessarily poor women). After the DWCRA programme started, SEWA did a survey for the government entitled 'Economic Activity of Women in Rural Areas' and prepared a block level plan with poor rural women's perspectives as the starting point.

The Fund for Poor Women in India

The Setting

As the women's movement gathered momentum in India and the 'space' widened for responding to the gender and equity issues taken together, a number of other small banks or co-operative credit facilities for and by poor women also emerged in the wake of experiments for development of poor women at the local/village level, e.g., the Nippani Co-operative Credit Bank in Karnataka. There are now nearly 40 of these already in existence, apart from the two major banks described in detail in the earlier section, and a great deal of experience is available in India in the operations of these poor women's banks and credit societies.

These banks, as has been described in SEWA and WWF, followed the process of organizing women for productive activities in response to a felt need by them. Every poor community had a need for savings and each has devised their own mechanism for saving as part of their survival system. In India, the mechanism is the 'chit system,' where everyone saves a small amount from their daily receipts and uses these funds, in turn, as a revolving savings fund. There are many different types and scales of chit funds in operation in India. Some involve saving in cash, while others may even entail saving in kind e.g., fist full of rice from the allocation for the daily meal. It is clear that, starting with the chit fund system, the habit of personal savings is growing among poor women's groups irrespective of whether there are formal banks or not. Their credit needs are small and range from initial survival credits to production loans. These experiments are not conventional 'delivered' rural or urban credit schemes.

As described earlier, in the initial stages poor women did not have access to credit from conventional banking sources. The innovative credit facilities referred to did not operate on the same norms as the banking system, but the repayment rate is at a very high level. A great deal of dialogue, discussion, awareness creation, organization and training precedes the grant of a loan to a poor women's group. Initially this preparatory work is slow and painstaking. The cost of this preparatory work cannot be borne by the small women's banks and is usually borne by the women's movement which precedes the establishment of the banking facility, e.g., SEWA, WWF and Nippani. Some new umbrella mechanisms are clearly required to reinforce these fragile on-going savings and credit facilities for poor women, which have been started with their own internally generated funds.

In the course of a joint IFAD/UNICEF mission to India in 1987, it became clear to the consultant in discussions with the Ministry of Human Resource Development and representatives of poor women's groups that there was a felt need from local women's groups, as well as the already established small women's banks for an umbrella institution to facilitate, oversee and support the whole issue of production and other credit for poor women.[12] In these discussions, it was also felt that DWCRA alone was insufficient to address the total concerns of poor women and provide a comprehensive support system.

The Joint-Secretary, Ministry of Human Resources which handles the programmes for women and child development, in consultation with the IFAD/UNICEF consultant organized a small workshop of persons who were actively involved in organizing credit for poor women to formulate the broad outlines of such a fund. The workshop analysed the problems faced by poor women in moving out of poverty into sustainable development, and recommended that a study team be appointed to assess the support system for the existing women's credit facilities. The study team was to formulate a proposal for the establishment of such a fund with broad objectives which would enable it to go beyond purely providing credit. The study team would draw lessons not only from the small banks and credit societies that had been established in India by women's organizations, but would also draw on the lessons of the Grameen Bank and the PCRW in Nepal.

Since the fund is still in its formative stage, the issues discussed at the workshop, the nature of the problems faced by poor women requiring credit, and the characteristics of an alternative credit system are set out here as presented in the Surajkund Workshop Report.[13] The study team has just completed its report and the proposal for the establishment of the fund is currently before the Government of India for a decision.

The Government of India was in the process of formulating a plan for women up to 2000 A.D and the Surajkund meeting was one of a series of exchanges which benefited the development of this prospective plan. The meeting identified the following issues for discussion:

1. What are the various elements and aspects in the conventional system of credit which were major constraints and which required alternatives? Based on this, what policy interventions, institutional support, programmes and operational systems can be developed to minimize the extent of struggle for others?
2. Can these be done within existing structures? If so, what is the nature of the reconstruction/improvements in conventional systems that need to be affected?
3. How can the innovative and alternative systems that have developed over the last couple of decades be built upon, so that it leads to a multiplier effect and provides qualitative competition and acts as a pressure point to conventional systems?
4. What are the processes that characterize the evolution of alternative systems, and which need to be promoted so as to create an environment and framework which will facilitate new and additional initiatives?

Points of Commonality of Credit Systems Organized by the Poor Women

Organization: All effective projects have emerged from and as a result of the organization of women for collective action. The problem is essentially not one of credit for poor women but that of addressing the problem of their powerlessness. An understanding of development, not merely in the economic sense, implies that women have to be helped to address the problem of their powerlessness. To the extent that this cannot be accomplished by isolated individuals, but through collective action, the organization of women around issues of common concern is a pre-requisite for effective and sustainable economic and social development. Provision of credit in the absence of this organization is not developmental but further erodes self-respect, dignity and collective action, and leads to a depletion of the already scarce resources and assets available to poor women.

The forms of organization, however, vary from project to project and are determined by the circumstances and needs, e.g., in SEWA, organization was along the lines of a trade union; in the Working Women's Forum, organization was on the basis of strategies and methods of a political organization; whereas in Nippani, existing indigenous credit systems like the chit fund were directly built upon.

Mutual Acceptance and Trust: Effective organization and group action is dependent on mutual acceptance and trust among all concerned—the rural women, the catalysts (both internal and external) and others involved. For trust and acceptance to emerge, the quest for knowledge, awareness and analysis has to be a joint process in which the catalysts or interveners accept that they themselves have to learn and be 'aware'. This joint action for learning and analysis results in altered descriptions of the situation, an altered perception of roles, in the acceptance and acknowledgement of a larger 'us' (as opposed to an 'us' and a 'they') and consequently in group action. This process takes time (about fifteen-twenty years in the case of the Uttarkhand experiment for example) and requires that a conscious and continuous process of action-reflection-action be the core or fulcrum of any intervention strategy with the specific services being introduced as and when necessary rather than having 'awareness building' as one of many activities and interventions foreseen. Training in such a context assumes an entirely different dimension and must be a constant and continuous activity. Both these imply that effective interventions must not be bound by time bound targets and activities but must have the 'space' to emerge and evolve.

A holistic approach to the problems of women, not merely the provision of credit: Credit alone has little impact on the economic status of poor women. A holistic approach incorporating the struggle for fair implementation of various legislations in their support; support in marketing, availability of raw materials, skill training, legal aid, health and child care, maternity and social security, and getting out of debt are some of the key elements that need to go hand-in-hand with availability of credit. The situation and problems of the poor women determine the immediate priority (and therefore the entry-point) as well as the mix of support systems that are needed. These needs and priorities need to be viewed dynamically and therefore response mechanisms need to be flexible to suit different situations and evolve over time. For example, among the lace makers of Narsapur, the other elements that proved imperative were skill upgradation, access to raw materials and markets, which not only helped increase incomes while ensuring a 100 per cent recovery rate but also helped to address the problem of exploitation by middle men. In other cases credit helped release other family members from bondedness and therefore improved the economic status. In SEWA, for instance, innovative group insurance schemes and riot insurance have evolved out of a holistic and flexible approach. Availability of credit emerges from a holistic approach and when facilitated in this context, it, in turn, leads to further strengthening of the group and effectiveness in addressing other issues.

Informal Sector: All poor women are part of the informal system of the economy which implies that their dealings are of small size, based on trust or dependence on known people and on verbal transactions rather than written communication. It also implies that women have little control (real or documented) over their assets and means of production and that since the margin of returns over the investment of their effort is small, women often resort to a wide variety of occupations and trades within the span of a year. Seasonality assumes a crucial significance in such a context, and timeliness of response becomes a very important attribute of successful intervention. Within this common context, the specific situation and needs vary. Women in different parts of the country and in different livelihood situations are at various points on the continuation of subsistence—commercial economy. Women in Uttarkhand, for example, are aware and knowledgeable about the factors that impinge on and influence their economic status but have little experience in handling even day-to-day money transactions. In their context, economic development manifested itself in the form of a struggle to ensure their rights of access and control over their environment. In contrast to the many thousands of micro-entrepreneurs in the southern states and in urban areas, the lack of ownership of means of production and/or working capital is a daily reality and erosion in their struggle for survival and credit assumes an immediate and urgent need. A holistic and flexible approach to intervention helps in addressing this diversity, while maintaining the common focus on women in the informal sector.

Training and Sensitization: Training and sensitization of catalysts for group action at various levels assumes importance. Training and sensitization requires a continuous approach and must address itself to facilitating and supporting all the core principles mentioned above.

Characteristics of Alternative Credit Systems

All alternative systems of credit are built on the strength of poor women and their creativity, their sense of responsibility towards fulfilling their obligations, a strong and pervasive habit of saving and their skills in managing small indigenous credit systems (e.g., chit funds). The responsibility of poor women towards their obligations is demonstrated in myriad ways: a 90–100 per cent recovery rate (which sometimes may require an extension of the time frame for loan repayment but never for loans to be written off) as well as in some cases, a spontaneous offer to pay interest. In addition, alternative systems, by their flexibility and timeliness of response, have invariably resulted in a liberation from money lenders for they offer the very same advantages that a money lender does, viz., easy accessibility during need. The effectiveness and success of alternative systems are due to a number of common characteristics, chief among which are:

1. Knowledge of all aspects of the borrower—her occupation, work conditions, family and social obligations, etc.— which enables a realistic assessment of need and repayment capacity;
2. Preference for improvement and upgradation of existing trades and occupations rather than introduction of new ones, since the former have invariably proved more viable;
3. A willingness and initiative on the part of the banker (or credit institution) to undertake a number of tasks, e.g., filling in of forms which ordinarily are left to the women;
4. Provision of a number of other support services (both economic as well as social) to enable women to address themselves to the complex problems and deprivations arising from proverty and powerlessness;
5. Timeliness and flexibility of response which allows for the seasonality and variety in poor women's work and occu-

pations. Alternative systems also provide frequently repeated loans to meet survival needs. Simultaneously they address the other needs (skill improvement, marketing, etc). This approach in the long term helps poor women to cope with the pressures of survival and work towards the goal of self-reliance;

6. An emphasis on reaching out to large groups of women while limiting the value of each loan within the absorptive capacity of poor women;

7. Participatory structure which provides women with effective access to decision making;

8. Development of alternative systems of identification and documentation to cope with the factors of illiteracy, lack of certification, etc., that frequently accompany poverty and powerlessness (e.g., using a photograph rather than signature as the means of identity verification);

9. On keeping administrative and operational costs as low as possible and relying on leadership generated from the women themselves for much of the operation;

10. Effective channels of communication between the women and the credit systems which enables the latter to adapt themselves to the personal constraints of poor women, such as, lack of literacy or difference in the understanding of time as the formal sector sees it and to the need for other support systems and respond effectively to their needs and priorities;

11. Organization of alternative systems of credit has followed two main trends—the establishment of societies and organizations within the co-operative framework and that of banks. One agency working on the principle of limiting the size of the organization has diversified as it has grown with an overall federated linking among the various societies.

Constraints in the Existing Formal Systems

The Surajkund group felt that for various reasons the conventional credit system had failed to respond effectively to the needs of the poor. The single focus on credit is inadequate and has invariably aggravated the problems of the poor rather than helped address them. Two examples were analyzed: one the Banking Regulation Act and the other the Co-operative Act.

The process of registration and certification is itself inappropriate. Conventional systems operate on the basis of formal certification by a third party as the basis of establishment of identity, ownership of assets, credit systems, etc. These are inappropriate for poor women who are frequently illiterate, have little ownership of assets and operate within the informal system. The presumptions that the poor must adapt themselves to the formal system rather than vice-versa is the main hurdle.

The formal system works on the assumption that borrowers have effective access to sound advice on the other aspects relating to a viable activity and that they have control on the broader factors affecting that activity. Neither of these assumptions are valid for the poor and, therefore, since the formal system does not address itself to these issues, it fails in meeting the needs of the poor

Formal systems do not provide a flexible, timely response which is crucial given the factors of seasonality and multiple occupations common to poor women.

Conventional systems lack the basic feature of organization of poor women to address the exploitative factors that erode their economic status and, therefore, have little long-term positive impact on the economic independence of women.

The multiple area of accountability (i.e., to the Co-operative Act, as well as, the Banking Regulation Act in India) creates problems for these new alternative banks and credit societies.

The conventional system does not recognize the importance of savings in the case of rural women or that savings grow faster than loans. The existing norms are: the proportion of lendings to savings need to be changed in favour of savings. The emphasis placed on lendings by the Banking Regulation Act creates unnecessary pressure, particularly since the absorptive capacity of poor women is modest.

Since rates of interest to be paid on savings are fixed, and since the alternative systems take no recourse to large loans to offset the small ones, they are unable to offer loans on DRI. They have opted for rates of interest (on loans) that are lower than commercial rates by restricting their operational costs. The concept of efficiency and viability needs to be changed with key emphasis on the number of persons helped rather than the quantum of loans dispersed, and on savings.

Acts governing the establishment of co-operative societies vary from state to state. It is therefore necessary to undertake a comprehensive analysis of the various Acts to identify the factors constraining effective involvement of and benefits to poor women. However, some of the aspects that have necessitated struggle are:

1. Rules and regulations concerning membership. Some Acts stipulate that a woman cannot become a shareholder if a male member of her family is already a shareholder. This is a constraint for women, particularly given the intra-family exploitation prevalent;
2. The ceiling fixed on lendings as a proportion of share capital. However, the key factor in the development of successful credit systems for poor women in the co-operative framework is characterized by a spirit of co-operation among all concerned rather than the co-operative system per se.

Policy Options

There is a need for overall comprehensive policy which recognizes that the problems of poor women in the informal sector needs independent attention in national plans and programmes. The policy must also acknowledge the concept of shared poverty (among men and women in different occupations). At least for a reasonable period of time, however, specialized institutions would be required to cater to the needs of poor women.

Follow-up Action[14]

The Surajkund Workshop concluded that there is a need for a support programme and instrumentality at the national level to promote and reinforce effective systems for the development of poor women (inclusive of their economic development). This instrumentality (called the Fund here, but whose name is to be decided) should be guided and run by representatives of poor women and voluntary agencies, to address itself effectively to its task.

The scope of the Fund would include:

1. Financial and other forms of support for the expansion and wider reach of existing effective alternative systems of credit;
2. Conduct and support to effective participatory development and continuous system of training and sensitization;
3. A research dimension, whose primary function would be to explore, facilitate and conduct participatory action research and analysis, based on which policy imperatives and actions (including legislation) to address the constraints in the formal system can be identified and advocated;
4. Creation of a situation to facilitate and support further innovation and experimentation.
5. A policy and advocacy dimension which, based on all of the above, would provide a basis for revisions in the formal systems. The fund would be established for a limited period of time (say ten–fifteen years). The magnitude of the initial capital would be to the order of US $15 million.

The report and the proposal for a Fund are expected to cover the following aspects:

1. (a) A brief background of the problems of poor women and lack of credit for poor women in the informal sector; (b) the emergence of new responses culminating in the establishment of alternative credit facilities or banks through their own efforts.
2. Justification for the proposal to establish a catalytic support fund, including its economic and social impact during the ten-year period of its existence.
3. The objectives of the Fund and its functions so that it can provide lines of credit to local poor women's banks to enable them to give development credits, social and survival loans and also assist in training and organizing poor women with whatever action or research that is required. The objective of sensitizing the existing banking system and re-orienting it to respond to poor women's needs must also be included.
4. Capital structure of the fund and its duration.
5. The management structure to ensure its independence. The management must be entirely in the hands of the trusted representatives of poor women.

6. The method of incorporation not as a public or semi-
   autonomous body, but as an autonomous body under the
   Co-operative Act or any other existing law.
7. Some broad operational guidelines for the first Board.
   Consideration may also be given to the Fund giving priority
   to the expansion statewise of the three existing banks/
   credit societies in Gujarat (SEWA Bank), Tamilnadu
   (WWF Credit Society) and Karnataka (Nippani Credit
   Society).

Once such a fund is established nationally, provided it is
managed sensitively and not bureaucratically, it can support processes that have been initiated by various poor women organizations with different entry points to establish their own banks
and credit societies to sustain a process of economic and social
development.

PAKISTAN

The experiment that led to the establishment of the Baldia Home
Schools was initiated by the faculty and students of the School of
Social Welfare, University of Karachi, as a response to the growing
problems of urban slums in Karachi. This experiment is also an
example where the original project started as a sectoral intervention (under the Karachi Slum Improvement Programme) via
the environmental sanitation 'entry point', but as the process
evolved, it went on to become a centralized operation organized
by poor tradition-bound women of the slum and squatter settlements in Karachi. The home schools then became the center-piece
for economic and social development by poor urban women in the
informal sector. This case clearly illustrates how committed
academics and students, by identifying with the poor, can act as
facilitators and catalysts in the process of alleviating poverty.

The Baldia Home Schools in the Kachhi Abadies of Karachi

The Setting

There is a sharp disparity between Pakistan's overall progress in terms of economic growth and the country's backwardness in terms of the quality of life indices of the majority of its population. The average annual growth of 6.6 per cent in GDP attained in the fifth Five-Year Plan period (1978–83) has been sustained over the sixth plan period (1983–87) and has been even slightly improved upon in the last two years, 1986 and 1987. The per capita income in this country is the highest in South Asia.

However, 45 per cent of the rural population is below the poverty line with a rapid growth of urban slums due to rural-urban migration. The numbers of the rural and urban poor are increasing, i.e., those with an income insufficient to ensure 2,300 calories per person per day. Sixty per cent of the children between the ages of 1–5 suffer from some form of malnourishment; and infant, child and maternal mortality rates are unacceptably high. Access to health facilities is inadequate. More than 62 per cent of the population do not have access to potable drinking water. Eighty-four per cent of the population does not have access to sewerage facilities; housing conditions are so inadequate that 81 per cent of the housing units have, on an average, 1.5 rooms inhabited by seven persons. The country's literacy and school enrollment rates are among the lowest in the world. The conditions of rural poverty are increasing the rural-urban migration. According to estimates of the National Human Settlements Policy Study (March 1983), there will be a trebling of the urban population by the year 2001 on present trends. Levels of unemployment and under-employment are nearer 50 per cent of the potential work force and are much higher than presented by the partial official statistics. Recent World Bank, UNICEF and ILO surveys and studies by Pakistan economists confirm this disparity between economic and social progress.[15]

These studies also indicate that past planned investment has not given benefits to the poorer farmers, the landless and other categories of the poor, e.g., poor women. The 'delivery' of inputs for rural development, even where intended for the poorer farmers, have benefited only the richer farmers. The small farm sector (below 12.5 acres of irrigated land) and 25 acres of Barani (rainfed) land, which accounts for 74 per cent of the total number of farms, have not benefited significantly from rural development or rural credit programmes. These credit programmes have also failed to address themselves to the needs of the landless poor and particularly those of poor women. As a result, both these categories are becoming increasingly dependent on the large landowners, the money lender and the traders who continue to exploit the poorer farmers and the landless and divert these 'delivered' inputs from the poor. The government has become aware of the significance of social affluence and private financial power in rural areas, and encouraged innovative credit delivery schemes. But even these schemes have not made a major impact on the poor. For example, 80 per cent of the credit allocated for such schemes did not reach the small farmers let alone poor women. Very few schemes are available to the urban poor.

The bureaucratic machinery, through which plans have been implemented, is not capable of ensuring that the benefits reach the poor, because of the fragmented sectoral approaches and overly bureaucratic procedures (despite which there is considerable waste and corruption). A lack of innovation and identity with the poor, which are essential pre-requisites for economic and social development for the benefit of the poor is also evident. The rural credit mechanisms, which have been established to benefit the poor are biased in favour of the larger farmers. Even the Agricultural Development Bank's Mobile Credit Scheme, after ten years, is still only experimenting with reaching the poor farmers and has hardly touched the problems of poor women.

It is in this context that a few innovative NGOs have experimented with participatory poverty alleviating approaches. Two of the better known are the Aga Khan Rural Support Programme in the North Western Region of the country and the Baldia Home School Programme in the Kachhi Abadies (slums and shanty towns) of Karachi by an NGO called BUSTI.[16] The latter is described here because it demonstrates the effectiveness of the participatory action-research methodology initiated by committed academics and students in enabling poor women, in an Islamic urban environment, to bring about a change in their condition. The situation of poor women in Pakistan is currently and has been in the past dictated by traditionalists. Most women's organizations active in Pakistan are controlled by elite ladies organizing service centers, industrial homes, and mother and child care centers which are in the form of charitable and welfare institutions and hardly touch the fringe of the problem. This programme is also illustrative of how the stage has been set in the Baldia Home School

Programme for expanding savings, credit and income generating processes with the social dimension also taken care of. The programme was initiated with UNICEF support.

The Process

The process evolved gradually, but started with the Department of Social Work of the University of Karachi sending its lecturers and students to the Kachhi Abadies, i.e., the slums and shanties with questionnaires to collect information in a conventional way, on the problems of slum and shanty dwellers. Gradually, these students and the faculty began to identify with the objects of their research and developed a commitment for going beyond observational research to action-research with the poor as participants.

With the help of other NGOs such as the Jaycees in Karachi, a full-time woman community worker and a part time technical adviser were recruited from the Department of Social Work to work on slum problems. Other committed University faculty and students, particularly from the Department of Social Work, also continued to associate themselves with the experiment. The men in the Kachhi Abadies resisted the entry of women community organizers into their homes. The community organizer then began a long and painstaking dialogue with the men using environmental sanitation as an entry point. This dialogue carried on for over a year creating an awareness among the men of the benefits of a simple soak pit (pit latrines), the construction of which would not only help keep the environment clean but also improve the health of their children. With UNICEF's assistance, a team of community workers, with the participation of men, began to construct soak pits in several Kachhi Abadies in Baldia Town.

The process of dialogue and action lasted nearly two years and included the participation of engineers, doctors and other technicians from the University. This created close contact and trust between the men, women and children of the slum community and the external social workers. Eventually, the women community workers were allowed to extend the dialogue to other social and economic issues pertaining to the home and to women. The community workers then prepared leaflets and handbooks on better child care, hygiene and sanitation for distribution in the homes. But when the reading materials were given to the women, they could not read and the minds of the older women were closed to any new ideas. However, the younger girls in the age group of fifteen to thirty, who were confined to the homes waiting to be married, demonstrated an interest in a literacy programme. Out of this effort the idea of the Home School was born. Under the auspices of the Turk Welfare Society (a grassroot NGO) a younger women's meeting was organized to build on the idea of the Home School and initiate an educational and literacy programme for women' and children to be carried on within the confines of the homes. The Home School was scheduled for those times suitable to the women and children, i.e., after their household duties and family chores were completed. An initial set of ten teachers were selected from among the young girls in the community, who had at least some high school education. They were given training in primary and pre-primary education. One of them was trained in adult literacy. Funds for teaching materials were collected through the Turk Welfare Society. By the end of 1981 the ten teachers were conducting classes for about 300 children in their homes and charging around Rs. 10 per month per child. The children were taught with charts and slates which were provided mainly by UNICEF and sometimes from the parent's savings.

Women in the community then started a service and craft center along with literacy classes. Women also began to help the community organizer in the sanitation programme. The demonstration effect of these Home Schools and the spiral of activities made other girls in neighbouring slums interested in setting up similar schools in their communities as well.

At this point, it was felt by the community organizer that the expanding programme required more protection as there were some persons who had not fully accepted the idea. Through an organization called All Baldia Meman Jamat ABJM (an educational institute) a larger meeting of the community was called to explain the process. The ABJM accepted to undertake and expand a training programme for the Home School Teachers offering their school building as a training center. The ABJM also launched a public campaign through posters and leaflets to attract girls educated upto high school into this training programme. The criteria for selection was that they should already be teaching in their homes, belonging to poor families and having a commitment to bring about changes in their condition. Women who headed their households, girls from ethnic groups where the soak pit projects were being constructed, and from ethnic communities where education for girls was traditionally discouraged, were also included.

By 1987, there were seventy-eight teachers operating Home Schools in Baldia and its vicinity. The Home Schools and the teachers required close monitoring and follow-up. Monthly meetings of the Home School teachers were planned with the community organizer and her colleagues. They met in groups of twenty and discussed all the problems of the Home School, as well as related community health and economic issues. The community organizer with her co-workers also visited each school once a month and tried to co-ordinate the Home School with the sanitation committees of men which had been established to expand the environmental sanitation and soak pit projects. Meetings were also organized with the mothers of the children attending the Home Schools. These meetings, apart from dealing with the problems of the Home School, also discussed problems of sanitation, health and hygiene, child care, nutrition and income generating activities. Thereafter, the teachers themselves formed an association called the Home School Teachers' Welfare Organization. It is now a registered and recognized NGO. Gradually, this welfare organization became not only a center for female education but also a center for economic and community activities for women. Immunization programmes were introduced through the Home School along with growth monitoring orientation for mothers, use of oral rehydration salts, and the follow-up. Each family was prepared to pay Rs. 5 per month to the teachers for this health programme. The home schools have been established in thirty-two Kachhi Abadies in Baldia Town as well as in four Kachhi Abadies outside Baldia Town. Twenty-six hundred children are currently enrolled of whom 1900 are girls. Twelve primary health care centers have been established within the programme with thirteen PHC workers and fourteen trained TBAs. The primary health care component is expanding to all the home schools. The establishment of the primary health care centers further consolidated the Home School organization in the community, as the poor men and women now saw it as being able to respond to a variety of their needs. Even education and health projects became income generating. This also helped to bring about an attitudinal change in the men who saw the value of the involvement of younger women in community development activities and their potential as group organizers and catalysts in the community. As motivators and community workers, these young girls were also earning an income in the process. They were also able to work close to home. This represented a new kind of work and income generating opportunity in the community, as opposed to a 'job' in the formal sector. A recent evaluation has shown that the quality of training imparted through these Home Schools is better than the training in other established schools.

The process described took place nearly eight years ago, building on traditional patterns laid down for women in local communities, painstakingly adapting them, breaking needless constraints, making poor women agents of social change in their communities and also enabling them to earn an income. Each Home School teacher now earns Rs. 150 to Rs. 400 per month. Each primary health care worker earns Rs. 100 to Rs. 300. The Home School teachers and health workers are multiplying the process to other Kachhi Abadies. The Home School Teachers' Welfare Organization has made a request to the Karachi Municipality for a plot of land to construct a Women's Development Center. While committed academics from the Department of Social Work of Karachi University and some of its Engineering faculty and doctors are associated with the process, the Karachi municipality, the banking system and the extension services of the government have yet to play a major supporting role in the process. The municipality is, however, recently becoming more supportive.

A great deal more advocacy and training is required for these institutions before they can be expected to provide a flexible support system for the process as it evolves. This eight year process was supported from 1981–1987 by one donor with a modest sum of US $482,000. A part of this was in the form of institutional support to the NGOs who pioneered the above process. An umbrella organization named BUSTI has now been established to carry on the work. There were small inputs to BUSTI from other groups such as the Habib Bank which paid the cost of the supervizing doctors. A recent development is an agreement by the women's division, Government of Pakistan, for the funding of BUSTI. The women's division has agreed to support the expansion of this type of work in Baldia and other Kachhi Abadies with a grant of US $800,000. While in the past there has been only limited direct governmental involvement it should be noted that the government itself provides some services in the Baldia area which can be availed by the home schools. The process of empowering women in the slums and shanties and raising their awareness has also resulted in their asserting the right to these services provided by the government.

A major lesson is that the process for enabling poor women to move out of poverty started with a sectoral entry point, i.e., the Urban Environment Sanitation Programme. The process then began to evolve into a more comprehensive economic and social programme for poor women. It is now of benefit to the community as a whole and can be multiplied. If the process that has emerged is properly understood and conceptualized, this experience could provide important guidelines for an alternative approach to poverty alleviation in Pakistan, with poor women as the subjects in the process. The Home School was the organizational base in this case, with BUSTI as an NGO intermediary. Nonetheless, there could be other intermediaries in other situations. The process itself could also have far reaching implications for the future design of the women's programme in Pakistan.

NOTES

1. Andreas Fugelsang and Dale Chandler (1986), p. 53.
2. For more details see Jowshan A. Rahman (1985).
3. Andreas Fugelsang and Dale Chandler (1986).
   Dharam Ghai, (1984).
4. For more detailed information on BRAC activities see Martha Alter Chen (1986).
5. See Shree Krishna Upadayah (1986); and (1987).
6. See Meena Acharya and Lyn Bennet (1981).
7. For more details see UNICEF (1985); and UNICEF 'Proposal for Noted Funding for Production Credit for Rural Women 1987–92', Kathmandu 1986; also IFAD Preparation and Appraisal Reports of 1986 and 1987.
8. Jaya Arunachalam (1987).
9. Nandini Azad (1986).
10. See *Shramashakti—Report of the National Commission on Self-Employed Women and Women in the Informal Sector*, New Delhi, June 1988.
11. See internal SEWA Reports and Newsletters:
    (a) Self-Employed Women's Association 1984.

(b) Banking with Poor Women 1984.

(c) SEWA Newsletters 'ANASUYA' and 'We, the Self Employed' edited by Usha Jumani.

Also Jennifer Sebstads (1988).

12. See Ponna Wignaraja, Phase I report on 'Collaboration between IFAD and UNICEF in Selecting Countries,' Rome, March 1987 (unpublished); and Report of the Brainstorming Meeting on 'Fund for Poor Women,' Surajkund, January 1987, prepared by Annupama Rao, Sharada Jain and Ponna Wignaraja for UNICEF and the Ministry of Human Resources (unpublished).

13. Much of the following has been extracted from the report of the Surajkund meeting prepared by Annupama Rao, Sharada Jain and Ponna Wignaraja and is published here as this report remains unpublished and contains valuable theoretical and practical insights into the problems and solutions of credit for poor women. The meeting itself, though organized as an informal consultation, turned out to be an 'Expert Group' meeting on the subject, because those taking part were participants in poor women's experiments and banks or action-researchers interacting closely with poor women. This is how expertise in this field should be identified.

14. The discussions and follow-up actions have been presented in detail in this book as it can provide useful guidelines both for an analysis of the credit problems of poor women and the articulation of meaningful responses. It also indicates the new kinds of macro institutions that need to be established.

15. (a) For evidence on rural poverty see: (i) Irfan and R. Amjad, *Poverty in Rural Pakistan*, ILO/ARTEP, Bangkok, June 1983 (Mimeo)
(ii) S.M. Naseem, 'Poverty in Pakistan: Some Preliminary Findings,' *The Pakistan Development Review*, Winter 1973 and
(iii) Akmal Hussain, *Strategic Issues in Pakistan's Economic Policy*, Progressive Publishers, Lahore, 1988, pp. 3–84.

(b) For evidence on changes in the quantity and quality of diet of the poor and poor peasants, and for an analysis of the mechanism underlying rural poverty, see: Akmal Hussain, 'Technical Change and Social Polarization in Rural Punjab,' Ch. 12, in K. Ali (eds.), *The Political Economy of Rural Development*, Vanguard, Lahore, 1982.

(c) For evidence on Pakistan's social indicators, see: *Pakistan Economic Survey 1983–84*, Government of Pakistan, Ministry of Finance, Islamabad and UNICEF Situation Analysis of Children and Women 1987.

16. See: (i) Quratul Ain Bakteeri and Shama Aziz, 'Poor Women in Urban Development: The Participatory Action Research Methodology in the Kachhi Abadies of Baldia Town, Karachi,' paper for the UNU South Asian Perspectives Project, Karachi, March 1987 (to be published).

(ii) Quratual Ain Bakteeri, 'An Integrated Strategy for Development of Squatter Settlements: a Case Study of Karachi,' (PhD thesis submitted to the University of Technology, Longhborough U.K.), 1987 (to be published).

(iii) Laique Azam, 'Squatter Settlements of Karachi: a Comparative Perspective of the Culture of Activism,' (PhD thesis submitted to the London School of Economics), 1984 (to be published).

Some Essential Features and Lessons from these South Asian Experiences

THE South Asian experiences briefly described earlier are merely illustrative of comprehensive programmes enabling poor women to move out of poverty into sustainable development. These projects have grown in scale and have continued over a reasonable period of time. Clearly, there are many other cases which can be similarly analysed and which will point to the fact that in the past ten years a new social response is being generated in relation to the problems of gender and equity. In some cases these responses are spontaneous, in other cases a facilitator or catalyst, awakens by appropriate catalytic action, awakens the spirit of self-reliance in poor women. A striking feature of the evolving South Asian poverty alleviating experiments is that while there are differences in each case according to the socio-economic and political context, there is also a great deal of commonality on the essential features and methodology. In this chapter these common features will be further described and the lessons learnt from these innovative approaches—for multiplying the process—will be highlighted.

ESSENTIAL FEATURES

In all the South Asian countries, where these comprehensive experiments in economic and social development by poor women have been carried out, the government—through their five-year plans; through other policy pronouncements on the need for assistance to poor women; through enunciation of special poverty alleviating strategies, through directives to banks; through decentralization of the administrative system; through the local or village level organizations and some encouragement to NGOs—have provided a policy framework, a support system and a 'political space' for these experiments to be initiated. They have also permitted the experiments to be carried on and even supported their expansion in a variety of ways. Thus the 'political space' has been found for innovating the experiments from which everyone can learn. This does not mean that some of these experiments go beyond the rhetoric of their language, or that they have been implemented with a political will. In their success stories there has been a hard struggle against vested interests and existing social structures. Nevertheless, there is a political space and the experiments themselves help to widen that space.

Some of the traditional government and credit institutions, which had failed to implement the conventional, integrated rural projects for the benefit of the poor, are now willing to provide the support system for alternative initiatives taken by NGOs and organizations of the poor at the village level. Moreover, some governments have shown willingness to support an umbrella organization, whether an NGO or an autonomous or semi-autonomous body, to act as a catalyst in the participatory development process, and function with a great deal of flexibility in co-ordinating the large number of small scale activities and dialogues involved. These catalytic umbrella organizations are designed to promote development in an equitable and sustainable manner in selected areas. They are also conceived, from the outset, to be self-liquidating organizations, able to work themselves out of a location within a reasonable period of time, say ten to fifteen years. The aim is to leave in place local organizations and institutions capable of facilitating continued progress into the future. Where governments are ineffective, these organizations perform the tasks of economic and social development by mobilizing, conscientizing and organizing the poor. Some co-ordination with government programmes is required if the experiment is to grow in scale with a reliable support system.

The intermediary institution, whether government, semi-government, a bank or an NGO, fulfills the following basic inter-related functions:

1. Sensitizing poor women to a range of awareness, organizational matters, and upgrading their knowledge base;
2. The organization of homogeneous groups of the poor women at the village level to meet common needs and to provide or obtain services through collective action;

3. The mobilization of savings to support the economic and social development activities, build assets and to serve as collateral for collective borrowing to expand further;

4. The introduction of new activities and knowledge to enhance net incomes and assets;

5. The development of strategies for the productive and sustainable use of the natural resources in the local area;

6. Integrate the survival and social needs of poor women into the total process;

7. Ensure that the real poor are the beneficiaries.

In performing these functions there has been a great deal of detailed collaboration and exchange of information between government organizations, banks, academic institutions and the people's organizations. Joint studies have resulted to support programme management, co-ordination, and to measure progress at the local level with a great deal of participation and generation of new information. In the locations in which these innovative approaches have been tried out, there are several location specific features which favour the rapid implementation and effectiveness of the experimented programmes. These include the formerly isolated existence of poor women; the latent energy waiting to be released through group action; the partial political and social vacuum which could be filled by the new type of poor women's organizations; the implementing NGO's commitment, as well as community and social orientation; and the building on small initiatives taken over the previous years by various public and NGO groups in sectors such as education, environmental sanitation and health. There is also, in these cases, a cultural tradition of co-operative activity and a high degree of homogeneity amongst the organized groups.

Further characteristics of the process that is set in motion are:

1. The activities are implemented at two levels: by the catalytic intermediary itself functioning as an NGO and by the village level organizations of poor women. Implementation is not by the traditional bureaucracy, but mainly by a new kind of poor people's organizations in which the poor become the subjects of the participatory process. The bureaucracy, if

flexible, provides an additional support system and does not try to implement the activities.

2. The open management style, the continuous dialogue at all levels, continuous participatory monitoring at the village level by the organizations of the poor women and a responsive problem solving approach, all help to take corrective actions as the process evolves and when the problems are relatively small.

3. The need for careful institution building and social infra-structure construction in the early phase, with production credit being gradually introduced as the process gets underway. The social infrastructure like health and nutrition has not been separated from the economic process. Savings, asset creation, investment and income generation are part of the total process and cannot be separated from human develop-ment. The process starts with group formation and awareness creation and establishing the fundamental conditions for survival, before sustainable economic and social activities can be initiated. A great deal of attention to details is necessary, and to the inter-linkages between several eco-nomic and social small activities. This kind of co-ordination is undertaken by the groups themselves, viewing all their problems in their totality.

4. The village programmes are planned from the bottom up starting with the poorest. Even the infrastructure projects are initiated by the organizations of the poor women them-selves, sometimes in collaboration with men's groups. The essence of participation is that the priorities are set by the poor themselves as subjects in the process. This is in contrast to conventional projects where standard pre-determined technical packages of improvements and infrastructure are offered to poor communities and even implemented on their behalf, perhaps with some consultation with the richer and more powerful elements in the community. This latter is purely an additive process, where 'participation', 'poor women' and 'environmental protection' are added on as new objectives to conventional top-down planning methods and the 'delivery' of inputs from above. In conventional planning the poor are treated as objects and not as subjects of the process.

5. The process has been initiated with personal savings of the poor women themselves and with essential small grant funding. Subsequently, a blend of loans and grants from a variety of sources formed the supplementary/complementary part of the financial plan for expansion and multiplication.

All these reflect an attempt at mass mobilization, even in a particular location, using people's creativity, local resources and local knowledge as major inputs.

LESSONS FROM EXPERIENCE

From these experiments a number of inter-related lessons can be learnt for evolving a programme concept and an approach to design and evaluate activities enabling poor women to move out of poverty into sustainable development. The lessons, as identified, not only show the inter-relationship of the issues, but also the complexity of the social process. Each lesson cannot be looked at in isolation, and have been presented here separately, only for the sake of clarity. Many additional lessons could of course be drawn.

Lesson No. 1

The women's movements in most countries have focused on the issue of poor women and a great deal of energy has been generated in addressing some of their problems. Second, governments and donors are prepared to support programmes for poor women, thereby creating an 'economic' and a new 'political' space for innovation and boldness of action. Third, credit is a cross cutting issue and not a narrow sector subject or just another input like fertilizer or tractors. As a result, the issue of credit can be used to generate a command over all resources and to look at the existing institutional framework. However, the process does not start with credit but with awareness creation and group formation. Since the vast poverty crisis cannot be solved by merely helping a few individuals, these three factors taken together have acted as a driving force for initiating and evolving successful comprehensive programmes and a new form of accumulation in a few countries. It is the programme perspective that is comprehensive; the specific activities evolve in response to the needs and priorities of poor women and an 'entry point' may be located in a specific sector or activity. Even if the process starts with a specific sectoral entry point, as was the case in the Pakistan soakpit project, it can evolve in a comprehensive manner through a participatory process and move to other social and income generating activities. The process can be multiplied depending on the available political space. The political space itself can be widened by advocacy, re-moulding elites, building countervailing organizations of the poor and through the influence of sensitive donors who are not motivated by their own vested interests.

Having said this, the limits of existing state structures to provide such innovative support systems, across the board, cannot be ignored. So also the extent to which elites can be 're-moulded'. Nevertheless, the lesson is clear that these alternative grassroots processes can serve to reinforce democratic and political processes, and help in building structures with social justice built into them.

Lesson No. 2

In initiating such a programme 'innovation' is the operative word. The conventional project approach and marginal tinkering with existing institutions and structures, adding an objective here and there and calling this 'integrated', does not work. An innovative approach is necessarily that which reserves past approaches and initiates new processes. These new processes are characterized by poverty alleviation, income generation, skill development, social awareness and investment activities, integrated into a process of creating a self-actualizing and self-reliant community. Self-reliance also implies a creative evaluational system and an ecologically sustainable process for development.

The innovations now have a material basis in the successful cases of new forms of capital accumulation and human development with equity. Therefore, it is not necessary to 're-invent' the wheel. A coherent approach and methodology is emerging which needs to be applied experimentally and, as the process evolves, to be further refined in different socio-political circumstances and adjusted to country specific and local conditions. This is not a matter of 'replicability' but of multiplying the process on the basis of experiential learning and a sensitive problem solving participatory approach, rather than a pre-determined, prescriptive and rigid bureaucratic approach to a standard 'model'. The question of replicability does not arise, but the process can be multiplied.

Lesson No. 3

The programme should involve clearly identifiable homogenous groups of poor women, i.e., the poorer of the small farmers and landless labourers, poor women in urban slums and shanties. There is a conceptual issue here. 'Rural' or 'small farmers' or 'women' per se cannot automatically be labelled poor. The gender issue must be qualified by the class and equity issues. Cultural commonalities are also important. Homogenous groups of poor women would need to be organized even on ethnic lines, before a technical package or credit can be introduced. Their survival and social needs would also need to be addressed simultaneously as part of a total package. Lack of conceptual clarity and proper in-built participatory monitoring of these issues has, in the past, led to easy diversion of resources meant for the poor to the rich, irrespective of gender.

Lesson No. 4

The poor women should not merely be tagged onto a technical sectoral package. The design should start with awareness creation, building the poor women's groups, conscientization, and then initiating a poverty alleviation strategy and process based on their needs, resources, knowledge system and capability, with a view to improving their condition to the next possible economic and social level. The technical package should be a response and a support package. Even this should be identified in relation to their needs, knowledge system and capabilities and with their full participation. Investment and credit should be preceded by social mobilization, conscientization and building organizations of the poor where necessary, so that they can mobilize local surpluses and also receive external inputs only when required. In other words, there is a stage when poor women have to overcome their immediate survival problems, become credit-worthy in the more conventional sense and be able to assert their right to it before formal institutional credit can be introduced. Otherwise, the credit can be tranquilizing or be siphoned out of their hands, before they can use it in a productive manner. The organizations of the poor should continuously monitor the results themselves. All this means a great deal of attention on preventing the need for default, initiating hundreds of small scale activities, building small assets, solving problems as they arise, ensuring that the agreed tasks are done and correctives introduced while the problems are small.

Lesson No. 5

The programme design should recognize that the poor do not divide their lives into the purely 'economic' or 'social' or 'credit'. The overall design should be capable of responding to the basic needs of the poor in an inter-related fashion, and look at issues of production alongwith health, rural indebtedness, and other inter-related social issues connected with production organization. Only the poor women, through dialogue among themselves, can identify their priorities. Each support programme has a set of guiding objectives (listed hereunder) but these should not be imposed in any particular sequence. The support system should have the capacity to first prevent erosion of the poor women's basic resource base—i.e., forests or other resources like water—and then support activities, in a flexible manner, initiated by the poor women.

The programme should also ensure that the people's surplus is kept in the people's hands. The marketing system or credit system should not be instrumental in continuously preventing the poor women from holding on to whatever small surplus they are entitled to by their own activity. The guiding objectives of the support programmes are:

1. Increased small scale agricultural and livestock production and income generation through home based activities for the poor need to be encouraged. There is clearly considerable 'economic' space and scope, particularly in rural areas, for intensification of crop production by cost effective methods of water management, improvements of soil, good crop husbandry, animal husbandry, mixed farming, community forestry (on a food, fodder fuel wood, medicinal herbs basis) recycling of waste, and use of renewable resources. A concept of household food security can also be evolved in the process. A great deal of knowledge to evolve a technical

package exists either in the people's knowledge system or in the research institutes, which is not being fully utilized. While research continues to deepen the knowledge system; sufficient information is available to initiate a process towards the achievement of this objective. Full utilization of the existing knowledge system needs to be built into each programme. Likewise, in urban areas there are a great many income generating activities in the informal sector which poor women can undertake, if properly organized on the basis of what they already know. Training of skills can come later if necessary.

2. Improved social conditions for the poor women can be effected through improvements in environmental sanitation, primary health care, nutrition and education. This set of objectives must take into consideration the reality already mentioned, that while economically some countries have moved into middle income status and show high growth rates, the social indicators could rank the country amongst the lowest. The reverse is also sometimes true: good social indicators but poor growth rates. The main point is that the poor do not see their lives only in material terms, and economic and social aspects have to be seen together in a holistic approach.

3. Moreover, preventive medicine and new forms of learning should also be a major part of the social process. The whole process should be culture specific and should not be dependant on crude transfer of technology or pure market processes with their inherent valuation preference and biases. To be culture specific, several processes used in the recent past will have to be reversed and the correct cost effective processes will have to be evolved with awareness creation, participation and retrieval of people's knowledge as integral components.

4. Expansion of small scale local infrastructure, industrial, construction and service oriented activities which provide forward and backward linkages into points 1 and 2 above, giving supplementary income to poor households, as well as creating full or part time additional income generating work for poor women, need to be evolved gradually as the process goes forward.

All these inter-related objectives need to be part of a continuing process, for the most part using local resources and knowledge, as far as possible with nearby markets so that the product and factor markets could serve to generate secondary multiplier effects with forward and backward linkages at the local level, and thereby serve to accelerate an autonomous accumulation process. The scale of activities also should be within the capacity of the groups of poor. Otherwise the benefits will not accrue to the poorest. As has been stated, the activities should be identified by the poor themselves with a high level of awareness. These objectives have to come in natural sequence starting with activities poor people are accustomed to and not by pre-conceived attempts at skills training, credit delivery, or setting up small income and employment generating industries in an ad hoc fashion.

Lesson No. 6

In order to achieve the objectives in the manner indicated and ensure participation of the poor women and sustain the process, it is clear that institution building at village/local level, as well as at the central government level is required and would need to be built into the design. The mere existence of a woman's division in a central government ministry or dependence on any NGO is not enough. A major effort at social mobilization is required, in which participation of the poor women as the subjects in development and not merely the objects becomes a key element. Three critical aspects for ensuring participation of poor women are:

1. Strengthening of existing innovative grassroots NGOs and participatory organizations of poor women and building new groups for participatory sustainable development activities at the village level. As identified, a few innovative NGOs are experimenting in the field and important lessons have been learnt from these experiments which can be multiplied. The work of these NGOs are often supported by committed members of the academic community. The lessons learnt from these experiences is that poor women in interaction with committed academics can be mobilized, conscientized and organized into groups for development action. It is a process of mobilization of the poor women into homogeneous

groups, mobilization of resources for both small group activities and later group construction and management of small irrigation and water projects, other small capital works, and group access to credit and marketing. This is the only way to ensure development with equity. It is compatible with the family farm concept, growth of off-farm employment and a variety of other community based activities as the local economy diversifies. It is clear that not all NGOs are supporting these tasks and some are more 'top-down', bureaucratic and charity oriented and do not address the equity issue as such.

2. Re-orientation, as far as possible, of the existing delivery mechanism of the government, making it a more flexible support system to reach the village level poor. The government does not have to implement all the activities. The poor are quite capable of doing a great deal themselves if properly organized and supported. This would require, on the one hand, policy dialogues and sensitization of the bureaucracy, particularly at the district level and below, making the procedures of the line ministries more flexible and deepening their impact on the support for village level poverty alleviating activities, and, on the other hand, strengthening the capacity of inter-sectoral co-ordinating mechanisms, if they exist. If they do not exist they may have to be created. There would need to be appropriate technical package and finance should be available, if necessary, to support the process and build on what the poor are already doing. There are a number of committed individuals in the bureaucracy or technical services who are prepared to make a new kind of commitment to poverty alleviation. They need to be identified and involved in the process. As social mobilization proceeds, the groups have an impact on the support system and can prevent the diversion of resources meant for the poor to the rich. This is where they act as a countervailing force.

3. Re-orientation of credit institutions for mobilization of local savings and supporting small income generating activities of the poor, with flexible procedures and strengthening innovative credit windows. This requires new kinds of bankers not only to take the bank to the poor, but also to commit themselves and identify with the poor. The credit institutions

have to ensure that the savings of the rural poor are mobilized and the rural surplus is kept in rural areas for the poor. The banking or credit institution needs to have a 'holistic' approach. It is not simply a matter of group lending and guarantee. What is needed is for the bank officers themselves to act as catalysts in initiating the formation of small action groups among poor women and village level organizations for the wider dialogue. Second, these latter organizations and the bank catalysts would need to assist in resolving the technical and social nature of the bottlenecks in the implementation of activities initiated by the poor women themselves. When the activities begin to generate income the bank catalyst must also ensure savings not only for loan repayments but also for future investment and asset creation to sustain the process. New norms and a flexible banking strategy suitable to each location and the specific women's groups have to be evolved. Traditional savings systems of the poor can be built on. However, initially, the poor women should not over-save as it could have an adverse effect on nutrition and health. Thus a very delicate balance has to be maintained and can only be ensured if the level of awareness is high.

Lesson No. 7

The process does not stop with strengthening NGO action, creating village organizations and reorienting the line ministries and the credit system to identify with the problems of the poor. Even where the process may have started spontaneously by the poor women themselves, it requires a new kind of continuous dialogue within and between the three above mentioned groups, leading to a series of small scale development actions. The process will require a major catalytic institution to co-ordinate and sustain the dialogue if the process is to be multiplied. In each case an innovative institution acts as a catalytic intermediary. As was seen, these intermediaries could be a government organization as in the case of women's development section of the Panchayat Ministry of Nepal, a bank as in the case of Grameen Bank in Bangladesh or the Agricultural Bank in Nepal, or an NGO as in the case of SEWA, or WWF in India, or BRAC in Bangladesh but all acting

with new norms and flexibility. Several institutions and intermediaries have to dialogue and work in a mutually reinforcing
fashion, with a new kind of motivation towards poverty alleviation,
based on commitment and empathy with the poor. This requires
new forms of communication between all the agents, right from
the initial stage.

In each case, one or two key committed individuals are required
to steer and facilitate the whole process in each experiment.
Sometimes a charismatic personality initiates and facilitates the
process. As the process evolves and organizations of poor women
are strengthened, these facilitators need to withdraw and move on
to other tasks of multiplication as may be necessary, leaving the
natural leaders to emerge.

Lesson No. 8

Training in innovative approaches for poverty alleviation is a
critical part of institution building for multiplication. Innovative
training/sensitization programmes would need to be properly
established as part of the new design and for reversing old processes. The existing staff of line ministries, banks and even some
NGOs cannot be expected automatically to provide an innovative
support system for poverty alleviation. Those in need of sensi-
tization/training are:

1. Facilitators, change agents or catalysts who can motivate,
   bring out the creativity of the poor themselves and organize
   them in small groups at the village level for participatory
   sustainable development. A great deal of attention would
   need to be paid to training the trainers of the catalysts, and
   to the content and methodology of training. Training in itself
   would have to be innovatively carried out, through action/
   research/reflection methods in a kind of praxis, where the
   barriers between trainer and trainee and research and action
   are also broken down. Training cannot be imparted by
   manuals and mechanistic methods and the content cannot be
   just skill training. This is why a methodology called Participatory Action-Research (PAR) (which will be described
   later in detail) has been evolved. When training is completed
   through this action-research process, some economic or

social activity would also have been initiated. These activities will be evidence of whether the training has been effective or not. For the facilitators and catalysts, these functions represent new kinds of paid work in lieu of formal jobs. As the process evolves, natural leaders emerge from within the poor community and the facilitator-catalyst can withdraw. The Working Women's Forum is a case in point where the natural leadership has taken over the movement and the credit society.

2. High level government officials and those who are to manage and support public institutions entrusted with poverty alleviation. As was mentioned earlier, there are individuals who can be identified, who are prepared to innovate and work with a high degree of commitment. But the procedures have to be revised and new norms introduced. This cannot be done in short and hurried courses. It is not merely a matter of giving them new information or manuals. Their commitment has to be reinforced with the reversal of past orientation and methods and training in new methodologies.

3. District level officers and staff of financial institutions who are part of the 'delivery' or support system, staff of more conventional research institutes and university departments. For these too, training, re-training and re-orientation has to be in-depth. The case of the PCRW in Nepal shows that this is not easy, but perseverance is necessary. Conventional research is different from inter-disciplinary action-research. It has to be understood that the poor are also capable of research and investigating their own reality.

4. Staff of donor agencies, likewise, need a great deal of re-orientation and training on how to support these innovative approaches. Most donor approaches and procedures are quite inadequate to the task of supporting innovative approaches which enable the benefit to accrue to the poor women. Donors also need to have conceptual clarity and be clear about their objectives and priorities. A more detailed discussion of this issue is contained in chapter VI.

Lesson No. 9

As has been mentioned earlier, innovative approaches have to start with the poor women, their creativity, knowledge system and resource base. Poor women have dignity, creativity and strength and are not waiting for charity as a handout. No government (or even banks, which are public institutions) even when it is efficient, has the capacity to deal with the magnitude of the task or myriads of problems involved with poverty alleviation, nor the financial resources to meet the needs of the large numbers of the poor, the majority of whom are women. The government (or banks) can, however, provide a sensitive support system in keeping with its policy pronouncements. Where these pronouncements are mainly rhetorical the disadvantaged group, in this case the poor women, if properly organized can assert the right to their share of the resources. They can also, through vigilance, ensure that the resources are not being diverted to the rich or the corrupt. Flexibility and responsiveness are key requirements in a support system, with the participatory groups maintaining the vigilance and monitoring the process.

For the government to provide a support system, not only new ways of functioning, new norms and new attitudes are required. Trust in the poor and commitment to poverty alleviation are critical elements in the attitudinal change that has to be brought about. These attitudinal changes cannot be legislated into being and can come with multiplication of experiments, new exchanges of information and training in which a new learning process/sensitization is involved. For these innovative approaches to work, this learning process has to be rigorously undertaken.

Lesson No. 10

As in the case of governments, sensitive donors also have to change their approach and procedures. Much of official development assistance, despite the rhetoric, is still poorly equipped for poverty alleviation focusing on grassroots level development with participation of the poor. When it comes to the issues of gender and equity together, while there is a great deal of general interest and support, the methodology for design and evaluation of programmes has not yet been fully understood nor reflected in most donor procedures. Some marginal flexibility exists in donor procedures, but these are still peripheral to their mainly conventional approaches.

Like governments, sensitive donors also can provide only a support system and additional resources when necessary. There is a recognition of the need to work with NGOs, but there is a tendency to 'use' NGOs to 'deliver' inputs rather than to catalyze a new approach for poverty alleviation. Donors (with few exceptions) too often bring their own perceptions, procedures, consultants and vested interests into the process. If the Grameen Bank expansion was a success it was because donors were not able to impose their procedures and followed the leadership of the pioneer effort. Donors have to re-train their own staff, consultants and their training institutions to better appreciate the recent lessons of experience with participatory poverty alleviation and the methodologies associated with it. Donors also have to learn and change so that they can help to operationalize the new methodologies to poverty alleviation, particularly for poor women, through the new institutions that are emerging as a result of these experiments. They have to learn to build and work with new kinds of intermediaries.

Lesson No. 11

Implied in these lessons is that the series of inter-related small scale activities which result from this poverty alleviating strategy cannot be encompassed in the conventional project approach. The project approach assumes that there is a beginning and a defined end and that all inputs and outputs are quantifiable. The activities in the new approach are inter-dependent with several linkages in the process. Finance and technical know-how are not the only inputs. The creativity of the poor, their knowledge system and local resources are important ingredients. The total resources, including local resources, recycling of waste and local energy sources must be looked at together with the financial surplus available locally. Poor women are guided in the use of resources mainly by considerations of minimizing resource utilization rather than maximizing benefits and profits in the short term. Finally, external resources when introduced would need to be a blend of grants and loan funding on concessionary terms. All successful cases of poverty alleviation were initiated with local resources, before a blend of grant and loan funding was introduced from external sources.

FROM LESSONS TO CONCEPTS

With the experiments described having been well established—
demonstrating sustainability, providing lessons and being multiplied—it is now possible to further conceptualize the methodology.
This conceptualization does not claim to represent a general
consensus among the de-professionalized intellectuals or the
activists involved. But it does attempt to generalize on the basis of
an observable reality which is in evidence in South Asia. As has
been mentioned, the methodology was originally conceptualized
in a series of three studies by a group of South Asian scholars on
the basis of the first generation experiments in poverty alleviation.[1]
The team started with a perspective, looked at some macro-micro
experiments and made the first set of generalizations. Then they
interacted with the activists in Maharashtra and further refined the
concepts with their assistance and participation. These concepts
and methodologies have been refined under varying conditions in
further experimentations in the last ten years. The concepts are
equally valid in dealing with all categories of poor, including poor
women.

It is necessary that the methodology is clearly and unambiguously
understood. Words like participation are co-opted and tagged on
to the 'delivery of inputs' processes, without reversing it. The new
methodology is not practiced with rigour and in the essentials. To
do this, it has to be recognized that good theory and practice go
hand in hand. The theory has to be abstracted from the reality,
and the practical methodology has to flow from this theory. A
priori theorizing, which ignores the necessary relationship between
theory and practice, is predominantly speculative. As has been
mentioned before, this would also require training/sensitizing of
the consultants and the staff of the various organizations involved,
on the basis of the lessons of experience, if they are not completely
familiar with the methodology of these innovative approaches for
project design and evaluation. But first they must have commitment. On the other hand, there are many who have this commitment
and can be involved. The application of the methodology has to go
beyond the rhetoric or lip service to the 'target' group, 'participation', 'poor women' and be conceptually and methodologically
correct. Evaluation of these new processes cannot be conducted
externally and only with conventional quantifiable data and statistics.

Sometimes, a part of the information can be quantified by a combination of methods including economic costs and benefits and the PQLI indicators.[2] But even here the results are not comprehensive and do not cover the whole process of social change and linked results. Evaluation itself has to be participatory and built into the process, and a series of qualitative measurements have also to be made for longer time horizons than the normal project cycles. The question of evaluation will be elaborated later in this chapter.

To summarize: the old framework of development, i.e., the growth model, trickles down with marginal reforms supported at the micro level by a conventional technocratic approach to project development and evaluation. Despite the fact that experience has shown the limitations of this approach in that the benefits do not reach the poor and marginalized groups, it is deeply rooted in the current operations of most governments and donor agencies, the integrated rural development approach and rural credit programmes. Casual references are made to target groups and participation, without any rigorous methodological or process content.

There is now a growing body of literature referred to, some of it unpublished, which has evaluated the integrated rural development projects and other such top-down poverty alleviation programmes that make use of the conventional micro-level methodology for project development and are based on cost-benefit analysis or minor variations of the same underlying principles such as the internal rate of return analysis. The evaluations indicate that a technocratically evolved package polarizes the village further, and the village rich get richer and the poor become further marginalized with a great deal of resources being wasted, unless some basic structural changes have taken place and the contradictions are not sharp. Even when this package is aimed at a 'target' group identified as the poor, and is carried out with greater efficiency in the 'delivery' mechanism with better co-ordination of bureaucratic procedures and with some attempt at consultation with the target group (often confused with real participation), it does not in itself ensure that the economic benefits reach the poor, let alone improve their condition in wider human terms.

It cannot be contested any longer that as long as the basic economic and social institutions in the village are controlled by the rich, a mere terminological separation of the poor from the rich

does not safeguard the interests of the former against the mani-
pulations of the latter. A purely technocratic thrust cannot bring
about the desired changes. The social formations at the micro-
level need to be studied before an intervention is attempted. On
the basis of these analysis some countervailing institutions have to
be built.

The problem of inter-dependence and linkages of several activities at the village level also seriously limit the conventional
project approach, which assumes a sectoral approach: that there is
a beginning and a defined end to the 'project', and that all the
inputs and outputs are quantifiable. The inter-dependent activities
must evolve taking into consideration people's awareness, and
cannot be formulated externally in a grand design or, in a pre-
determined fashion, supported by an aid package. One further
point worth mentioning at this stage is that small-scale rural
economic or social activity is guided mainly by considerations of
minimizing resource utilization rather than maximizing the benefits
and profits in the short term. This is very natural in a situation in
which there is a lack of access to resources and a need to minimize
waste. Such activity does not respond to normal investment
criteria though there can be considerable economic and social
benefits over time. Thus, it is necessary to question the value of
the conventional cost-benefit analysis theory and the project
approach under these circumstances either for designing poverty
alleviation activities or for evaluating them, particularly, when an
alternative approach and methodology, even if it is not as elegant,
is available and more reliable for the total process. When it comes
to the question of poor women and their double burden the
conventional project approach, even with its limitations, is a long
way from coming to grips with the real issues involved.

Any strategy of development involving large numbers of poor
women (or any other vulnerable group) has to begin by bringing
about unity among them. Unity among the poor women and a
spirit of co-operation cannot be legislated into existence or hurriedly
undertaken. Disunity among the poor (women and men) arises
from asymmetrical dependency relationships that tie the poor
individually to the rich. This, then, generates dependency attitudes and a vicious circle is initiated with disunity built into it. In
the case of poor women, the patriarchal system creates dependency on men. There are also other contradictions within all the

categories of women and within the groups of poor women themselves, across the board. Hence, unity formation has to start with homogenous groups. Under these circumstances, before the poor women can benefit, their dependency on the rich has to be reduced by giving them independent staying power in a conflict-ridden social environment. Then, they have to resolve some of the other contradictions by funding common interests that bind them. In some situations where there has been land reform or where other co-operative values exist, the above contradictions may not be sharp. For poor women with their double burden, they must overcome both the poverty syndrome, as well as the patriarchal one.

The question, then, is how to break out of this vicious circle, and here is where 'another' approach for the designing and evaluation of poverty alleviating programme comes into its own. It is really a process which should be understood in terms of an inter-related and varied set of activities which are undertaken in different stages. The first stage is that which begins to unite the target group: in this case poor women, or a part of it, to set a positive spiral of activities in motion. The experiments analysed show that positive interaction among poor women can be generated and sustained. The steps towards this end are as follows: (a) separate out the poor women's groups by understanding the contradictions in the social environment; (b) work on their minds to actuate co-operative values; (c) sensitize cadres for initiation and multiplication of activities (d) initiate co-operative or group activity among the target group or a sub-sector of the group, starting with a non-confrontational activity, building organizations of poor women; (e) as the co-operative base of the activity progresses, further activities can be initiated to promote positive values in the minds of the target group and critical institutions, including fora for discussion of common issues and the savings fund. These, then, ensure that the participation of poor women is further strengthened. A visual representation of this process is set out in the diagram described.

Taken together, the above steps constitute a movement towards the creation of a self-reliant base for the poor women's groups and a process which permits them to de-link from economic and psychological dependence, thereby building on their own creativity and promoting self-reliance. Activities must evolve in the carefully

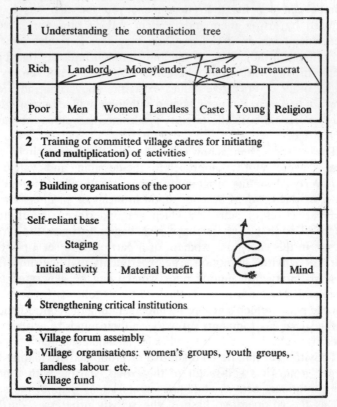

An Approach to Micro-level Development—A Visual Representation for Building Organisations of the Poor

1 Understanding the contradiction tree

Rich	Landlord	Moneylender	Trader	Bureaucrat		
Poor	Men	Women	Landless	Caste	Young	Religion

2 Training of committed village cadres for initiating (and multiplication) of activities

3 Building organisations of the poor

Self-reliant base

Staging

Initial activity   Material benefit   Mind

4 Strengthening critical institutions

a Village forum assembly
b Village organisations: women's groups, youth groups, landless labour etc.
c Village fund

staged manner and subsequent stages must be built on the collective experience of the previous stages. They cannot be formulated in a ready-made package, anticipating all the stages and assuming that all phases will proceed according to a preconceived technical plan designed from the 'top' without the involvement and understanding of the group. Central to this process is the need for the poor women to raise their level of consciousness. In the initial stages they would need to form their own organizations and thereafter work with or integrate into men and women umbrella organizations. Once this participatory self-reliant base has been built, external technical and financial inputs of one kind or another can be better received and absorbed and will not skew the benefits. The sum total of all this constitutes the process approach.

As has been mentioned, the process of building a participatory self-reliant base cannot always be a spontaneous one. Given the deep-rooted dependency relationships, the poor lack the capacity to take initiatives individually for improving their lot. The intervention of a catalyst or initiator is necessary to break this vicious circle. Such change agents and facilitators are fundamentally different from typical government rural development officials or extension workers or even the conventional rural volunteers. They need to be committed individuals who can identify with the rural poor, mobilize them, conscientize them, and help them organize themselves for participatory self-reliant development, if they cannot do so spontaneously. The identification and sensitization of such change agents now becomes a critical part of initiating or launching poverty alleviating programmes. It is worth repeating that evaluating itself is built into the process, with mid-course corrections in a continuous and participatory manner by those who are involved, and the process cannot be predetermined from the top or by outsiders.

STEPS IN INITIATING A PARTICIPATORY ACTION-RESEARCH EXPERIMENT

Further Elaboration of the Concept of Participatory Development

The experience of developing countries, in both the capitalist and socialist frameworks, indicates the need to consciously create grassroots institutions through which the people can act as a countervailing force to the systematic tendency of dependence and inequality (as in peripheral capitalist economies) and to the tendency towards centralization and bureaucratization (as in planned economies). This is where participatory development can have immediate relevance and far-reaching implications for poverty alleviation and sustainable development.

What is the essence underlying the PAR concept? The basis of this idea is the view that in many poor countries—and within these countries—the contradiction between the rich and powerful and the poor is not specified in simple terms (such as the capital/labour contradiction which may not be simply specified in terms of the wage relation). Since classes are not clearly articulated and the labour process is characterized by pre-capitalist forms, the poor are involved in a wide range of contradictions with the rich. For example, the poor tenant may be dependent on the landlord, not just for the possession of land, but also for credit, tubewell water, tractor rental and transport for carrying the produce to the market. Again, the poor peasant may have apparently no surplus available to buy fertilizers, level his land or get irrigation water. Yet the poor in a particular village may collectively have access to unutilized dispersed resources which, through organized effort and use of upgraded indigenous technology, could provide them with these inputs. Similarly, organized pressure by poor women on the local administration or landlords could get them cheaper credit, better health facilities and rent bargains. In short, in the nexus of contradictions between the rich and the poor, in a situation where the local state apparatus is not uniformly strong, there may be considerable space for the poor women to develop locally effective countervailing forces. It could be argued that in the circumstances indicated above, it may be possible to undertake small actions for specific development at the village level, viz., food production, small-scale manufacturing, small-scale irrigation projects, organic fertilizer manufacture, use of indigenous technology for the provision of clean drinking water, basic hygiene and preventive medicine. At the same time, these grassroots organizations by mobilizing their members could pressurize the landlords or the local administration for better tenancy rights, elimination of unpaid labour services, or better rental bargains. Poor women, if properly mobilized, conscientized and organized, are in a position to do all of this and also deal with the problems of patriarchy.

A participatory grassroots process implies that in achieving these relatively limited tasks, the poor women would acquire a greater awareness of their reality, increased technical expertise, using and building on their own knowledge system, and develop a scientific awareness of their economic, political and physical environment. At the same time, the achievement of specific objectives for improving their resource position through collective effort would impart greater confidence, help bring the poor women out of isolation and reinforce community consciousness. Ideas regarding the upgradation of indigenous technology organizations and the conceptualizing of experience could be provided by participatory action-researchers. These researchers and change agents would be a new breed of 'organic intellectuals' bringing to bear a 'new professionalism' based on the concepts and methodology outlined here.' They would be deeply absorbed in the culture of the poor women and also be equipped with scientific training. Such action-researchers, while engaged in the struggle alongside the poor women, would be interacting with their creative ideas and at the same time helping the women to conceptualize the results of their collective social, political productive efforts. Finally, PAR as a methodology could help rediscover the folk literature and use it to reconstruct a sense of community identity. Such consciousness could eventually charge the contemporary creative quest of the community as a whole to a major sustainable development effort.

If the grassroots organizations were linked across space and sustained each other through exchanging ideas, they could contribute to the eventual emergence not just of a new consciousness but also of new kinds of structures. Within such structures, decentralization of power and mass participation in economic/social decision-making could become a real possibility. In the short run, as has been mentioned, this process could act as a source for countervailing power to the mechanisms of inequality and repressive control. In the long run, when structural changes at the macro-level occur perhaps for reasons which the process itself had no direct control on, such organizations could form the institutional basis for developing further community consciousness and unleashing the further creative potential of the people. There is increasing evidence that with the decline of formal state institutions and loss of contact between the marginalized populace and the elites and bureaucracy, grassroots groups are performing vital community functions—not only for survival but also for development. A new kind of non-party politics is emerging as part of a new political process. Non-party means groups working in wider societal terms: in other words, struggle groups working with alternatives, but not necessarily with narrow party politics and their outmoded ideological confines. These are also the seeds of new democratic formations.

A word of clarification is necessary. The wide variety of micro-grassroots experiments in South Asia described here represent a new factor—a wide range of experience from which to learn. However, they are not homogenous or based on a common ideology. They are sometimes the results of romantic and idealistic approaches taken by charitable institutions, religious organizations, the 'small is beautiful' people, which have tried to teach the people to do 'good' things, often treating the village as a homogenous entity or 'community' to begin with. Gradually these processes can get hardened. Second, there are ideas introduced by radical political parties looking for a political constituency. They have been able to mobilize poor people to anger at the workings of the exploitative system, but have not always been able to sustain a spontaneous people's movement and/or a grassroots level experiment. Third, there are experiments which are a spontaneous response by the poor themselves as part of their struggle. Some of these represent 'seeds of change' while others are mere 'bubbles'.

At this stage, it is important to make a distinction between a 'seed' and a 'bubble'. A 'seed' can be identified with such broad criteria as equality of access to resources; equality of social, political, and cultural rights; real participation in all social decisions affecting work, welfare and politics; the end of the division between mental and manual labour, and the use of technology appropriate for this purpose. It is, however, not merely a matter of stating these objectives. Genuine participation, awareness creation and the effort to change social relations must be built into the process. One can keep adding to this list: local orientation, self-production, self-management, autonomy, solidarity and innovativeness. A 'bubble', on the other hand, is a 'soft' process and may not last for a variety of reasons. However, 'bubbles' should not be dismissed too hurriedly. They may represent 'entry points' to change, and some of them can be transformed into 'seeds' through additional sensitization programmes, training of sensitive intervenors and cadres, and an effective support system. The essential point about a 'seed' is that it is the outcome of a process of mobilization, conscientization, and organization which starts in a small way but could eventually lead to structural change and sustainable development.

The need for conceptual clarity is greater as no poor society is following a pre-determined historical pathway. No society can any longer lay claim to ideological purity. As a result of the emergence of a large state sector in many capitalist countries, and the use of the law of value in resource allocation in socialist countries, new conditions pertain. The different pathways and transitions to poverty alleviation call for new perspectives and analysis and the use of new interdisciplinary action-research methodology as has been outlined here.

The steps in initiating an innovative design

1. People's creativity the starting point: self-initiatives of the poor form the essence of a process of participatory development, where the poor operate as conscious subjects of change. They reflect on their life-situations, and take decisions to bring about changes to improve their social and economic status. The underlying assumption is that the poor are creative and are capable of taking self-initiatives for their development, but social processes have often operated to deny opportunities for the practical expression of people's creativity. A meaningful development process must lead to a liberation of the creative initiatives of the poor and of poor women who are in the majority of this category.

2. From objects to subjects: conventional top-down models for development, explicitly or implicitly, treat the poor as objects of change and the relation between the intervenor and the poor often takes the form of a subject acting upon an object. It is assumed in these top-down models that the poor have no knowledge-base or that their knowledge is irrelevant/unscientific, and the poor have to be told and instructed as to what they should do. The outcome is a delivery approach—that is, an attempt to bring development to the poor through deliveries of knowledge and resources from outside. As has been seen, these models do not provide for the additional burden of poor women. Fundamental to the initiation of a process of participatory development is the break up of this dichotomy of subject and object, and the transformation of the relation into one between two knowing subjects resulting in a creative tension between two knowledge streams, namely poor people's experiential knowledge and the formal knowledge introduced from outside. It is a dialogical process of creating change. This is also the essence of participation.

3. Investigation and analysis of reality by the poor: poor people

can be expected to undertake self-initiatives for change when they become conscientized, that is to say, when they become critically aware of their life-situation (the reality of life) and begin to perceive self-possibilities for changing that reality. Hence, the first step in the generation of a process of participatory development is to assist the poor to critically reflect upon, analyze and understand the socio-economic reality in which they live. Reality has to be posed to the poor as a problem to be investigated and as a challenge to transform. The reality that the majority of the urban rural poor face is poverty and underdevelopment: in particular, low levels of production, income and consumption, and the inability even to retain a part of the surplus they generate. Hence, the problematization of the reality must lead to an investigation and analysis of the totality of life in poverty and underdevelopment. The assumption here is that there is considerable potential for the poor to improve their lives which remain underutilized. Such potential for development should form the focus of problematization and subsequent analysis by the people.

4. Exploration of self-possibilities for actions: when the poor carry out such investigations and analysis they also begin to perceive self-possibilities to deal with the factors in their poverty, hence to change the reality. Alternative possibilities of action will be explored and the feasibility for such actions will be examined using the poor people's own knowledge and experiences and drawing from the knowledge available from outside. Resources, requirements and constraints for each action will be carefully studied. This is a process of the poor's own planning at the grassroots level. In the case of poor women, the knowledge system and internal dimensions are even more relevant.

5. Organizational consciousness: in order to initiate actions, the poor need to organize themselves in a manner (as decided by them) that best suits their purposes. They may decide to build new organizations of their choice or use existing organizations over which they have effective control as instruments of action. The important point here is the availability of organizational mechanisms and support systems in which the poor have confidence, over which they

have control, and which they can use as organs for their actions. Poor women would need to build separate organizations initially, to take care of the double burden and then link into the general organizations of the poor.

6. Initiation of actions: the poor tend to make a beginning with those actions which they can undertake with their own resources and which they feel could be implemented with success. They tend to start with fairly simple actions. The resources required for such actions are mobilized within the community itself, through collective actions to generate funds. The success of these initial actions gives them some experience in self-initiatives and also enhances their confidence in their abilities to bring about changes in their life-situations. They then embark upon more actions and go into larger and more sophisticated actions which involve claiming and using resources from outside. When they reach this stage, they begin to make claims and bargain for resources available from the social system (e.g., extension services, credit facilities, training and infrastructural facilities) so that their own resource base is strengthened and supplemented, thereby improving their capacity to initiate more actions. There is, then, an interaction between the poor groups and the socio-economic system with the poor making claims, bargaining for improvement in their access to social resources, while at the same time mobilizing their own resources to further the development process. As a result of this assertion, the socio-economic system will now begin to respond to the needs and requirements of the poor and to serve their interests better.

7. From action to reflection: reflection on actions, that is, to review and evaluate the ongoing actions as a regular practice is undertaken by the poor groups themselves and constitutes an important element in a participatory development process. Reflections on actions are needed to learn from experience, for early correction of mistakes, to identify problems and constraints and to seek ways to cope with them, to assess the benefits accrued from actions and to explore possibilities of improving the on-going actions as well as initiating new ones. Reflection enhances the poor's knowledge and understanding and helps to improve the quality of their actions.

8. Capacitation of the people: as the people's self-development process unfolds, people will begin to improve their capacities to conceive development ideas, plan, implement and manage development actions. A wide range of opportunities will be created for the practical expression and development of talents and skills that lie dormant among the poor. Leaders, intellectuals, animators, managers, etc., will emerge from the action process reducing over a time the dependence on outside catalysts. The poor will tend to become increasingly self-reliant in their thinking and action and begin to develop autonomous capacities for action. The women's movement has raised women's consciousness and now the gender and equity issues have to be responded to not only at the philosophical level but also through concrete development actions undertaken collectively.

9. Diversification and multiplication of actions: initially, the poor women's groups will naturally tend to start with the problems and issues of immediate concern to them and which they can tackle with confidence. With increasing conscientization and experience gathered in action planning, they will tend to diversify their actions to include other aspects of their socio-economic lives. Self-initiatives are educational experiences which expand people's horizons. New problems, issues and needs will be identified for investigation, analysis and initiation of actions. The success of one action creates the possibility of undertaking another, setting in motion a flow of successive actions. Furthermore, the process tends to multiply from one group to another and from one village to another. Successful actions of one group demonstrate to others in a village the possibilities of self-development. Moreover, after a point, people's groups tend to develop an urge to expand the process among others, for they begin to realize that it is only when several groups join hands and begin to act together that they will have the strength and the bargaining power to tackle larger issues of common concern to them. The logical outcome of this process is an empowerment of poor women, the development of their capacity for self-development and the emergence of the poor women as a counter-power within the socio-economic system capable of asserting their rights and claims to improve their lives.

Role of the Animator

As has been mentioned, a process of participatory development (as described above) rarely emerges as a spontaneous phenomenon. The poor, including poor women, need to be stimulated and assisted to initiate such processes. In order to undertake self-initiatives for change, the poor need to understand the socio-economic reality in which they live, perceive self-possibilities for bringing about changes in that reality, develop the capacities to translate the possibilities into concrete actions and to manage the actions. This is not a matter of 'skills' training in the narrow sense of technical skills or a manipulative process in the name of 'participation'. All categories of the poor need to develop their intellectual skills (to investigate, reflect upon, analyze and understand) as well as their practical skills (to organize, implement, and manage actions). This defines the role of the outsiders, namely to assist the poor to bring out and acquire the intellectual and practical knowledge needed for their self-initiated development process. The role of the outsiders may be conceived as consisting of two main elements, namely animation and facilitation.

1. Animation: is a process of assisting the poor to develop their intellectual capacity to investigate the reality of their life-situations, analyze the relevant issues, understand the factors creating poverty and deprivation and through such understanding to perceive self-possibilities for change. They are animated when they understand the reality and perceive possibilities for changing that reality. The outcome of animation is conscientization. Animation is the outcome of a specific mode of interaction between the outsiders and the poor. The essence of this interaction mode is the evolution of a subject-to-subject relation between the two parties (replacing the conventional subject-to-subject relation). The poor have a knowledge-base rooted in experience, practice and living with nature and society. This knowledge has its own validity and relationality. On the other hand, outsiders bring with them knowledge derived from formal education. These are two different knowledge streams each having its own scientific basis. The delivery approach to development seeks to transfer formal knowledge to the poor and disregards the poor's own knowledge as unscientific or irrelevant. It is a

subject to object relation. On the other hand, a participatory approach seeks to achieve an interaction between the two knowledge streams creating a mutual learning process. It is an interaction between the two worlds, capable of systematizing the knowledge of the poor, creating new knowledge and generating seeds of change. Animation seeks to break the dichotomy between subject and object and to evolve, as far as possible, a relation between two equals.

Such an interaction mode requires the adoption of a dialogical approach and even these steps cannot be taught or applied mechanically. Teaching, instruction and transfer of skills will be replaced by discussion, dialogue, stimulation of self-reflection and analysis, and sharing of experience and knowledge. The starting point for this purpose should be an attempt to initiate a dialogue with the people on the reality of their life-situations. The reality that people face (poverty, underdevelopment and deprivation) should be posed to the people as a problem for their investigation, as a challenge for them to respond. By raising key questions such as: why do we have low incomes? why is our production low? why do we buy our needs at high prices and sell our produce cheap? can we not find new kinds of work in the informal sector? what access do we have to different kinds of resources? why do we eat certain kinds of food? The animator has to stimulate/provoke the people to come out with ideas, issues and factors that they perceive as barriers in improving their livelihood. Dialogue with the people must lead to a re-evaluation of poor people's own basic perceptions of issues pertaining to their life-situations.

Dialogues enable the poor to systematize their own experiences. Besides, the interaction with the animator enables them to improve their knowledge-base by absorbing the relevant formal knowledge brought in by the animator. The outcome is a synthesis of their own and formal knowledge. From such problematization, analysis and the knowledge creation that follows, they will begin to perceive self-possibilities for change which form the basis for their actions to change the reality. Hence, actions are rooted in the investigations and analysis carried out by the people themselves assisted by the animator. This approach may be contrasted to the normal run of development projects where the underlying social analysis for projects is carried out by outside professionals and the poor are at best involved in the implementation phase of the projects.

2. Facilitation: animation is a necessary but not necessarily a sufficient condition to enable the poor to undertake and manage development actions to transform their realities. There are a host of factors which operate to keep the poor passive rather than active. Given their behaviour patterns (often non-innovative and non-experimental in nature) and lack of experience in undertaking self-initiatives for change, it will take time before they begin to develop the confidence in their abilities to bring about changes. Hence, an external input in the form of facilitation is often required to assist the poor to initiate actions for changing their conditions. Animation by breaking mental barriers begins to show possibilities for change. Facilitation is an attempt at assisting the poor to overcome practical barriers to action. The animator with his formal education, wider knowledge of socio-economic contexts, and links with the governmental machinery and service delivery personnel should be able to assist the people to cope with their practical problems. Such facilitation can take several forms such as:

   (a). Assisting them to acquire basic management and, where necessary, technical skills, building on their own knowledge.
   (b). Assisting them to develop contacts with formal service agencies, institutions and bureaucracies relevant to their action programmes, and to develop skills and knowledge required to deal and negotiate with them.
   (c). Assisting them to improve their access to material resources, such as, credit available within the socio-economic system.
   (d). Assisting them to translate their developmental ideas into concrete activities and programmes and to work out the implementation plans (a kind of consultancy role).

3. Progressive redundancy ('Self Liquidation'): an important characteristic of the animation and facilitation roles should be its transitional character, that is its progressive redun-

dancy over time as the poor develop their own capacities to initiate, undertake and manage their development. The animator's interaction with the poor must lead to capacity build-up among the people, and a crucial test of an animator's success must ultimately be his ability to render his role redundant over time within a given community or village so that he is released to start similar work in another village. Self-liquidation (the ability of an animator to phase out from a given village) becomes important in two respects: (a) to ensure that the poor become self-reliant, that they develop the capacity to manage their actions without critical dependence on outsiders and (b) to ensure multiplication of the participatory development process such that the animator is released to move into other villages to start similar work.

This is a fundamental characteristic of the interaction mode for participatory development as distinguished from other modes of intervention implied in the notions of bureaucracy, vanguardism and paternalism which, in one way or another, tend to perpetuate the role of the intervenors. It is the generation of internal animators from within the village communities that enables the external animator to make his role redundant over a time. Poor people's development processes create a wide range of opportunities for the people to develop their dormant skills and talents. Investigation and analysis of reality, exploration of self-development possibilities, translation of the possibilities into concrete action plans, implementation and management of actions, development of links with formal agencies, bargaining for resources and services, and reflection and review of actions are among the many activities that the people would be actively involved in a process of participatory development. Involvement in such a wide range of actions provides a training ground for animators and facilitators to emerge from the poor themselves. These are organic skills (organic intellectuals, planners and managers). The external animator must identify such emerging ability, hold meetings and discussions with them and assist them to improve their knowledge and ability so that they develop the capacity to eventually replace him. The ratio of internal to external animators must progressively increase over a time which is in fact an indicator of the success of a project of this nature.

It may be noted that self-liquidation does not necessarily mean a complete withdrawal of the external animator from a given location. It should rather be taken to mean the evolution of a state of non-dependence on him, with the poor able to act more or less autonomously such that they are no longer dependent on the external animator to initiate, undertake and manage development actions. The external animator may continue to keep contacts with them, provide consultancy services at their requests, and assist them in other ways, but the animator's constant presence is no longer a requirement. He shifts his role from that of an animator to a visiting consultant and perhaps a trusted friend.

EVALUATION

In the foregoing sections the steps for initiating a participatory experiment, whose basic objective is to enhance the status of the poor women (and for that matter poor of all categories) and enable them to move out of their poverty, has been enunciated. In this process the poor are creatively self-engaged and assert their rights which is also a part of self-reliant development.

Irrespective of whether a government agency, a bank or an NGO initiates the experiments or whether they emerge more spontaneously, and irrespective of whether the activities start with a particular entry point, its evolution must be seen as a self-generating process where each stage is built on the collective experience of the previous stage. This is how the process is made sustainable. Thus, this collective experience needs to be periodically assessed and systematized. This is the task of evaluation.[7]

Since participation is central to both the approach and design, with poor women as the subjects and not merely the objects of the process, participation is also a natural corollary of the evaluation process.[8] In this sense evaluation is part of the internal dynamics of the process, as well as an assessment of progress from the standpoint of the perspective from which the objectives are derived—in this case enabling poor women to move out of poverty into sustainable development. To the extent that the poor women have participated in the process, it is also easier for them to evaluate it. This also helps to de-mystify evaluation and relate it to the daily tasks and work that all participants need to undertake. This kind of evaluation also pays attention to detail.

Figure 1
Sociogram for Evaluation of Rural Development Projects

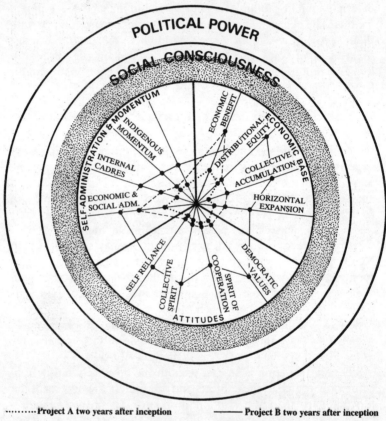

.... **Project A two years after inception**   ———— **Project B two years after inception**

- - - - **Project A five years after inception**   ▨ **Project B degree social consciousness achieved**

Source: G.V.S. De Silva, W. Haque, N. Mehta, A. Rahman and Ponna Wignaraja, *Towards a Theory of Rural Development*, Lahore: Progressive Publishers, 1988.

Conventional evaluation requires an outside evaluator who, in a sense, exercises control over the process. But in a situation of participatory development where the action-reflection process is a continuous one, internal evaluation provides the necessary control, raises further awareness and the capacity for self-management. It is this kind of evaluation which also leads to corrective actions and to subsequent development actions. The internal motivational objective is to raise the poor women's understanding of their experience through collective assessment, improved articulation, problem solving and commitment to the tasks they have set for themselves. They also learn from their total experience and derive a political resolve towards group action for achieving their objectives. Individually, they cannot go very far given the magnitude of the problems they face. This is also what is meant by empowerment.

The specific criteria to be used as the focal point for such participatory evaluation purposes cannot be laid down externally in a prescriptive manner. However, the experiences that have been narrated, and the lessons that have been derived crystallize a number of criteria or values that are of strategic importance for the realization of the objectives. These values, which have been enunciated in describing the case profiles, are grouped together, however, recognizing that the set of values that the participants may choose for themselves will be specific to the phase of the activity (e.g., staging). The totality of these strategic values is thereafter viewed within the framework of the fundamental objective, namely, to enhance the political status of the poor women in the society and enable them to move out of poverty into sustainable development.

The set of criteria are all inter-related and mutually reinforcing. But they are still distinct as values. They deserve to be presented separately not only for their own sake but also, and more importantly, because they contribute to each other's growth and thereby to the total process. By presenting and discussing them separately, attention is focused upon the need to promote each of them in such a way so as to stress not only individual contributions but also their joint contributions. They are not all quantifiable, but they are measurable and changes are observable by the participants in the process. Circumstances may offer one or other of these values, individually as the one easier to promote under specific circumstances, which in turn could set the total process in motion. Finally, the whole process may be retarded or, even worse, backslide, if for any specific reason one or more of these individual values trail too far behind, and vigilance against this possibility must therefore be exercised by all the participants.

Five clusters of inter-related criteria or values are listed below. They are:

1. The basic institution
2. Attitudinal criteria
3. Criteria for economic base
4. Criteria for social aspects
5. Self-administration and momentum.

The Basic Institution

The basic institution, a value by itself, that poor women need to create is the forum for systematic deliberation by the groups of poor women on all issues that concern them. This may consist of at least one weekly meeting where everyone participates. The meetings may initially be informal, allowing for the gradual evolution of a formal structure. As this structure evolves, it may be assessed from time to time in terms of the contribution it is making to the mobilization of constructive ideas, to removing inhibitions in the way of free exchange of thoughts, and to the structuring of discussions for more efficient deliberations. Thereafter, matters such as income or health or family planning can also be brought into the evaluation.

In addition to the weekly forum, which all members of the group are encouraged to attend, forums for different sub-sets of the poor women and others in alliance with them are also important. The more people—men, women, youth, different castes, or various cross-sections of these sub-sets—who acquire the practice of getting together for constructive discussion of questions of common concern and mutual interest, the better. It is out of this process that new types of participatory village level organizations emerge which benefit the poor. These cannot be prematurely legislated into being. They must not be confused with the formal decentralized structures created by governments from the top.

Attitudinal Criteria

The establishment of a self-reliant activity base, if successful, will itself contribute to promoting positive attitudinal values. Conscious attempts to diagnose, assert and mutually stimulate such values brings them to the fore and contributes to turning them into a driving force for further action. In other words, these values bring about a realization that the groups can effect change in their condition. The following are some of the more important values:

1. Sense of solidarity: meaning an affinity among the poor groups that makes them stay together and turn to each other for material and emotional support, a concern for each other's well being, and an urge to have constructive dialogues with each other about issues of individual, mutual and common concern. This is why there is a need for homogeneity.
2. Democratic values: meaning a concern that the specific views of each should be listened to, a respect for each other's views and a desire not to impose decisions on others but to try to arrive at a consensus.
3. Spirit of co-operation: that is, not only getting together to decide on joint activity and to act accordingly, but also to go beyond one's formally assigned responsibility to take constructive interest in the work of others and assist them in performing their tasks. This spirit of co-operation may be extended not only to the participants but also to those who may not yet have joined the group, but whose inclusion in the process, through the demonstration of the economic and social value of the activity, remains one of the objectives.
4. Collective spirit: meaning an urge to see common interests of the group as a whole and to seek fulfilment by contributing to the promotion of such interests.
5. Creative spirit: meaning an urge to innovate, to seek new resources, to seek and innovate new technology, to make organizational and administrative innovations, to experiment, to solve problems and not to run away from them or expect others to solve them.
6. Spirit of collective self-reliance: one of seeking maximum fulfilment in mobilizing the group's own physical and mental

resources, looking at external resources as a secondary and supplementary means only. Not seeking external resources at terms dictated from outside, not accepting external charity, and a resolve to repay all external debts.

Criteria for the Economic Base

Economic benefit: It is axiomatic that the participatory development project must bring economic benefit to the participants in due course. Without this, economic staying power is not increased, and dependence on the traditional exploitative economic base is not reduced. Furthermore, at the level of subsistence or below subsistence, where the poor are basically struggling with life, material incentives should be an important motivation to mobilize them for co-operative effort. But material benefits cannot be looked at in isolation.

Distributional equity: The economic benefit must accrue to the members of the group in a way that is assessed by the participants to be fair. Failing this, the activity itself will generate divisive contradictions among the participants and frustrate the fundamental objective of reducing such contradictions.

Collective accumulation: The activity for development should generate a process of collective accumulation, i.e., there should be an agreed arrangement by which a portion of the economic benefit is pooled as collective savings for the building of collective assets. Such assets, which are the visible symbols of the collective, would enable growth of the activity base, contribute to the paying off of any external debts which is necessary for self-reliance, and expand and strengthen further the material basis of collective solidarity. This should not prevent personal savings or individual asset creation over and above this collective accumulation.

Horizontal expansion: The activity should expand horizontally, in the sense, both of expanding the size of local participation and of multiplication in other areas.

Developing linkages: In order to reap the benefits of multiplication systematically, and also to establish systematic, mutually stimulating and supportive relationships with other self-reliant efforts that may already exist elsewhere, social and institutional linkages with all such ventures need to be formed. Periodic joint 'workshops' for exchange and systematization of experiences should be fostered for such a purpose. These linkages also create additional activities and new kinds of work.

Criteria for the Social Aspects

As has been mentioned, poor women look at their lives in its totality and the economic aspects cannot be separated from the social. But for analysis it is useful to have the kind of review as in the UNICEF Status of Women and Children Reports or a PQLI index which gives an assessment of the nutritional status, health indicators, level of primary education and literacy rate inverse of the infant mortality rate i.e., the expectation of life at birth. Other social indicators can also be added, such as, participation in public bodies, leadership development, and the changing perceptions about the status of poor women and their awareness. However, these criteria need also to be applied not only in macro aggregate terms but also at the micro-level. Further, these have to be adjusted for difference in quality of life enjoyed by different sections of the poor. These indices should be relatively simple so as not to needlessly complicate the evaluation process and to minimize the conceptual and methodological problems that could arise if overly sophisticated indices are used.

The recent work at the Centre for Development Alternatives in Santiago, Chile, has attempted to define a human needs based index.[9] They have emphasized that basic human needs are quite few and can be measured, even if not completely quantified, and that basic needs are not culture specific and have been the same historically. A corollary to the above is that what has changed is the way in which basic needs have been satisfied in different cultures and in different periods of time. Apart from the earlier social indices which are not ignored, CEPAUR has listed the following human needs: subsistence, protection, affection, understanding, participation, leisure time, creation, identity and freedom. The inter-relationship between the economic and social indicators is established, for instance, by relating subsistence and physical health. If a poor woman does not eat, she falls sick. If she falls sick, she cannot work. If she does not work she cannot earn an income and thereby gets trapped into a vicious cycle affecting her total life.

Self-administration and Momentum

Experience in economic and social administration: An attempt
should be made to systematize the experiences in economic and
social administration that the process itself generates, so that these
may be applied in other areas as the project multiplies, and further
administrative innovations may be built upon such systematic
experiences. This implies techniques of self-management by small
groups.

Generation of internal cadres: For its further development and
multiplication, as has been mentioned, a process must generate
internal cadres, who are to play the leadership role in mobilizing
the poor for various economic, administrative and value-generating
tasks of the project, who will be rooted in the daily lives of the
poor and who will demonstrate exemplary personal values. They
will also be the 'change agents' or catalysts in multiplying the
process and linking with similar activities in other areas.

Indigenous momentum: The process should acquire indigenous
momentum of its own in material, institutional, psychological and
leadership terms and thereby become truly self-reliant and sustainable in an overall sense. A crucial test of this is whether the
process can continue without loss of momentum if the original
initiators, whether external or internal, and any external resources
are withdrawn. No amount of progress in any other sense can be
considered fundamental if the process would receive a serious
setback at the withdrawal of its external initiators and external
resources.

Overall Evaluation

The question may be asked: can such different criteria as listed
above be aggregated in order to obtain an assessment of overall
progress of the process?

As has been stated, the different criteria may all be considered
important and mutually reinforcing. There is no room, therefore,
for a linear trade-off between them, and the use of relative quantitative weights for aggregating them into a single indicator of
progress as is done in conventional social cost benefit analysis.
One digit cannot be added for participation in an internal rate of
return computation. Some criteria may have greater priority in

certain stages of development of the process than others: but, among the criteria appropriate for each stage, there must be significant progress in terms of each for balanced development of the process as a whole.

Moreover, an aggregate of the above criteria alone would be akin to a 'physical mixture,' which would, however, be unable to indicate whether the necessary qualitative change is taking place. The basic question to ask is whether, as a result of progress being made in the several dimensions discussed above, a change is taking place in the social consciousness of the target group. The development of social consciousness, which consists of (a) an understanding of exploitation in the society and (b) liberation from psychological dependence on those which makes exploitation possible, requires social education—analysis of experience, concrete action, reflection, and deriving lessons from experiences of other societies. Without social education, a mere decrease in the dependency relation in the economic base will not reduce dependency in the superstructure or raise social consciousness.

Finally, there is the question of the fundamental task—empowerment of poor women. The test for this is whether the principal process of exploitation, of which the poor women are the major victims, is being reduced by virtue of the increasing strength which the group derives from the process, and whether conditions are being created to move towards asserting the group's power as direct producers in society and for enjoying the benefits.

The methodology of evaluation set out here does not mean that outside or external evaluation is not necessary or possible. What it means is that the role and training necessary for an outside evaluator is changed. Outside evaluators themselves have to be participant evaluators. By having identity with the total process and in interaction with the participants they ask new questions. They could also have a facilitating role to play while evaluating. Coming into a complex process, hurriedly, with a few standard rules of thumb, using only quantifiable indicators and trying to evaluate the interrelated and inter-disciplinary process with questionable statistics is too simplistic. It is no longer considered very helpful either to the participants or to those in the support system. A new professionalism is required. Here too, just as in the design stage, a new kind of training and sensitization needs to be imparted to those who are trying to evaluate innovative poverty alleviating processes for their own purposes, whether they be staff of government agencies, banks, academic institutions or donor agencies. The internal participatory evaluation plays a far more important and necessary role than the formal external evaluations in these innovative approaches for poverty alleviation.

An outside evaluator also often brings his own perspective and world view into the evaluation process.[10] The evaluator's world view and commitment to the process has to be made explicit, before the evaluation can be meaningful. An outside evaluator, in order to be effective, needs to go to the field with a deep understanding and identification with the objectives and the underlying approach, undertake concrete field investigations of the reality followed by reflection and analysis jointly with the participants and then form a systematic understanding of what is observed regarding the process as a whole. If the empathy and commitment of the external evaluator is not there and if the participatory process is not undertaken, the external evaluation can also distort the process.

With the lessons in perspective, and with the concepts and methodologies which evolved from the South Asian experience, the study then proceeded to look at some of the experiences in Africa and Latin America (albeit selectively and within the limitations of the time available) to assess to what extent the lessons learnt could help to initiate innovative processes and build on, where possible, on-going activities.

NOTES

1. See 'Towards a Theory of Rural Development,' and 'Bhoomi Sena: a Struggle for People's Power, op. cit.
2. These indications are elaborated later in this chapter.
3. This annex is based on the experience of the Participatory Institute for Development Alternatives (PIDA), Sri Lanka and was prepared for the UN University/UNDP Interaction Programme for Senior Action Researchers in South Asia (see 'Re-focusing Praxis,' Dossier No. 5, United Nations University South Asian Perspectives Project) by Ponna Wignaraja, Sirisena Tilakaratne and the PIDA action researchers. The methodology of the project design and evaluation was first written up in 'Towards a Theory of Rural Development,' and further tested in the 'Bhoomi Sena,' study by Wahidul Haque, Niranjan Mehta, Anisur Rahman, Ponna Wignaraja and G.V.S. de Silva (see *Development Dialogue*, 1977: 2 and 1979: 1). The methodology has since been further refined and experimented with at PIDA and several other institutions over the past few

years. These efforts have helped further refine the underlying concepts and methodology under varying socio-political conditions.

4. See also Robert Chambers (1983), op. cit.

5. It is not possible to state the steps in a manual form, as this is too mechanistic. However, it is possible to restate some concrete steps which are an essential part of the process. If any of these steps are left out the process itself becomes soft and 'bubbles' rather than 'seeds' are generated. Such a listing has been found useful when training catalysts and internalizing the process.

6. The information for this section has been gleaned primarily from the monthly meetings of the PIDA action-researchers and from the experiences of action-researchers in some of the other experiments described.
See also S. Tilakaratne (1985).

7. See 'Towards a Theory of Rural Development,' op. cit. (pages 71–136) for a more detailed discussion of 'Micro-level Development: Design and Evaluation of Rural Development Projects'. The main clusters of evaluation criteria are given in the 'Sociogram' at the end of the above study. Whilst some refinements have been introduced to the basic criteria enunciated by the group of South Asian scholars, the original presentation is still valid and hence re-stated here.

8. See report of the Institute of Development Studies, University of Rajasthan, 'Women's Development Programme of the Government of Rajasthan: A Review, (prepared by Sharada Jain, Mamta Jaitly, Kavita Srivastava, Nirmala Nair and Kanchan Mathur) Jaipur, 1986.

9. Desarrollo a Escala Hymana, CEPAUR/Dag Hammarskoljd Foundation, *Development Dialogue*, 1986 special issue (soon to be published in English), Uppasala, Sweden.

10. Roland Hoksbergen, 'Approaches to Evaluation of Development Interventions,' *World Development*, Vol. 14, No. 2, 1986.

Potential for Innovative Approaches in Africa

THIS chapter is situated within the current debate on the African crisis, and on the attempts to find answers, either by Africans or others, to the permanent poverty crisis that is being perpetuated.

In Africa, too, conventional institutional approaches for poverty alleviation have yet to benefit women, let alone poor women.[1] Some marginal comprehensive programmes exist, but few of these demonstrate the depth or scale of those described in South Asia. On the credit issue, co-operative credit societies are somewhat more successful as far as women, particularly women entrepreneurs, are concerned than the formal banks, but they too have not systematically addressed the specific concerns of poorer women.

Some of these initiatives—even where they have attempted to be 'innovative' and recognize the complexity of the problems faced by poor women in Africa and the double burden: that of being women and of being poor—are still relying on fragmented sectoral approaches and 'delivery' of inputs, like credit to the poor and skills training for income generation, and primary health care or literacy improvement. Many of them add a women's component into the same kind of aid or investment package that is technocratically evolved, identify women as a target group and add participation at the end.

The intermediaries offering the delivery of these services are for the most part the bureaucratic structures, banking institutions and charitable institutions, who have only very marginally, if at all, changed their approaches, attitudes, procedures and norms. Donors trying to work with these institutions and with their own priorities and procedures only compound the problems. The shortcomings of these conventional programmes and their constraints will not be repeated in this section as there is a growing body of literature, even in Africa, on this aspect and the problems identified are similar to those encountered in other regions.

What is important is that these evaluative studies, which have gone beyond the critique of past approaches and their additive methods, now recognize that to enable poor women to move out of poverty the approach to programme design and the micro-processes need to be looked at afresh by all concerned.[2] It is also recognized that the micro-processes should start with a proper conception of the felt needs of the poor women themselves, and with an identification of the newly created awareness. This means reversing old methods and initiating and supporting new more spontaneous processes, or designing catalytic programmes as referred to in the previous section, in a step by step manner with the poor women as the subjects. The lessons and the methodology learnt from South Asia can be multiplied in Africa as well. The fragile experiments that are beginning to emerge can be deepened, made into more comprehensive responses and expanded. In the following sections a few selected cases under different socio-political circumstances are analyzed from this viewpoint.

The cases selected are: the Development Education Programme of the Catholic Diocese of Machakos in Kenya; the Joint Nutritional Support Programme in Tanzania; the Savings Development Movement in Zimbabwe and the Six S Association in Burkina Fasso. There are a few other cases which also could be studied where participation and sustainable development is becoming evident as in the experiments of ORAP in Zimbabwe and CONGAD in Senegal. The network of participatory action-research in Africa has also attempted to identify a few of the other cases which even though fragile have some of the distinguishing features. The four cases illustratively described in the following sections, are, however, sufficient to demonstrate the potential for innovative approaches enabling poor women to move out of poverty into sustainable development, using the methodology and the processes under varying socio-political circumstances, emerging from the lessons of the South Asian experience.

KENYA

The Development Education Programme of the Catholic Diocese of Machakos

The Setting

Since independence, one strand of Kenyan development was influenced by the philosophy of Harambe. According to Harambe, people in their local environment were required to initiate development activities based on their felt needs and with contributions from their own labour and savings. The role of the government was to provide a support system of extension services and additional finance. This process was to ensure cost sharing in development between the government and the people. This approach was partly motivated by a realisation that the government would not be able to carry out the major task of poverty alleviation as a capital intensive top-down process, because of the magnitude and complexity of the problems, lack of capital and experienced manpower. To facilitate this form of grassroots mobilization and participation, the government established several institutions like the Provincial Development Committees and District Development Committees. The people, on their part, organized themselves and formed many parallel community-based groups with the objective of pursuing their own development.[3]

It is in this context that women's groups, created by themselves for working collectively and communally come into their own. Women's groups have existed in Kenya since the pre-independence period. For many of these, the whole village was the operational unit and the groups were not necessarily homogenous or confined to poorer women. An important characteristic of the pre-independence groups was their informal nature and their function as mutual aid women's work groups. Today, some of these women's groups have a more defined organizational structure, and the activities that are encouraged are not only those which are beneficial to the felt needs of the group but also to the community. Women's groups undertake a wide diversity of income generating activities, such as, cash crop farming and poultry keeping. Some of them have established group revolving funds, such as savings clubs. With these savings they are also able to undertake larger community activities like tree planting, construction of schools, roads and bridges and adult literacy programmes. Some of these women's groups are supported by NGOs. In Kenya, most NGOs are not poverty oriented. Many are branches of foreign NGOs. They are charitable organizations which now adopt development projects and act as a channel for external assistance and are not always distinguishable from the bureaucratic 'delivery' processes. Some of them are marginally able to reach the poor with fragmented inputs. However, very few have taken a comprehensive approach for enabling poor women to move out of poverty into sustainable development.

It was in this setting that the Development Education Programme of the Catholic Diocese of Machakos was started as an innovative approach for poverty alleviation.[4] The Catholic Diocese functions as an NGO and covers the entire district of Machakos with an area of 14,000 sq. km. and a population of 1.6 million people. This is a semi-arid district. The intellectual underpinnings, undoubtedly, come from the newer strands of liberation theology emerging from within the Catholic Church itself.

The Process

In 1974 the Diocese appointed a full-time lay Development Co-ordinator which marked a new approach by the Church, away from the charity orientation of the past and focused on development for the poorer sections of the community. The first task of the new co-ordinator was to organize a community survey in order to identify the needs of the poor in the Diocese. The survey was popularly referred to as the 'listening community survey of generative themes' and covered family, education, subsistence, recreation, beliefs and values, and patterns of decision-making (socio-political). Adult literacy was identified as a high priority need and a pilot programme was started in 1975. Literacy classes became the 'entry point' for discussion of other concerns of the poor in the village. In this manner, though the programme started with literacy classes, as it evolved it began to encompass several other aspects involving the totality of the lives of the poor.

A women's programme was started under the literacy programme in 1978. A variety of other programmes were also added, such as, tree planting, co-operative farming, savings and credit schemes, bakeries, co-operative grain stores, consumer shops for small farmers and water projects. A water engineer and an agronomist were recruited to provide technical support and extension services. But the focal point continued to be the Development Education Programme, which in turn generated social programmes like primary health care, family life, small homes for disabled children, soil conservation and afforestation and leadership training.

The essence of the Development Education Programme is awareness creation and creation of the methodology of participatory development. The principles underlying the methodology are:

1. No education is neutral and therefore it should seek to avert suffering, alleviate poverty, discredit inequalities, open the potential for adequacy in life and abhor injustice;

2. All education and development projects should start with concerns of the poor and participatory research becomes a part of the process;

3. An animator facilitates the process and participants are recognized as having the capacity to think, reflect and take creative actions;

4. To find valid solutions to complex problems of development with equity; everyone needs to be both a learner and a teacher and a mutual learning process needs to be initiated.

The Development Education Programme identifies natural women leaders from the activity groups. These are given further training in group dynamics; handling conflicts; creating awareness in relation to their reality—why the poor do not need to be poor and what they can do themselves to overcome their poverty; how to market their produce—not to sell cheap and buy dear, not to sell their staple food—and how to finance their survival and social needs without increasing crippling debts.

This initial sensitization/training is resulting in the formation of groups visibly strengthened for other development activities. As the process evolves, leadership formation programmes, development action group formation and other forms of communication (posters, plays, songs, proverbs, etc.) are added to the dialogues. Amongst its other activities the DEP also extends credit to poor women.

To minimize economic risks for the poor women, the DEP also operates its own small revolving funds which give survival and follow-up funding in special cases to permit the borrowers to overcome unforeseen calamities. Skills training is imparted, when necessary, for community activities. Innovation has been a guiding principle in all DEP activities and the process which started with literacy training went on to awareness creation, group organization and a series of sustainable economic and social activities. The programme has now expanded to other districts in Kenya. As the programme expands and multiplies, it is being deepened and systematically supported by a church-based NGO.

From their experience so far, the NGO has identified the following elements that are crucial to a participatory poverty alleviating experiment:

1. Effective leadership, i.e., one that is committed to the poor group, shows respect for their ideas and experiences, are trustworthy and accountable and have a high degree of creativity and leadership capacity. These can be generated from within the poor community or, initially, by outside facilitators.

2. High degree of awareness among the participating groups of the poor, particularly in relation to the social forces at work and the root causes of their poverty. From this level of awareness they can also see the potential to bring about changes through their own efforts.

3. Self-organization into small homogenous groups: these groups are initiated by the leadership. There should be social homogeneity to avoid domination of the groups by more powerful individuals.

4. Support framework: as the small groups could not survive without a sensitive support system, which is not dominating or creating a new kind of dependency, the NGO intermediary provided this initially. This support system responds to the needs of the groups as and when additional resources or inputs are required. The support system functions flexibly and operates with new norms. At a later stage the intermediary could also work in the interface between government extension services, banks and the organizations of the poor, as was done in some of the South Asian cases.

5. Small Scale Projects: effective participation and sustainability where the groups begin activities that are familiar and then move to larger actions as they feel the need. The initial small activities utilize local resources and knowledge and are managed within the capabilities of the poor. As the process evolves the groups can collectively undertake more challenging community activities.

6. Less dependence on bureaucratized professionalism: overdependence on outside expertise reinforces 'top-down' processes and defeats real participation. Where external expertise is required, this has to be introduced through an interactive participatory process where everyone learns and changes.

7. Minimized risks: effective participation that starts with the knowledge people have also attempts to minimize risks rather than maximize profits. Persons living at survival and subsistence levels cannot afford the luxury of taking high risk with unknown methodologies and experiments, particularly when many of their own time-tested methodologies are also scientifically valid.

These elements reflect an attempt at reversing past approaches and creating the maximum potential for involving the marginalized and the poor, ensuring that they benefit. In order to grow in scale a larger support system and additional resources are necessary.

Multiplying the Process

An opportunity exists in the district of South Nianza, where the Machakos Development Education Programme has expanded and where the Government of Kenya with UNICEF support has a programme for training advisers and extension workers for working with groups of farmers, mainly women contract farmers, in food production. These could also later be involved in home economics and primary health care. A programme is also being initiated for training community health workers. An inter-sectoral dialogue with the central ministries and at the district level on women's programmes is also being organized. These elements can be complementary to the Development Education Programme of Machakos in South Nianza. If the two programmes can be sensitively linked they can reinforce each other.

Collaboration between the Diocese of Machakos initiative in South Nianza and the above mentioned women's programme could not only reinforce the total process for enabling poor women to move out of poverty in this district, but also provide the missing links for a comprehensive and innovative participatory approach. To achieve this, the following steps taken from the concepts and methodology in chapter III are suggested.

A brainstorming workshop to:

1. Assess the lessons from experience of the two programmes in South Nianza to enable poor women to move out of poverty into sustainable development;
2. Evaluate the Machakos NGO experience and the methodology of participation of poor women now being practiced in South Nianza;
3. See how collaboration can be arranged between the two programmes and a common perspective be evolved for an innovative comprehensive collaborative programme design for poor women in South Nianza.

For a meaningful design to emerge, the participants have to be carefully selected (committed academics and students can play a significant role as in the Pakistan or Bangladesh cases). More than one session of the workshop would be required, with interactions of the workshop members with the poor women currently involved in the DEP programme both in the district of Machakos and in South Nianza, to fully understand and internalize their experience. The NGOs should take the leadership, with government and donor agencies responding by providing the support as requested. This was one of the essential features of the BRAC, and Grameen Bank experience in Bangladesh.

Once a perspective and a broad design is arrived at, the next step is to expand the participatory base institutions of poor women by the training of additional women catalysts with careful selection of the trainers. Here the experience of the DEP should also be built upon and their training programme expanded, with small selective and well timed donor support. These catalysts would be more than technical extension workers. They would be group organizers and those who link the group with organizations providing inputs, when the need arises.

The next step would be for the catalysts to expand the process of group formation and activities, building on the process for poor women already initiated by the NGO. This expansion has to be carefully nurtured, again keeping to the outlined participatory methodology. A long enough time-frame must be provided for the expanded process to unfold, with participatory evaluation built into the process at each stage.

The fourth step is for the government and banking support systems to be reoriented so that they can respond flexibly to the needs of the poor women's groups as they are articulated. This can be done through advocacy programmes for district line ministry staff, the training of extension workers, taking the bank to the poor and training bank staff. The training imparted should follow the DEP model and not be confined only to fragmented sectors and technical skills training. With the increasing awareness, the poor women's groups themselves will begin to assert their rights to additional resources and the reorientation can help to provide a flexible response.

What this means is that instead of having several separate sectoral and training programmes in South Nianza or even at best expecting the linkages to occur automatically, collaboration can be established on the nucleus of a comprehensive programme that has been initiated by an innovative NGO. This is one method which may be able to help release the creative energies of large numbers of poor women and provide the support and co-ordination for the whole range of small economic and social activities generated by the groups. The NGO could even act as a link between the groups, the additional support system provided by government agencies and banks. The kind of role for the support system is similar to the one in Nepal in relation to SFDP and PCRW processes, and the one in Bangladesh in relation to the Grameen Bank and BRAC processes respectively. Given a meaningful time horizon a major innovative approach and programme can be developed and multiplied in other districts of Kenya as well.

Since experience has also been gained by the NGO, which is itself evaluating the process and expanding, this kind of collaboration can help speed up an on-going alternative comprehensive process of poverty alleviation focused mainly on poor women. Donor's advocacy could help to build a flexible external support system in the line ministries and banks in South Nianza. Second, this support system could also provide timely institutional and technical support and resources to the NGO, where necessary, to enable it to expand. Where one donor's resources are not sufficient it should be possible to involve other sensitive international financing institutions or bi-lateral donors in the process, with one of them as the lead agency for co-ordinating other donor's interests. This will help to protect the process and prevent too many varied donor procedures and the diverse interests of various donors from distorting the process. As more donors get involved, it is essential that they do not bring in their own procedures and evaluation criteria which could distort the participatory process at the level of the poor women themselves.

The steps suggested are basic but not prescriptive in that the initial brainstorming workshop, to establish collaboration on a comprehensive suggested design, will determine the next steps. The process as it evolves will also take into consideration the context of Kenya and South Nianza in particular. The continuous exchange of information through dialogue that will take place between the poor women's groups, the NGO, the government agencies, banks and donors will enable problems and bottlenecks to be solved as they arise. To the extent that a period of experimentation with the DEP has permitted the NGO to expand on its own, now provides an opportunity for other organizations to support such an activity. There would be many further lessons to be learnt by all concerned from such a comprehensive experience growing in scale. The original brainstorming group can transform itself into a participatory external evaluation group.

TANZANIA

The Iringa Model

A second case has been identified in Tanzania where the potential exists for a sector intervention by the government, supported by UNICEF and WHO, i.e., the Joint Nutritional Support Programme (JNSP) in Iringa, to go beyond its sectoral confines into a more comprehensive economic and social programme, enabling poor women to move out of poverty into sustainable development.

The Setting

Since independence, the cornerstones of the philosophical underpinnings of Tanzania's development have been freedom, equality, and justice. What distinguished this from more conventional development strategies adopted by most other African countries was the emphasis on mobilization, organization and active participation of the population in development. The emphasis on 'mass oriented' development through people's participation has generated significant structural changes throughout the society, especially in rural areas. In the areas of health and education, significant progress has been achieved.

The experiment in social change is not yet complete and has suffered from diffusion. After the initial experimentation with people's participation, the bureaucracy was made the main instrument of mass mobilization. The villagization (Ujaama) programme was made compulsory. Without an intermediate step of specific conscientization of the masses for development action, new learning processes and the re-moulding of the elite, it was inevitable that the early creativity of the people and leadership which was released was diffused, and only a weak 'top-down' process resulted, with people geared, for the most part, to the delivery of resources and expertise from outside. The Ujaama villages, which were the embodiment of a commitment to organize the rural population into socially and economically viable self-governing collective production units has not resulted, though some of the values and organizational arrangements exist, even in a fragile form. Apart from the achievement in education and health mentioned earlier, some community action, egalitarianism and participation are in evidence. Furthermore, not all external interventions in Tanzania helped to reinforce the strategy and this also contributed to weakening the thrust towards greater equity. It was in this context that the Joint Nutritional Support Programme was initiated experimentally in the Iringa region. This programme was not specifically designed for poor women, nor did it include the comprehensive social and economic package that could respond to their needs. However, the process initiated by the JNSP has the potential for serving as an 'entry point' to such a comprehensive programme.

The Process

Building on an earlier programme which provided drinking water in the Iringa region, what is now called the 'Iringa model', the

JNSP was initiated as a multi-sectoral primary health care programme. It was based on the concept that increased food production alone will not automatically improve the nutritional status of the poorer sections of the community. The major components of this model are monitoring of the nutritional impacts; advocacy and communication; provision of primary health care, e.g., immunization, improvement in child feeding practices; re-orientation and training of the regional administration; and sensitization of the villages for greater awareness of health and nutrition related issues.

It has been recommended that additional components should be included in the expansion.[6] These include greater emphasis on social mobilization, group formation and participation, household food security including home gardens and traditional crops, integrated training programmes and basic income generation activities and innovative savings and credit schemes. The issue of participation of poor women in such an expanded programme becomes both relevant and critical.

The JNSP now covers one third of the Iringa region. Using a nutrition focused conceptual approach to improve the health and nutritional status of children and women, and training of village health workers, the Iringa programme, in the three years of its existence, has been able to demonstrate remarkable results in reorienting the administrative structures and training of young women to conduct growth monitoring, and sensitizing the villages to the programmes of immunization and primary health care. Building upon these experiences similar programmes are to be started in other parts of the Iringa region and in the neighbouring regions of the Southern Highlands. While the JNSP in Iringa has achieved a great deal of what it set out to do in the health nutrition field, there is a great deal more that such a programmatic thrust can achieve in economic and social development for the poor, particularly poor women.

In Tanzania, from another parallel programme 'Planning Rural Development at the Village Level', new experiences are being learnt on the training of catalysts, group organization and initiation of participatory development action. This programme, initially conceived differently, has now been re-designed by a consultant from the Participatory Institute for Development Alternatives (PIDA) in Sri Lanka, (loaned by a UN agency to Tanzania). The methodology of participatory action-research (PAR), which releases the creative energy of the poorer sections of the community, can now be utilized in the Iringa model as well. The Iringa expansion should also focus on groups rather than individuals, with greater emphasis on poor women's groups. There is a potential among primary and secondary school leavers, who can be trained as new kinds of catalysts, animators, and group organizers for initiating social and development activities in the villages. In the original Iringa experiment it was young women who were trained as primary health care workers and growth monitors. Even this category of persons can be now sensitized and brought into catalyzing production and income generating activities, as well as health care. In other words, the same sectoral catalyst can function as a development catalyst.

The traditional banking system could also be brought into the process. Existing 'tontines' or savings clubs among the poor women can provide the initial resources for a series of small scale economic and community activities. In the initial stages, until the banks could be induced to create special windows to provide supplementary group credit for poor women, a small revolving credit fund can also be created by the poor women's savings to initiate the process for enabling poor women to become creditworthy through the process outlined.

In this way the 'Iringa model' which is now primarily a health nutrition sector programme can be extended conceptually into a programme of economic and social development in the Tanzanian context enabling poor women to move out of poverty into sustainable development.

An opportunity for donors

Unlike in the case of South Nianza in Kenya where an NGO was involved, what is now being suggested relates to several fragmented Tanzanian Government programmes supported by many donors.

One donor's recent activities in Tanzania included a health programme (Immunization and Essential Drugs); a JNSP (primary health care and nutrition); and a basic services programme in Iringa, Moragaro, Mtwara and Ruvuma. A programme in planning at the village level and other selected activities in community development, child care, education, communication, social welfare and social statistics were amply supported by two donors. A food production programme in the Iringa district was funded by an international financial institution. Despite all these interventions there was no significant programme for poor women. Although the above programmes naturally touched on women's concerns in varying villages, their social and economic programmes were not linked.

The government was planning to expand the Iringa model, in its original JNSP format, to the rest of Iringa region, and, funds permitting, to the other three regions of the Southern Highlands of Tanzania—Ruvuma, Mbeya and Rukwa—in separate phases. In this context, the suggestion is that the expansion should not only be spatial but should also include economic activities, particularly those relating to household food security, and a stronger social mobilization process based on training of facilitators and animators for mobilizing and organizing the poorer sections of the community for a more comprehensive social and economic development. Since there is now a clear recognition of the role that poor women play in food production in Africa and in achieving household food security, this component also needs to figure significantly in any expansion of a sectoral programme in a particular geographical area.

This presents an opportunity for designing a major innovative approach by building on these fragmented building blocks, to enable poor women to move out of poverty into sustainable development. This kind of comprehensive programme can be undertaken initially in the Southern Highlands, since the focal point to be referred, for many of these programmes is the Prime Minister's Office. Second, a high level committee cutting across various ministries and chaired by the Prime Minister already exists for the JNSP. This machinery could be used for a wider purpose as well. Third, with the experience gained with both the JNSP, the local level planning project and the food production activities, a more comprehensive programme involving poor women in the Southern Highlands could be undertaken. Fourth, there is considerable political space in Tanzania for such an innovative approach.

As in the case of the Kenyan South Nianza programme (*a*) a perspective would need to be evolved; (*b*) catalysts would need to be trained for establishing groups and base institutions of poor women and to build on their savings capacity; (*c*) the government support system for food production and other income generating activities would need to be put in place along with the health, nutrition and education programmes with advocacy and sensitizing so that a responsive and flexible support system is put in place. NGOs, the academic community and the banks would also need to be brought into the process.

Here again the government or donor is not expected to plan and implement all these activities. What needs to be done is to help initiate a process by which the concerns of poor women can be responded to with a comprehensive programme in one area building on some of the elements that exist. One sensitive institution needs to give the lead and effect the co-ordination, as was done in Nepal's PCRW. With this perspective and methodology elaborated and with various lessons from Tanzania itself, the programme needs to catalyze a process along the lines of those undertaken in Nepal, Bangladesh or India, or a combination, whichever is most appropriate to the Tanzanian context.

ZIMBABWE

Savings Clubs and the Savings Development Movement

Reference has been made of the capacity of African women including poor women to save through 'Tontines' for their survival and social needs. The following section illustrates how this cultural characteristic which also reflects a co-operative spirit can be an 'entry point' for a comprehensive programme to enable poor women to move out of poverty into sustainable development in a country like Zimbabwe. Most 'Savings' Clubs' do not, as yet, specifically address the equity issue, as such, and the special additional concerns of poor women. Savings' clubs, however, can provide an 'entry point' into the process and lessons that address the double burden. The lessons from the Working Women's Forum or the SEWA in India can also be adopted in this context.

The Setting

Agriculture is the main activity in Zimbabwe. During the colonial period, African peasants were systematically deprived of land, both qualitatively and quantitatively. As poor male Africans went in to wage labour, the women's subsistence in agricultural production increased in Zimbabwe, as was the case in other African countries. However, women did not hold land rights. They also had little access to extension services and credit. Since independence, however, there are no longer any formal legal restraints on women's access to these facilities. The banking system, however is, very traditional and is mainly collateral based. As women generally have no land, poor women in particular have no collateral for receiving credit from the banks. Even the establishment of the Agricultural Finance Corporation after independence did not result in poor peasants receiving credit, let alone poor women. The corporation had no clear policy regarding poor women. The few women who obtained credit did so through group borrowing and by virtue of being female heads of households with collateral. The Post Office Savings Banks was an instrument of savings, but not for credit.

Two movements of relevance emerged in Zimbabwe. Both of them were located in the traditional tribal social formation and the co-operative values and spirit of mutual aid inherent in it. These values were stimulated by the Independence. The first is the co-operative movement. Following independence, demobilization and the return of refugees, many ex-combatants, and political prisoners joined by other men and women from urban and rural areas started several co-operative activities. In the first five years after independence, with the resulting release of people's energies, over 800 producer co-operatives were started as a response to the problem of unemployment and poverty. This co-operative movement was supported by the Zimbabwe project which had been originally established in 1978 in the UK, with a view to assisting Zimbabwean refugees in Mozambique, Botswana and Zambia. After independence the Zimbabwe project re-established itself in Zimbabwe with the President of Zimbabwe as its patron. It has offices in Harare and Bulawayo and runs a training center outside Harare. The training, however, is mainly of a technical nature focusing on skills training. Some training in health, nutrition and education and fuller participation of women in co-operatives is also being carried out. With limited resources, the Zimbabwe project is trying to gear itself to respond to the multiplicity of daily problems and developmental needs which are faced by the members of the co-operatives. They have not established links with the traditional banking system, which is still reluctant to lend to ex-combatants and the poor in rural areas who are members of the co-operatives, even on market terms let alone in an innovative manner with new norms.

The second movement is the Savings and Development Movement. This was initiated in the late 1960s by a small group of volunteers who tried initially to start credit unions in Zimbabwe at the suggestion of the World Credit Union International Association. The credit union concept did not take off as the administration of loans was found to be more complicated than originally thought and the persons who started the unions had little training. Instead, savings clubs were formed based on the traditional 'Tontines' or rotating savings associations, in which, as has been mentioned, groups of women organized and saved to meet unforeseen needs. In the 'Tontine', members contributed certain sums of money periodically and each member received a part of these group savings at agreed frequencies to meet their needs. Members of a 'Tontine' who have an immediate need for funds can negotiate a loan on payment of interest to the member whose turn it is to draw on the fund. This traditionally was a flexible and rapid means of raising funds based on personalized relationships and mutual trust. The cost of operation is minimal since workers are volunteers and reliance is placed on local knowledge and peer pressures for processing the loans and securing repayment. It was also a system which linked savings to credit.

With the failure of the initial attempt at forming credit unions, their efforts were redirected at encouraging savings' clubs to save money as a short term alternative to the use of credit. As the number of savings' clubs increased, the Savings Development Movement (SDM) was established as a loose umbrella organization providing broad supervisory services and technical assistance, and channelling other services to savings' club members as they moved from saving to investment in income generating activities. The savings' club members are mainly women with men constituting only 3 per cent of the membership. The system, however, did not make a distinction between rich and poor women and the savings' clubs included both groups. In other words, the savings' clubs were not comprised of homogeneous groups of poor women with common interests. However, it would be possible to build an alternative poverty alleviating strategy on the on-going process.

The Process

The first savings' club was established in the Chiweshe communal area in 1963, with the help of a Catholic missionary who was working in that area to promote rural development. Twenty women and men started the club with token savings at the first meeting. Regular savings were made compulsory in the following year. Initially, no withdrawals were permitted. Gradually more clubs were established.

Independence gave a filip to the process and the establishment of the savings clubs was initiated on a more systematic basis. The Savings Development Movement (SDM) was then established and provided a loose catalytic instrument for expansion as well as for securing technical assistance. It also provided some other supervisory services.

The SDM consists of elected areas, district and provincial committees which help clubs holding savings to invest them in local productive activities, thereby generating rural development and mobilizing local resources for it. The committee also acts as a loose link between savings' club members, extension workers, local government workers and other development workers. The savings clubs have become a cost effective channel for communicating technical and other information to the women. The SDM, which has a small management group of ten members, keeps records of the activities and has tried to link members with financial institutions. It does not interfere with the day-to-day management of the savings clubs, nor does it handle the savings. But it does run training courses for the savings' club members in fields such as book-keeping, leadership and management training, and nutrition and primary health care. The SDM also arranges for a supply of agricultural inputs, such as, fertilizers, insecticides and equipment.

Savings clubs are generally initiated by an SDM member or even by an extension worker. The membership is generally from the same geographical area within a single village or cluster of villages and each club averages approximately thirty-five members. The members are not necessarily a homogeneous group of the poor peasants, though in Zimbabwe some egalitarian values prevail after independence, reinforcing some of the collective values of the tribal system. On joining the savings club each member makes a commitment to save a certain amount of money each week. No single member can dominate the club with savings larger than 10 per cent of the total. At present there are over 5,700 clubs with a membership of 200,000. However, not all the clubs are a part of the Savings Development Movement.

Clubs are initiated with the purpose of saving money, but as the savings grow and immediate family needs are met, economic activities such as subsistence farming, poultry keeping, piggeries and other activities have been undertaken with the funds. These then become mutually reinforcing savings and investment activities for further income generation. A great deal of dialogue and awareness is created around the process of savings and the use of savings and investment. The information exchanged is mutually beneficial and educative.

Each club has an Executive Committee comprising of a Chairperson, Secretary, Treasurer and three or more committee members who can substitute in these roles. General meetings are held on a fixed day every week and records are kept of both savings and withdrawals. The funds are deposited in a financial institution.

The meetings take up all inter-related problems of the members— economic and social—and discuss solutions. As the economic activities expand, women members form into groups or co-operatives for larger collective production or marketing activities. Gradually, from purely on-farm and subsistence agricultural activities the groups are moving to non-farm activities. Some construction activities are undertaken collectively by the collective purchase of building materials, organizing the necessary labour and finance, and training members in the skills required. Sewing groups are being established to make school uniforms. Other home-based activities, including food processing have also been initiated.

Moreover, some clubs have been allotted government land or communal land for expansion of their collective activities. A number of savings clubs are also involved in making bulk purchases of inputs like fertilizers thus eliminating the middle men and getting better prices or saving on transport. Clearly, a spiralling of activities towards meeting a multiplicity of local needs is becoming evident.

Savings clubs in Zimbabwe are demonstrating the possibility of becoming an effective alternative to institutional credit for rural women. The organization also provides, as has been mentioned, a cost-effective method for transmitting technical information, raising awareness of the inter-relationship between economic and social problems and identifying local solutions. The process also builds a sense of solidarity, self-reliance and organizational capability. For the poor women, this can become not only an instrument for raising their income and productivity in a situation where institutional credit was not available but also for improving their material and social well-being and of their families, and would give them a new sense of dignity.

However, if the savings clubs are to become an instrument for enabling the poor women to move out of poverty into sustainable development, then the Savings Development Movement would also need to have a coherent and comprehensive programme design based on a clear perspective and commitment not only to the gender issue, but also to the issue of equity. The poor women would need to be organized into homogeneous groups so that their interests are served. Otherwise, while the poor women may marginally benefit from the savings clubs and have their survival needs met, they could still be polarized and trapped into a permanent poverty crisis while the richer among the women in rural areas benefited. The lessons from SEWA and the Working Women's Forum, which worked with the poorest women and built on the 'Chit System' or indigenous savings associations of poor women, are applicable. If the poor women are to benefit, the methodology outline in chapter III would need to be systematically followed.

Re-designing the Programme

Through the government's social programmes some of the club members also benefit. However, the Savings Development Movement, as an NGO, could design a programme like BRAC with a view to ensuring that it evolves an instrument for enabling poor women to move out of poverty into sustainable development. It can initiate a programme designed towards this end. Through this programme it would need to initiate a rigorous process of training new kinds of catalysts or animators, form homogeneous groups of poor women with their own savings fund, help to build a sensitive and responsive support system and ensure that both the economic and social needs of poor women are met. The design for such a programme has to be undertaken in a systematic way, with the methodology indicated in chapter III.

  As has been mentioned, the Savings Development Movement* and the savings clubs have much to learn from the WWF and the WWF Credit Society and the SEWA and the SEWA Bank. It can also be assisted to expand its social component and to build a savings and credit window specifically for poorer women which can experiment even on the lines of the Grameen Bank, and then expand.

---

  * As in the case of the savings clubs in Zimbabwe and the 'Chit System' in India, savings associations also exist in several Arab countries, where they are known as 'Gameya'. These can also be 'entry points' for addressing the special concerns of poorer women.

As has been mentioned, these savings associations are organized informally by all classes of people including poor women. They too are based on the voluntary contributions of members and on a rotation system by which each member gets the use of the group's savings in turn. In addition, in an Islamic environment the system has the advantage that no interest is paid on credit and loans. It is also a part of the mutual aid system which is a part of the cultural tradition in many poor countries. There are no overhead costs to be met and peer or group pressure ensures repayment. In the case of richer members, the savings associations are consumption oriented. Among the poor they are mainly for survival and unforeseen expenses.

There is potential in Egypt—where, for instance, the savings clubs are called the Jam Iyyat Iddikkar, as in the case of the Working Women's Forum in Tamilnadu or the Self-Employed Women's Association in Gujarat in India, or in the case of the Savings Development Movement in Zimbabwe—for the savings associations to become the basis of a savings and credit system among poor women, not just for consumption or pure survival needs, but also for sustainable economic and social development. For the potential to be brought out in the particular cultural setting it will require the evolving of the same process which includes a perspective, identification of an intermediary, the initiation of an action research programme, the training of catalysts, awareness creation and building homogeneous organizations of poor women which can respond to their social and economic needs. It would also require building a sensitive and flexible support system. There is sufficient experience from the examples given earlier, from other countries like Bangladesh and Pakistan to demonstrate how the process might be initiated experimentally in the Egyptian cultural setting.

For further information on Egyptian Savings Clubs see:
  – Van den Akker Piet, 'Savings Clubs—the Egyptian Experience', 1986 (unpublished).
  – Geertz Clifford, 'The rotating credit association: a middle rung in development' *Economic Development and Culture Change*-vol. 10, No. 3, April 1962.
  – F.J.A. Bowman, 'Indigenous Savings and Credit Societies in the Third World' *Savings and Development*, No. 4, 1977.

BURKINA FASO

The Six S Association in the Sahel

The Setting

In the Savannah region of Burkina Faso, the dry season is a period of migration for the young and older men and women from their villages in search of work and additional income for family survival. This migration is a time consuming and costly process. There are exceptions, however, where innovative alternatives have been initiated through dialogue and continuous consultation between some of these younger persons. These alternatives have not only permitted the younger people to stay in the villages, but have also resulted in the promotion of village development activities.

For this purpose groups have been formed and a variety of small economic and social activities have been initiated within the drought prone villages themselves. Various community infrastructural activities are undertaken, such as, digging wells, building culverts and dykes to conserve rainfall and other sources of water; clearing tree stumps and other minor construction activities. These spontaneous groups are culturally homogeneous and not based on economic motivations alone, e.g., the 'Groupment Naam' or Self-help groups where the underlying assumption is that the poor farmers can do a great deal for themselves given a little support when needed. The persons involved demonstrate both a personal and a collective commitment. Building on this commitment, the groups initiate an activity, first with their own resources and creativity, then expand into other activities with supplementary resources and inputs from outside. A problem they have faced is the need for an umbrella organization to provide them with a systematic flexible support system, when they needed it. One such organization that has emerged is the Six S Association (which translated means 'Making good use of the dry season in the Savanna and the Sahel').[6]

The Process

The Six S was initiated by a committed and experienced intellectual, who settled down in his own village Quahiagouyia in Burkina Faso, in 1974, with a view to using his experience and contacts for the benefit of peasants in some of the poorest villages in the country including his own. He understood the process of spontaneous group formation through 'animation rurale' or awareness creation and the need for a new kind of umbrella support organization by those who wanted to be more self-reliant. He also understood that it was important to work within culturally conditioned structures if development efforts were to be sustainable. Forms of organizations based on imported models would not work in that context.

The objective of Six S was to provide a sensitive and flexible support system to some of the groups that had formed spontaneously. In their spontaneous emergence, the groups were very diverse and government and donors alike had attempted to provide some support to them, but in accordance with their own criteria, rather than in response to the felt needs of the groups. Therefore, there was too much control, supervision and bureaucratic rigidity.

The Six S, on the other hand, promoted the establishment of an umbrella association for some of the groups in 1976 with a different approach. The association was composed of those groups who wished to be more self-reliant and develop their own creative responses to their adverse circumstances in the drought prone areas and not be constrained by rigid government and donor procedures. The association was to operate flexibly and support the group (or individual activities) with a funding and training scheme. The association would itself mobilize these funds from the more sensitive donors and use them with new norms for the benefit of the village poor.

The groups who formed the association then elected area committees, who were responsible for deciding the use of the funds, overseeing the accounts, monitoring the process and ensuring repayment where loans had been granted. Thus, though the Six S was flexible, financial discipline was maintained in the supported activities. A local area head was appointed from one of these groups. This person is responsible for organizing regular meetings of the groups for exchange of information and experiences and for carrying out an in-depth dialogue among group members on their problems and solutions to them. Each area committee decides the criteria for assistance in grant or loan form. In some cases loans are interest free, in some cases 7 per cent interest is charged. In other cases, loans are made in kind with repayment also in kind e.g., lending one cow to a group or individual in exchange for one calf two years later. The group is responsible for ensuring repayment. The groups are also encouraged to form their own savings funds.

The process, as it has evolved, has resulted in the creation of a flexible fund by the association which is able to mobilize and re-channel resources from outside, with new norms. The initial funding for the Six S has been contributed by the Swiss Government, French and Swiss NGOs and by German and Netherlands NGO co-financing agencies. The donors have provided these resources to Six S, with a great deal of flexibility, in support of the process as a whole and not on the basis of conventional project lending. The funds can be used for a wide variety of purposes, designated by the area committees in response to the needs of the groups. The donors have not pre-determined the use of the funds. The funds can be used for training of catalysts or sensitizing government officials and extension workers or be used for economic and social development activities. A formal project by project approach is not taken by the donors as they have entered into three year renewable agreements with Six S. The Swiss Government and the German co-financing agency have already renewed their agreements.

The expansion process is catalyzed by trained and paid facilitators who have a commitment and an empathy for this kind of work. Their training includes building of trust and confidence in people and in bridging the generation gap. The facilitators also help to move the groups from smaller economic and social activities on to somewhat larger community activities which are beneficial to the village as a whole.

Some of the more dramatic community activities that have been undertaken are:

1. The establishment of a Cereal Bank, with input from two donors. Farmers also contribute their surplus grain to these banks and withdraw grain in times of need. If there is a drought, they are given longer periods to replenish (repay) grain they may have borrowed over and above their contribution.
2. The building of larger barrage dams in the Sahel to hold the

rains. This has been done by use of communal labour mainly women and with labour intensive methods.

3. The organizing of a common purchase system for fertilizer, seed, agricultural tools, wire mesh and for the construction of wells.

4. Grain mills have been installed, with as much success as the Cereal Banks.

The Six S process is expanding both within Burkina Faso, as well as in Mali and Senegal.

NOTES

1. See: i) Reports of the African Development Bank Seminar on 'Women's Access to Credit', Abidjan, Ivory Coast, 1986.
   ii) SIDA Evaluation Report 'Mobilising Rural Women in Kenya,' Stockholm, 1987.
   iii) ILO/DANIDA Report on 'Rural Development and Women: Lessons from the Field,' Geneva, 1985.
   iv) Jacqueline Novogratz (1987).
   v) IFAD (1987).
2. See USAID (1987); Bernard J. Lecomte (1986); and Jacques Bugnicourt, 'L'administration rurale en Afrique,' in *Revue Africaine d'administration publique*, No. 11, Paris, July–September, 1979. Mary Racellis, 'Transforming the African Crisis into People-based Development' paper for Conference on Training for Social Development Methods, Association for Social Work Education in Africa, Addis Ababa, 1985, (unpublished).
3. See Peter Wanyande, 'Popular Participation for Development: An Examination of the Organization and Role of Women's Groups as Institutions for Popular Participation in Kenya,' paper for the SID Workshop on Participatory Grassroots Development in Africa, Dar-es-Salaam, 1986.
4. See Francis W. Mulwa (1986).
5. See Ponna Wignaraja, Phase I Report on IFAD/UNICEF collaboration, op. cit.
6. See: i) Ledea B. Oeudrago (1977).
   ii) Bernard J. Lecomte (1986).
   iii) Report of the Federal Ministry for Economic Co-operation 'Study of various methods promoting self-reliance' Bonn, 1984.

Initiating New Programmes
in Latin America

T HIS chapter has been written in the context of the current debate on the impact of the economic crises and adjustment policies on poor women in Latin America, and on the reviews that are being conducted of external assistance for women's programmes.

Studies undertaken by several UN agencies and others point not only to the reduction in the per capita GNP and quality of life indices of the poor in the 1980s in all Latin American countries, but also to the double burden that poor women suffer as a result of the extremely skewed land and asset ownership patterns, modernization strategies in the agricultural sector, and migration of younger persons to urban areas and across the borders.[1] The burdens on poor women are further compounded by those factors resulting from other aspects, such as, the cultural undervaluation of their work and contribution to society and their continued exploitation. Nearly 50 per cent of the 200 million women in Latin America live in conditions of dire poverty.

The IFAD study on 'Rural Women's Access to Credit', referred to earlier, confirms that in Latin America and the Carribean, as in other regions, conventional banking and credit mechanisms are based on collateral and therefore bypass women and poor women in particular. Even official efforts made by special institutions like Rural Development Banks do not reach poor rural women. Rural women entrepreneurs, however, who have land or other assets and develop independent activities, theoretically have access to credit, but still face the same constraints either due to lack of commitment of the top management, institutional rigidities, attitudinal biases of the bank's staff or lack of information and understanding of how the system works by the women themselves. All these difficulties are compounded for poor rural women.

The IFAD report also recognizes that specific delivery mechan-

isms for credit to poor women, in particular, will need further
specification and experimentation. It also recommends that harder
evaluation, both of women's participation and resulting benefits
would have to be made to ensure that the benefits reach the
specified target group, i.e., poor women.

Several donors have initiated reviews of their regional programme for women in development in Latin America. The women's
movement has catalyzed interest in women in development activities and advocated national level activities. An initial review
revealed that there were too many scattered activities, mainly
meetings. Several women in development projects were funded
and a wide variety of scattered and sectorally fragmented activities
were in evidence in many countries.

The evaluations of these projects and undertaken activities
showed partial successes and failures from which many lessons
could be drawn. It was found that each donor was supporting
fifteen to twenty different kinds of activities in the region, including
income generating projects, appropriate technology projects and
training for various types of women functionaries in health,
peasant and urban women's organizations. Most of these were ad
hoc and fragmented activities within countries. For income
generating activities, funds went directly to women's groups
engaged in basket weaving, dress making or food processing.
These resulted in weak delivery processes and the groups broke up
after inputs were received. The programmes were directed at
women who were poor as compared to the elite rich women, but
not necessarily to the poorest. Little was done to identify the real
poor in the Latin American context either conceptually or in
practice.

With the lessons from these evaluations in mind, many existing
programmes are recently being reformulated. In reformulating
these programmes many donors, while continuing to advocate
greater interest by Latin American Governments in women in
development activities, also attempted to concentrate their interventions in a particular geographical area and address the total
concerns of women in that area. The sharper focus on women did
not necessarily mean that the gender and equity issues were
addressed in an unambiguous way. As analyzed in the African
cases, there are, however, several examples where programmes

and activities supported by NGOs or governments can be deepened to achieve these twin objectives whereby poor women are enabled to move out of poverty into sustainable development.

By looking at the process initiated in the two countries like Colombia and Mexico, one by the government and the other by an NGO, it may be possible to identify if there are further innovative elements that may be necessary in the designs of the processes which could better enable the poorest of women in these countries to move out of poverty into sustainable development. In identifying these elements the analysis will attempt to go beyond the question of assisting women in general in poorer regions of the country to focus unambiguously on the issue of the concern for poorer women within the poor regions.

Here again the lessons from South Asia could be helpful in ensuring that real 'seeds' have been planted, as these Latin American programmes begin to expand and grow in scale.

COLOMBIA

In Colombia, in the 1980s a number of new programmes in support of emerging concerns with the situation of women in development were started. One was the 'Income Generation Project for Independent Workers' in the Southeastern Zone of the city of Cartagena. Credit was supplied through a government poverty alleviating programme to street vendors in the informal sector, whose only means of obtaining finance was through the informal credit system at interest rates of up to 10 per cent per day. With the lessons of this programme, an attempt is now being made at replicating the process at the national level. The programme in 'Basic Services, Income Generation, Employment and Productivity' in the urban area of Bucarmanga is one such attempt at replication. A second programme was to complement the national policy of 'Participation of Peasant Women in Rural Development' in co-operation with the Ministry of Agriculture, by promoting and institutionalizing the organization of rural and indigenous women. The process initiated in Cartagena will be analyzed to identify the innovative features which have been introduced in the government policy and its implementation, and the further elements that are necessary to deepen the process.

Income Generation Project for Independent Workers

The Setting

The project was located in Cartagena, the capital of the state of Bolivar in Colombia. During the past 30 years the city had undergone significant growth both as a result of an expansion in tourism, as well as the establishment of an industrial area. However, unemployment in the formal sectors was increasing, but there was considerable potential for employment generation in the informal sector.

The southern zone of Cartagena is considered one of the poorest urban areas in the country. Fifty per cent of the population does not have access to clean drinking water, electricity and other public services. At least 50 per cent of the families have monthly incomes of less than the minimum wage of US $91.8 per month. According to standards established by the government, only 20 per cent of these can purchase the minimum basket of goods necessary for the average family to survive.

The majority of the area's population is black, among whom there is a cultural tradition of assigning the central role in community life to women. Many families are also headed by women. More than half the independent (self-employed) workers in the informal sector are women. It was in this setting that the government initiated a women's programme, working through a non-profit community organization, called Centro de Desarrollo Vecina (CDV), created by the government to co-ordinate the efforts of a number of public agencies in the southeast zone of Cartagena. The objectives of the CDV were:

1. To provide basic services in the area of education, health care, family and infant assistance, skills training, sports, cultural and recreational activities;
2. To promote an active, organized and conscious participation of the community in the identification of its needs and the search for solutions;
3. To improve the skills of workers and management capabilities of small entrepreneurs, as well as to promote the creation of micro-enterprises through provision of training, technical assistance and financing from public agencies.

In the area of income generation, which is a major part of CDV's mandate, the activities of CDV involve skills training, credit to individuals and community groups, and technical assistance in management, production and marketing.

The Process

The process for income generation started with donor advocacy programmes which drew the government's attention to the need for addressing the concerns of women. This was followed by the identification of the area for intervention, i.e., the Southeast zone of Cartagena which was one of the poorer regions of Colombia and the implementing agency, the CDV. It was, however, a government programme, with the government playing a key role in the process.

The primary objective of the intervention was set as the improvement of the socio-economic conditions of the independent workers, the majority of whom (60 per cent) were women, and their families, through an increase in their incomes and the development of their own organizations. These objectives were intended to address the lack of access to financial resources, inadequate skills and lack of organization among themselves as they compete in the market place.

The project then identified the target group of street and market vendors and small shop owners in the low-income neighbourhoods of the Southeastern zone and the micro-producers in the city's informal economy.

In order to achieve these objectives the CDV has adopted the methodology of establishing solidarity groups. The groups are formed by promotional efforts of the staff of CDV. Groups of three to five persons having a similar type of business and based on friendship and mutual trust are grouped together. Once constituted, the groups go through a series of three orientation meetings, where they get acquainted with the project objectives and the solidarity group concept.

During the orientation, the CDV project staff interviews each participant to get acquainted with the situation in her business and family, obtain data for evaluation purposes and to help in drawing up a credit application. The CDV promoters then visit group member's places of business to gather additional information. A social worker gathers information about family needs, which can be attended to by government institutions that co-ordinate activities with the CDV in areas of health and education.

After group members have drawn up a credit application, a committee made up of the CDV representative, the promoter and the social worker reviews the request and within two weeks the request is granted. The loan is given to the solidarity group for an individual or group activity, but the group is collectively responsible for repayment. Groups that repay loans on time are eligible for further loans.

Follow-up and training is carried out through monthly meetings with group members. The meetings discuss a variety of problems affecting the business, solutions are also discussed and progress is evaluated. During the first six months the groups receive training around concepts of co-operation and solidarity. Thereafter, they are trained by the national training services (SENA) in basic accounting, cost control, marketing, and quality control. SENA has also created a National Confederation of Micro-Entrepreneurs from around the country for the provision of training and technical assistance.

A savings programme has also been initiated with the two-fold objective of inculcating the savings habit among the participants and to create a community fund, from which they can take additional loans to meet family emergencies.

An evaluation of the impact of the programme has yet to be made. The following achievements between 1983–1986, however, can be identified:

No. of solidarity groups formed	251
No. of independent workers involved	856
No. of orientation meetings	176
No. of loans to solidarity groups	1,317
No. of loans to individuals	5,019
TOTAL amount of loans	Col. $46,821.05
Amount recovered	42,612.14

The figures indicate that loans are being repaid.

The total cost of the project for the period 1983–1987 is US $351,000 of which one donor has contributed 42 per cent or US $147,200, matching an equivalent amount through the CDV.[2] The

Catholic Relief Services contributed US $51,000 and the Canadian Government contributed US $5,300.

It is clear from the process outlined that the advocacy on behalf of women in development has paid off and the government is attempting to address some of the concerns of small women entrepreneurs in the informal sector in poorer geographical areas, to incorporate them into the market and to replicate the model experimented with in Cartagena, in other urban areas, such as Bucaramanga.

The model responds to the needs for credit by independent small women entrepreneurs. A small revolving fund administered by CDV has been created to provide credit, at reasonable rates, to small women entrepreneurs who otherwise would have been continuously exploited by money lenders and who were not able to borrow from the conventional banks. In the process the savings habit has been inculcated and an awareness of available social programmes has been created.

The recipients of credit and the social programmes are organized into groups to receive these inputs, and promoters and social workers working for the government ensure that the inputs are 'delivered' to the target group. Groups are formed mainly to receive credit and other inputs, though some sports and cultural activities are also undertaken. Technical and skills training are imparted in support of the management of the economic activity undertaken.

It would appear that in a situation where women and the poor of all categories did not have access to credit from the formal credit institutions, or to health care programmes, education and other social services, this experiment has introduced some innovations into the 'delivery of inputs' approach for poverty alleviation. For example, the catalyst promoter, the solidarity group, the revolving fund, the linking of training of recipients to credit and small enterprise management and the use of CDV as an implementing agency, etc.

However, the question still remains whether the beneficiary group is the real poor and the poorest or is it the small entrepreneurs, women included. Conceptually, in a Latin American country like Colombia, with its social structure, skewed asset holdings and exploitative economic and social relations, 'Bario' (lower income neighbourhoods) or 'Rural' per se cannot be equated with poor. In barios and in rural areas there are those that are richer and wield influence and others who are deprived in every way. The programme analyzed clearly recognizes the existence of this large permanent layer of the deprived and the tendency for it to reproduce itself. The intervention in Cartagena, as has been designed, however, may still only be touching the better off or the richer of the poorer women (and men) in the Barios. As such, the programme could demonstrate how the government might establish a more flexible credit and social support system for this category of persons (women included), but not for the poorest. A few very poor families may be identified in a token fashion and receive a loan or a social service, but, apart from the limitedness of the coverage, this gesture does not lead to a sustainable process.

If the programme was, in effect, intended for the poorest, then it has to start with them—organizing them into homogeneous groups in an unambiguous way, releasing their creativity, using their knowledge system and with their participation as subjects of the process and not as the objects. If greater conceptual clarity is not introduced the programme, as it is now designed, could end up polarizing the barios even more and further marginalizing the poorest.

A second conceptual issue that needs to be clarified is the content of a participatory process. What is the element of participation, even for the richer of the poor women, let alone the poorer of the women in this programme? Real participation cannot, any longer, be confused with some 'consultation' and 'group discussion' in what is essentially a top-down process where the objectives and credit as an instrument is pre-determined from the outside. Mobilization and conscientization cannot be confused with some 'consultation' or 'advocacy' or 'social marketing'. The three orientation meetings are not sufficient for bringing about a required attitudinal change. With groups being formed to receive an input like credit, they could easily break up, if there is insufficient conscientization.

A third issue that should be addressed is to determine whether the process that has been initiated is a 'seed' or a 'bubble'. In either case the analysis should go deeper into assessing whether the process is merely a marginal corrective, in an otherwise iniquitous system, or whether it can be an 'entry point' which can be deepened with the lessons learnt from other regions, which could enable the poorest of women to move out of poverty into sustainable development.

The programme, however, can be deepened. This can be done on the basis of an indepth socio-economic survey, which is undertaken in a participatory manner with committed academics and the poor interacting with each other, with the methodology elaborated in chapter III. The first step is to identify the socio-economic formations within the Barios and who are really benefiting from the current intervention. Second, from this identification the programme should state in an unambiguous way, who the specific beneficiary groups are—are they small women entrepreneurs, or the real poor?

If the beneficiary groups are to be the poorest women, then the design and the process should follow the steps also outlined in chapter III. A new design should be formulated, with appropriate variations in the selection and training of new kinds of catalysts and facilitators, the group formation process, identification of the needs of the poorest as they see them, and the building of a flexible support system with new norms. A new intermediary, one who has the perspective, may also have to be found. In other words, in expanding the programme to other cities, the process should be somewhat different and based on a new and as yet unformulated design.

In Colombia, it would appear that there is considerable scope for initiating new experiments (from which everyone can learn) to move poor women out of poverty into sustainable development. There is also economic space, in a basically rich country like Colombia, to take a somewhat longer time horizon and let the process evolve with the participation of the poor themselves. Such an experimentation with hard innovative approaches for povety alleviation, supported by sensitive donors when necessary, is all the more critical in the context of the adjustments that Colombia is being called upon to make with major cutbacks in its social and economic development efforts and its impact on the poorest sections of the people, particularly the poorest women.

MEXICO

In Mexico too, as has been identified in other Latin American countries, the current economic crisis is affecting the urban and

rural poor women very adversely. It is increasing their marginalization and further reducing their capacity for survival. Their
survival capacity had already been eroded over recent decades by
the transformations that had taken place through the introduction
of high technology farming systems into the rural areas. These
transformations have turned farm families into landless labour,
paid workers, or into migrants. In this context several NGOs
concerned with the deteriorating conditions of poor women have
experimented with innovative approaches for bringing poor
women (and men) out of poverty into sustainable development.
The experience of one of them 'Promocion del Desarrollo Popular'
is dicussed here, as it represents a new kind of NGO intermediary
in Mexico, which is pursuing an innovative approach for poverty
alleviation within the political space that is available for NGOs in
Mexico.

Promocion del Desarrollo Popular

The Setting

In Mexico, in the past fifteen to twenty years as the polarization
between the rich and poor began to deepen, several Non-Govern-
mental Organizations began to emerge to identify and respond to
the needs of the poor. Some of them were a part of the progressive
sections of the Catholic Church, inspired by the liberation theology.
Others had functioned within the old framework of development
and were now experimenting with innovative approaches in
response to the deepening poverty crisis. With the growing
evidence of marginalization of the poor, and poor women in
particular, these NGOs were taking a critical look not only at their
own operations but were also re-evaluating the more traditional
organizations meant to safeguard the interests of the poor, like the
trade unions and co-operatives. Furthermore, there were NGOs
being formed in the wake of new social movements, e.g., the
ecological movement and the ethnic movements.

These new category of NGOs were not rigidly ideologically
oriented, nor were they linked to traditional political parties of the
right or the left. They did not have pre-conceived solutions to the
whole range of problems faced by the poor. These started as small
spontaneous grassroots efforts trying to establish by themselves

new processes which were rooted in the popular culture and knowledge systems of the poor. They then built new umbrella organizations, which could provide a support and information system to reinforce the survival struggles of the poor, to prevent further damage to their capacity to survive and to enable them to move out of poverty into sustainable development.

These umbrella NGOs which supported the new micro-processes were very different from conventional macro-institutions and bureaucratic planning organizations and even old style NGOs. These new initiatives did not direct or impose an ideology or promote development from above. They supported initiatives taken by the poor themselves and shaped their responses accordingly. Where there was inertia, they helped to release the creativity of the poor by their catalytic interventions. Some of these had identified with the gender and equity issues and were seeing new opportunities for sustainable development in creative initiatives taken by poor women. Committed academics and new kinds of professionals also associated with these NGOs.

Through these new kinds of NGO intermediaries and the interaction between committed academics and the poor women, not only are some of the survival and social problems being ameliorated but new forms of asset creation and accumulation processes are also taking place. The processes initiated are different from the conventional links between labour and capital. They involve labour saving and hardship saving technology, which results in a change in time use. Group activities under these circumstances not only further releases the creativity of poor women, but also creates technology appropriate to their needs, throws up natural leadership, and generates new gender spaces within which poor women can function. These new formations and processes are still to be fully understood in all their dimensions, but a major lesson was learnt when the earthquake struck Mexico City in September 1985. It was these NGOs, particularly those working with poor women's groups, which responded immediately and initiated the rehabilitation and reconstruction effort. After three years of additional experience with coping with an emergency of such major national proportions, these NGOs had a better capacity than before to support the efforts of poor women to move out of poverty into sustainable development. The process of evolution of the Promocion del Desarrollo Popular (PDP) and their methodology of operation is set out below.

The Process

The PDP has been working un-interruptedly in Mexico since 1960 as a progressive Church based NGO.[3] Its fundamental commitment is to work with the largest segment of the population, who are poor, exploited and with few opportunities of achieving minimum levels of well-being. It has evolved on the basis of both its successes and failures and accumulated a body of experience in economic and social development by supporting base-level organizations of the poor, particularly poor women. It has also a deep understanding of awareness creation and conflict resolution.

Its early experience gave PDP an understanding of the limits and possibilities of traditional rural workers' movements, trade unions, co-operatives and popular urban movements. With this experience it began supporting new social movements like the women's movement, youth movement, the ecological movement and the human rights movement, which reflected a new social awareness among the poor and deprived.

The PDP's organization is very simple. It has a core group of approximately 20 facilitators and action-researchers. They function as participatory mini-teams in various locations. Each team is broadly co-ordinated by an area co-ordinator and a general director. The mini teams include ad hoc technical persons and representatives from the base organizations they are working with at the grassroots or from other collaborating NGOs. The mini-teams support the base organizations of the poor in a flexible manner, exchanging experience or knowledge with them. The PDP center offers an umbrella or a 'hammock' (i.e., something that shapes itself according to the user) to the whole network. It also provides 'seed money' for initiatives taken by the base level groups for health, economics, housing, training, communication and related activities. As a result the PDP has now strengthened base groups working in alternative health and nutrition, rural production, improvement of technology, art, culture, information and communication.

Apart from its own support programmes the PDP encourages and supports other similar NGOs and organizations in Mexico who are dealing with survival challenges, cultural identity, and indigenous knowledge systems, and are evolving alternative development strategies. This collaboration also initiates a participatory process of information exchange and self-criticism among the NGOs who are involved in alternative development. PDP has recently made an inventory of 400 such NGOs. It is also loosely linked to several regional and international NGO networks and provides training and information exchanges for such NGOs between countries in Central America.

A major part of PDP's work relates to organizations which are made up predominantly of poor women. For instance, in the state of Guanajuato it supports the 'Centro de Desarrollo Auropecuario' (CEDESA). This organization works in one hundred small villages in which the majority of men have emigrated to the United States. The women headed households have to cope with an inter-related set of survival issues like food, health, water and environmental concerns. Often the poor women need to negotiate with the government agencies wherein the PDP and CEDESA act as intermediaries. A network called Peasanta Actions has been organized to foster solidarity among the poor rural women's small organizations in the state, and enable them to assert their right to various basic services, such as, health.

PDP has developed a team for health assistance. The focus is disease prevention and the use of available local medicinal herbs, clean water, solar energy and better soil conservation for growing traditional foods. They support the work of the catalysts who are 'barefoot doctors' and the poor women who have emerged as natural health workers and leaders in their own communities. PDP is now organizing training workshops with these groups of catalysts in order to multiply the process. The training methodology is based on the participatory action-research (PAR) methodology, referred to in chapter III. Training involves the mini-teams and members of the base organizations discussing together and reflecting on the causes of various diseases, the action that can be taken to overcome them and the appropriate support that is necessary from outside organizations, whether it is one like PDP which has identified with them or the governments. Even when health is an 'entry' point, the inter-related economic, and social aspects of the total lives of the poor women are also brought into the reflection/action/reflection process. Apart from Guanajuato, PDP is also working in the states of Chiapas, Oaxaca and Morelos and Mexico City with health as an 'entry' point for enabling poor women to move out of poverty. Extension of credit is another 'entry point' used by the PDP in its total process for development.

As a result of the earthquake in September 1985 several small family enterprises, small backyard workshops and other activities involving poor women were destroyed. The PDP immediately using its earlier experience with providing 'seed money' to support small activities, created a revolving fund in a bank to provide soft loans to these micro-enterprises at the grassroots. To date nearly 100 such enterprises have been supported, 50 per cent of them managed by poor women. The revolving fund has been in existence for nearly two years with a high rate of repayment on loans.

PDP is now organizing a solidarity network for training and sharing of experiences between the users of the fund. This is not conventional skills or technical training. The objective is to generate a continuous learning process, one that links training to education and organization, through systematic reflection, analysis and action in the search for alternative strategies for the poor in the informal sector. The suddenness of the earthquake called for an immediate response by organizations like PDP. Now they are in a position, through this new organizational/education programme, to begin another phase of mobilization, conscientization and organization of the poor, particularly poor women, to enable them to move out of poverty into sustainable development.

Throughout the 25 years of its existence PDP has received small grants from a variety of sensitive funding agencies. With its austere style and combination of use of local resources, new professionalism and committed volunteers, it has hitherto been able to optimize the use of its financial and human resources. The initial external support was for institution building. Today, PDP's activities and locally generated resources cover most of the institutional costs. However, as its activities expand, as a result of its support to base organizations of poor women, funding constraints could prevent such an innovative organization from functioning at its fullest potential.

Institution Building

Poverty alleviation is a complex task. New institutions are emerging in Mexico and need to be supported. Older institutions need to be re-oriented. Just additive and marginal tinkering with conventional institutions, bureaucracies and procedures are not enough. New kinds of facilitators and catalysts need to be trained so that the process can be multiplied. The PAR methodology requires the establishment of new light structures if more and more committed academics are to interact and associate with base organizations in designing, evaluating and sustaining innovative approaches and experiments. This would also require an inter-disciplinary approach which can retrieve the people's knowledge system, and give it scientific validation—an important ingredient in the process. New kinds of networks and credit institutions will need to be evolved with the participation of the poor themselves. In Mexico, such an alternative bank can be built on the experience of the 'Tandas' or savings' associations of the poor women and the experience with the PDP credit fund. The institutions that are required cannot be spelt out in a prescriptive manner. The process itself will identify the institutions that are required and their character. To the extent that in Mexico the process itself has begun to evolve through innovative NGOs and committed academic groups, the light structures that need to be reinforced and institutions to be built can more easily be identified.

NOTES

1. See: i) UNICEF Study on 'The Invisible Adjustment: Poor Women and the Economic Crisis,' Regional Programme on Women in Development, UNICEF Regional Office for the Americas and the Carribean, Bogota, 1987.
   ii) ECLA Regional Annual Report, Economic Commission for Latin America, Santiago, Chile, 1987.
   iii) Lola Roche, Maria Claria Gomez and Alegandro Acosta, 'Consolidating Income Generation Projects for Women in Latin America,' Bogota, December 1988 (unpublished).
   iv) Orlando Fals-Barda, trans, 'Knowledge and People's Power: Lessons with Peasants in Nicaragua, Mexico and Colombia,' ILO, Geneva, 1985, (mimeograph).
2. See UNICEF Internal Report entitled 'Income Generation Project for Independent Workers of South Eastern Zone of Cartagena,' Bogota, 1987.
3. See: i) Luis, Lopezellera, '20 Years of Experience: Promocion Del Desarrollo Popular,' PDP, Mexico City, 1986 (unpublished).
   ii) Internal Reports of PDP published and unpublished.

A New Sound from Sensitive Donors

THE PROBLEM FOR DONORS

T HE lessons learnt from the South Asian experience can equally inform donor approaches in providing support for poverty alleviation.

Official development assistance has yet to work out its equation both with poverty alleviation in general and with the kind of grassroots social action by poor women, in particular, in order to overcome their double burden. A variety of innovative approaches were described earlier. While some marginal evidence exists to the contrary, donors are as yet poorly equipped to support participatory processes—enabling vulnerable groups and the poor to move into sustainable development—and grassroots development experiments which are an essential part of poverty alleviation. These are due to lack of conceptual clarity, technical difficulties, procedural difficulties and lack of political commitment. While some donors have overcome these difficulties at the margins of their operations, they have yet to bring the lessons from their successes to the center stage.

Most donors have difficulties in following in detail the logic of concepts like 'the poor', 'participation', 'self-reliance', and process approach which are integral parts of an alternative conceptual framework. These words are often used rhetorically without conceptual clarity or detailed working out of the implications of the concept in the implementation phase. Second, technical, administrative and procedural difficulties arise in relation to the type of actions to be undertaken with donor support. These relate to the methodology, design and evaluation of programmes and projects, the need and quality of expertise, the time-table for action and speed of implementation. Third, the process approach which starts with the poor themselves raises a great deal of difficulty for donors. Their natural partners are governments, and even where a donor may be sensitive the government or its bureaucracy may be the stumbling block in working with other intermediaries. The process approach and participation by the poor requires new kinds of intermediaries like NGOs and alternative banks, all working with a great deal of flexibility, new norms and political space. Fourth, narrow donor financial accountability often results in needless sophisticated controls, careful adherence to narrow budgetary procedures and required predictable results. In the process approach one activity leads to another with continuous evaluation built into the process. Not every stage can be predicted in advance. Finally, effective poverty alleviation implies, at the least, a sharing of power with the poor and the necessary political consequences. It also means allowing the poor access to resources which were hitherto being used by the rich. In other words, the process requires the building of at least a countervailing power. This is what is meant by empowerment.

The question that this chapter seeks to answer is how have some sensitive donors, in supporting the analyzed programmes, sought to overcome the constraints and complications mentioned above. The successful participatory approaches in South Asia, described earlier, show that a donor who has insight into the problem, conceptual clarity, a committed and trained staff with the energy and perseverance to stay with the process long enough to over-come the difficulties, the confidence to enter into a new kind of dialogue with governments and the poor groups, and makes maximum use of the procedural 'space' that exists within their own organizations, has contributed in a significant way to the parti-cipatory process which has enabled poor women to move out of poverty into sustainable development.[1]

HOW THEY WERE OVERCOME

The innovative approaches for poverty alleviation—such as, savings, credit and asset creation for poor women which have evolved in South Asia and which have led to poor women strength-ening their capacity for survival, meeting their social needs, entering into income generating activities for further improving their economic and social condition and that of their families, and sustaining the process—have been supported sensitively by a few donors. In several of the described South Asian cases, their role in this new accumulation process stands out.

The positive contribution by these donors, even though still at the periphery of their total operations, will be further analyzed to see what lessons can be drawn from this experience both for expanding their own efforts and for informing other like-minded donors. Their role can be discussed in the first instance in relation to how these experiments came into being, who initiated them and how. The critical question is how did the donor support the process.

The South Asian cases analyzed show that there are three kinds of possible intermediaries which are themselves catalysts, and/or provide support systems which enable women to move out of poverty. These intermediaries could be an NGO as in the case of SEWA, WWF or BRAC in Bangladesh, or a government agency especially designed and established for this purpose as in the case of the Women's Unit in the Panchayat Ministry in Nepal, or a new style bank as in the case of the Grameen Bank in Bangladesh. Sometimes in a country as large as India it was found that a major new institution like the Fund for Credit for Poor Women may have to be created combining the characteristics of an NGO and an alternative bank with government support before a donor could act meaningfully. In Pakistan, the initial catalysts were committed academics and university students, who were later joined by NGOs. This chapter is intended to show how sensitive donors have worked with a variety of these intermediaries, supported their processes and the expansion of the experiments permitting them to grow in scale. Apart from this positive support, this kind of donor action also helps to reverse the damage from conventional approaches.

The donor involvement in supporting these innovative experiments and enabling them to grow in scale shows that, in these cases, they have performed a creative and flexible support role, and worked through new kinds of intermediaries, irrespective of whether that intermediary has been an NGO, a government agency, or a bank. The donors have given this support in some cases through their women's programme, and, in others, through other more sectorally oriented programmes. Herein lies a major point of departure. The particular donors have not tried to be an implementing agency at the grassroots, or only worked through the formal government bureaucracy with very rigid rules.

One donor, for instance, supported the Grameen Bank and the ADBN's Small Farmer Development Programme by introducing the social sector dimensions into what would otherwise have been purely credit or income generating programmes. In the case of an NGO like BRAC, several donors have supported the BRAC initiatives and helped it to expand. In the case of India, while donors have not supported SEWA or the WWF with large funding in any significant way, some of them are now encouraging the creation of a major support system at the national level which can help the SEWA, WWF and similar total processes to consolidate, expand in their own areas and multiply in other parts of India as well.

In the case of Pakistan, a donor supported a group of committed academics, students and NGOs through its urban programme. The sectoral 'entry point', in that kind of traditional environment, resulted in the commencement of an innovative programme to enable poor urban women to move out of poverty. As the home schools in the kachhi abadies of Karachi evolved and moved into additional income generating activities, new social needs were identified by the poor women to which donors could respond through their credit or primary health care and education programmes, thereby incorporating poor women's concerns further into its sectoral programmes.

In the case of the PCRW, donors helped to design an innovative programme for poor women to suit the particular circumstances of Nepal, building on its previous experience with the ADBN's Small Farmer Development Programme. A new government institution, operating innovatively, was thus created to address the concerns of the poorer women in rural areas, both their social needs as well as the income generating aspects.

All of this has been done with the government's concurrence or tacit approval, using to the maximum the existing 'political space'. Herein lies the second point of departure—a new kind of dialogue and advocacy in relation to recipient governments. But this required donor commitment and sensitivity, trained persons who could support formulation of designs with conceptual clarity, and conduct these delicate dialogues with governments, NGOs and banks who in turn are committed to the basic object of poverty alleviation and removing the double burden of poor women.

SOME SPECIFIC CASES[3]

The three cases mentioned below, two in Bangladesh and one in Nepal illustrate in greater detail how one donor organization functioned in relation to an NGO, a bank and a governmental department respectively. The detailed internal processes in these cases have already been described. Here, the donor intervention will be further analyzed.

BRAC: An NGO

The Oral Re-hydration Programme, which had been developed by the Cholera Research Laboratory in Bangladesh and the International Center for Diarrheal Diseases Research, was experimented with by BRAC as far back as 1979. Initially, a donor mounted an advocacy campaign for this cost-effective primary health care practice, after further testing its validity. In 1982, donors funded part of this BRAC programme for spreading the methodology. Here was a situation where BRAC evolved the home based technology and donors put the package together and advocated it.

Donors also indirectly supported BRAC in co-operation with the government. Recently, BRAC agreed to co-operate with the government in its extended national immunization and Vitamin A distribution programmes. BRAC participated in a three component child survival programme—oral rehydration, immunization and Vitamin A distribution in one third of the country which was not covered by OTEP. In the project area with 3.4 million households, BRAC workers continued to teach ORT to village women and also assisted the government to immunize all children against the six killer childhood diseases and all women of child bearing age against tetanus. They are also helping the government to systematize its twice yearly distribution of Vitamin A capsules to all children aged 6 months to 6 years. Under this programme, BRAC also implemented a comprehensive primary health care project in 6 upazilas.

Some donors have maintained a small but close and continuous relationship with BRAC. They have also responded to BRAC's leadership and assisted in a number of activities initiated by BRAC itself. For instance, in 1972, one donor provided a large number of DNDS kits which were provided to BRAC's emergency medical programme under its relief and rehabilitation activities. From 1973–1978 it gave financial support to the publication of over 60,000 copies of a Bangla language monthly development journal entitled 'Gonokendra' which were distributed amongst various development institutions including primary schools and rural farmers/co-operators. In 1973, the Jamalpur women's project was designed and implemented for 4,000 destitute women. In 1974 there was a famine in the Jamalpur municipality and adjacent areas. Core activities of the project included food for work through the supply of wheat, child feeding and functional education. In 1978, financial support was given to a pilot project entitled 'Study Service' whereby sixty post-graduate students of Dhaka University were oriented to rural development activities for three months. The donor also utilized BRAC training services and functional education materials for its various assisted projects.

In these ways the donor has linked its own mandate in the primary health care sector to BRAC's programme for poor women and helped to reinforce BRAC's total economic and social programme for poor women. With this step-by-step approach in building a partnership, the donor is now able to help BRAC move to scale on a number of fronts which respond to poor women's needs even though the entry point was a sectoral one.

Grameen Bank: A Banking Institution

Until mid-1980, in its initial operations, the Grameen Bank was concerned mainly with the extension of credit services to the landless to promote income/employment generation, without responding to the social needs of its members, even though these issues came up in the dialogue with the bank workers.

After observing the Grameen process, the co-ordinator of the women's development unit of a donor in Dhaka initiated an informal dialogue with the founder of the Grameen Bank and herself.[4] In her words:

During a series of joint discussions held between the founder of

GB and myself, a variety of concerns, were brought into focus on expanding the parameters of the Bank's operations in relation to the needs of poor women beyond the purely economic. For example:

1. Providing loanee groups with more skills to enable them to better understand and follow banking rules and procedures;
2. Providing them with functional education to upgrade their existing skills and enable them to perform their multiple roles of participants, beneficiaries, producers and consumers;
3. Offering members a forum and providing the necessary mechanism through which a Basic Service strategy could be advocated; and
4. Strengthening poor women to enable them to take care of the special needs of their children.

It was in response to these concerns that a Trainer's Training Programme (TTP) of the GB was conceptualized and developed with the donor's support, beginning its activities in July 1980.

It needs to be emphasized that the Grameen Bank was itself reflecting the felt needs of the poor, as indicated to it from the dialogues of the bank's workers with the poor women, and the donor played a supporting role.

The programme aimed at training female bank workers and loanee group leaders to play a vital role in the strengthening of women's groups along three major dimensions: (a) train GB group members in organizational procedures, banking services and credit management; (b) raise the level of social awareness among village women; and (c) develop viable loanee co-operative groups to undertake activities such as PHC, child nutrition, sanitation, literacy and family planning. In other words, the donor's intervention at this juncture permitted the Grameen Bank to go beyond credit operations and take a holistic approach and respond to both the social and the economic needs of poor women.

The bank's village groups became the forum for discussion of primary health care and nutrition concerns of the poor. Training became an entry point and the new change agents/catalysts were able to understand both village level banking with new norms, as well as the social dimensions. The trainers were being trained to train both categories of change agents—the barefoot bankers and the community workers.

Starting with this activity, this particular donor's support to the Grameen Bank has expanded as follows:

Period Covered	Donor Inputs (US$)
1980–1982	52,000
1982–1985	251,000
1985–1988	683,300
1988–1993 (proposed)	1,192,400
Total	2,178,700

With these gradually increasing levels of expenditure, the donor's collaborative involvement with the Grameen Bank evolved as follows, with a great deal of continuous dialogue between the particular donor and the bank:

Period 1980–1982

In addition to training the trainers the donor helped support:

1. Community level workshops to introduce social development components to the village level women group leaders. The subjects related to PHC, nutrition, child care, personal hygiene environmental sanitation, use of safe water, etc. During this period 600 women group leaders and women bank workers were trained in these workshops to serve 10,400 women and 20,800 children. Due to this training the increased demand for basic services was reinforced amongst the Grameen Bank members in a natural way.
2. Exchange of visits within districts and zones for bank personnel and group leaders to share experience.
3. Regular national workshops and policy dialogues.
4. The donor also assisted in compiling and printing case histories of the women Grameen Bank members and translating it into English for wider dissemination and as part of an experiential and shared learning process.[4]

Period 1982–1985

The activities of the earlier period were continued and in addition
the donor began providing Grameen Bank members with the
following support services:

1. Tubewells and alum for safe use of water;
2. Seed-saplings for promoting family food gardening;
3. Immunization of children and women;
4. Printed ORS jackets on passbooks as memory-aid;
5. Iodated salt for prevention of IDD;
6. Children's learning centre for promotion of female
education.

During this period 4,500 women group leaders and 150 female
bank workers were trained to service 50,000 women and 150,000
children. Another important dimension of the training was that a
demand was generated from amongst the GB members to train
male members in social development. Thus the GB started (with
its own resources) a one-day orientation on social development for
the male GB members. Under a donor assisted project a national
workshop was organized where sixteen decisions were taken relating
to refining of the women in development activities.

Period 1985–1988

24,500 landless women group leaders and 1,500 female bank
workers/programme staff were being trained to serve 600,000
women and 1.2 million children and support services were
provided, as in the previous period, on an expanded scale.

Period 1988–1993 (proposed)

The project title has been changed to highlight socio-economic
development along with the training. With the donor's assistance,
training will be provided to 60,000 women group leaders to serve
750,000 women and 1.5 million children. In this period the bank
will take over the bank workers/programme staff training and
finance the training with its own resources. The bank has internalized the functional education programme and this will continue

in the old villages, assisted by the donor in a self-sustaining manner. Revolving funds have been accumulated for ORS, seed-saplings, alum, iodated salt and tubewells, out of the sale proceeds as the Grameen Bank, in principle, does not distribute anything free of charge.

Over the years, the bank has been assisted by the donor to establish linkages with the national basic services programmes, particularly with the Health Department for immunization of children and women bank members.

The following detailed picture has been presented to demonstrate how a donor with small discreetly placed assistance has systematically reinforced the Grameen Bank process over a reasonably long period of time by:

1. Following the leadership provided by the bank and expanding its own support keeping pace with the bank's expansion;
2. Introducing the social dimension not only to complement the bank's economic dimension, but to permit the bank to respond to the totality of poor women's needs and generate a truly cost-effective, self-sustaining, poverty alleviating process.

Finally, in this process, a holistic approach has been added to an already unconventional bank and turned it into a stronger development bank of the poor. All this has been done within the donor's wider mandate and available instruments and procedures. This partnership has been built painstakingly. The difficulties encountered should not be minimized, but the positive results speak for themselves and can be multiplied. Some other donors participated in parallel. Others have come in after the groundwork was laid to permit further expansion of the Grameen Bank. International financial institutions like IFAD have built on this foundation.

PCRW: A Section in a Government Department

A particular donor involvement started, in this instance with its support to the SFDP, as a predecessor programme to PCRW. The donor saw SFDP as an alternative to the conventional Integrated Rural Development Programmes with the IRDP's 'delivery' of inputs and 'trickle down' approach. Apart from the more clearly articulated target group of the small and poorer farmers of the SFDP, the donor's interest was enhanced by the potential in the SFDP as a bank to respond to the problem of poor families, not only with credit but also in relation to malnutrition and family health.

This is another instance where the donor related to a banking institution even though that was not its normal channel for extending assistance. In this case, the Agricultural Development Bank showed a sensitivity to the poverty issue and attempted to provide credit to the poor for income generating activities. As the participatory process and group dialogue evolved, the social and survival needs of these poor families emerged as a priority but, being a bank, the ADBN could not respond with their own resources directly to these needs. The ADBN then approached the donor for assistance in undertaking a programme preparation study which could inform them on how to incorporate the social dimensions into its credit operations. A local Nepalese research consultancy firm undertook the study which was funded by the donor, and which took one year to complete. The report was in the form of a project document and had guidelines for UNICEF as well.

It required two years of dialogue between the donor and the ADBN to understand their respective roles and to have the ADBN accept their full responsibility for the social dimension as well. The line agencies of the relevant ministries had also to be brought into the process, functioning as a support system to reinforce the process. The donor also undertook to train the women's group organizers in the social aspect while the ADBN continued to train the men group organizers.

As the women group organizers went about their task of organizing groups, spontaneously felt needs were articulated at the field level for primary health care, safe drinking water, home gardens and other basic amenities. When the line agencies failed to provide extension services or the technical problem became too complex for them, the donor stepped in to provide support to ADBN to permit it to recruit the necessary expertise particularly in the social fields and integrate them into the bank staff. As the involvement deepened, the donor found that the bank's SFDP and the groups were a better intermediary than the line ministries for promotion of child survival, sanitation, primary health care, nutrition and drinking water programmes.

Out of this experience the need for focusing on poor women's groups rather than the family subsistence became more sharply articulated within the donor organization. Its staff's awareness also had increased as a result of the continuous dialogue with ADBN, referred to earlier, in relation to introducing a social component into ADBN's Small Farmer Programme and in helping to 'problem solve' all aspects of poverty alleviation on a continuous basis. As the training programme for the women's group organizers got underway, the donor's experience in designing and evaluating the training helped to further deepen its understanding of the conditions in the field. The donor's dialogues with ADBN was also continuous at the field level, where ADBN gave leadership and was the formal implementing agency, with the donor providing flexible back-up support, monitoring, ensuring follow-up, organizing advocacy and policy dialogues with government officials. This was the body of experience and concepts that the donor later on brought to bear on the creation of a separate women's programme in the Women's Development Section (WDS) of the Panchayat Ministry, which was its focal point Ministry in Nepal.

The donor was able to move confidently into helping to design a bold new comprehensive approach to poor women in development in Nepal because of (a) its experience in SFDP, (b) a series of studies on women's issues which were prepared for the Nairobi Women's World Conference, and (c) the conceptual and operational clarity that had begun to emerge. The conceptual clarity related to: how to identify poor families, train women catalysts who could organize poor women into homogeneous groups and sensitively identify their felt needs, operationalize the concept of improved status of women not only in economic terms but also in social and survival terms, develop a down to earth process of dialogue and advocacy at all levels, including the highest political level so that the governmental extension and support system could be made responsive, and finally the methodology of experiential learning and training which included process training and group reflection and action, leadership training and skills absorption, starting with the people's own creativity and knowledge system.

To summarize the donor agency's involvement in PCRW in the period 1981–86:[5]

1. Support to designing PCRW project in the women's development section of the Panchayat Ministry.
2. Funding the training of the women development officers and helping in site selection.
3. Providing support services in the form of equipment, etc., for the women's development section at the district level and assisting the WDS through a continuous problem solving dialogue.
4. Provision of adult literacy and library material.
5. Provision of consultants for on-the-job training.
6. As the PCRW got underway, providing continuous monitoring and evaluation so that problems could be corrected while they were still small.
7. Provision of social input which often was the entry point into the process, not credit which emerged only later as a need.
8. Assistance in participatory action-research into the time saving, labour saving devices and income generating activities for poor women.
9. Organizing policy dialogues and advocacy campaigns.
10. Organizing inter-country visits, study teams for policy planners and implementors.
11. Conducting a mid-term evaluation.
12. Providing moral support and encouragement for greater flexibility of operation on the part of the government department so that it functions responsively like an NGO with new norms, yet maintains a necessary minimum of formal accountability, recognizing that the poor themselves, through their participation, are being trained to be continuously vigilant and monitor the progress as part of the participatory process.
13. Collaborating with other donors in providing additional loan and grant funding.

To perform these tasks the donor staff itself had to learn and undergo a new kind of experiential training in the new methodologies of project design and evaluation, and be able to have an understanding of the process. Second, they had to undertake detailed, painstaking and time-consuming tasks (not necessarily an implementation role) that are required in initiating and sustaining a major new participatory experiment of this kind. As in the case of the Grameen Bank, IFAD has now come in to assist in the expansion of PCRW to new districts and also to deepen the process, particularly the re-orientation of the banking system and the line ministries.

There are four major conclusions that have been drawn here from the donor's role and involvement in these cases in South Asia which could provide lessons for meaningful donor support to participatory poverty alleviation programmes elsewhere as well.

Some donor has been able to provide a creative and flexible response to the need for an innovative approach for poverty alleviation for poor women, through one or a combination of the programmes and instruments available to it. It has required, evolving a perspective, committed staff, patience and time. The investment in financial terms has been relatively small and these small catalytic grants have eventually resulted in substantial additional financial resources being mobilized through other donors and the government when necessary for multiplying the process. These initiatives are now providing a demonstrational effect for sensitive governments, donors and the academic community for alternative and poverty alleviation and development possibilities.

In all cases, the available political, economic and social spaces have been widened as a result of this kind of donor involvement and advocacy. The donor has also helped in institution and capacity building for poverty alleviation. It has effectively demonstrated that a donor can work with a variety of institutions—the intermediary can be an NGO, a bank or a government agency—provided they also have the right perspective and commitment and are able to function with new norms. The government bureaucracy does not have to plan and implement all development actions. At some point the government, however, needs to provide sensitive support systems if the participatory development processes are to multiply and expand on a national scale. The Grameen Bank is a case in point.

As in the case of the PCRW in Nepal, or the case of BUSTI in Pakistan, a donor helped build the new institutions, and then supported them through its various programmes. It worked closely with the intermediaries to overcome the constraints and problems encountered by these innovative approaches during the initial five years. The donor encouraged participatory evaluation and the taking of continuous small creative actions and also assisted in the external evaluation in a participatory manner. The donor also supported the process involved in raising the awareness of poor women regarding their needs and priorities and helped create a collective consciousness through group action. As a result of these combinations of supportive actions, the expansion process could be carried out quicker.

From these experiences several further refinements have been made to strengthen the conceptual and methodological aspects for innovative approaches enabling poor women to move out of poverty into sustainable development. The combined experience of a donor in working through NGOs, banks and government agencies in South Asia can now be systematized and can provide guidelines for helping in institution building for a support system for similar processes elsewhere, under varied circumstances. While the identical experiment cannot be replicated per se, the process itself can be multiplied.

Finally, where a donor assists with grant funding in the initial stages of designing and sustaining an experiment, with other donors, like the international financial institutions, financial aid can come in to support the expansion at a later date, after the pioneer effort has been a success. This can also lead to new forms of collaboration between donors right from the outset. The question of collaboration between donors will be the subject of further analysis in the last chapter of this book.

INITIATING THE MULTIPLICATION PROCESS

A donor's role and involvement in supporting these innovative experiments and enabling them to grow in scale raises the question of whether donors cannot do more. In the South Asian cases donors have demonstrated that they can perform a creative and flexible support role. Second, the question can be raised, is it not possible to multiply the processes initiated in one country, in other countries as well?

Today all donor programmes have a women's component. For the most part, as has been stated, while the objectives are broadly stated, when it comes to activities and budget most women's programmes include a series of items which do not add up to a comprehensive package in any given geographical location. The approach is also, for the most part, one of 'delivery of inputs' in an essentially 'top-down' governmental bureaucratic planning process with the expectation that more efficient delivery will reach poor women. Despite the evidence of the limitations of this approach in reaching the poor, often it continues to be followed un-critically.

The lessons of experience however, show, that each of these programme items may constitute an 'entry' point to a more comprehensive programme. But, in many cases such an approach, programme concept, design and inputs have not been clearly perceived as a comprehensive economic and social package, to enable poor women to move out of poverty. Some donor programmes address only the gender issue without addressing the 'gender and equity' issues together, thus leaving out the poorer or the poorest. Other programmes address the social or economic or training or credit aspects separately and in a fragmented way. Some donors have little experience in dealing with banking institutions and deal with NGOs concerned with poor women only in an ad hoc way. Fifth, some of the women's programmes are isolated even within the donor organization and are not always co-ordinated with other major programmes, which are inter-related. Hence, a sectoral entry point does not move out of its narrow sectoral confines to address larger development concerns or take a holistic approach, without which the total concerns of poor women cannot be addressed.

There are, of course, exceptions, some of which have been analyzed. These exceptions are still at the margins of most donor strategies. The central message of this book is that with very little additional effort, the exceptions can become the rule and then brought to center stage in donor approaches.

It is now recommended that each donor, who has not done so, initiate one major new comprehensive programme in support of a process for enabling poor women to move out of poverty into sustainable development using the basic concepts, design and approach adopted in the cases analyzed in South Asia. Such an initiative would require a co-ordinated approach within a donor organization, with a sufficiently trained staff and time to support the evolution of the process. Several donors have stated their intention to go beyond fragmented or isolated gender activities, and with the methodology that is becoming increasingly clear they should be able to do more and help multiply the experiments.

Such a major programme can be initiated *de novo* or it can be built around an existing sectoral programme or even a partial women's project. In the case of the PCRW in Nepal a rural development programme was initiated *de novo*, building on the earlier SFDP experience with the Agricultural Bank. In the case of the kachhi abadies of karachi, a sectoral intervention under the Karachi slum improvement programme with the soak pit as an 'entry point' evolved into a process enabling poor women in the urban slums to move out of poverty. In the case of Mexico and Kenya, major new initiatives can be initiated through NGOs. In the case of Tanzania, the suggestion is for a programme like the JNSP to be an 'entry point' for the evolution of a major component addressing the totality of the concerns of poor women. There may be other instances where a women's programme itself could be designed or re-designed. In other words, all donors have several programmatic instruments for multiplying the basic process enabling poor women to move out of poverty. With the available body of experience they do not need to re-invent the wheel or continue to make the kinds of mistakes that are still occurring or be so tentative about the methodology.

In chapter III the development process that was observed in the 'success' cases and which can be multiplied has been identified and conceptualized. As was categorically stated, this was not the result of *a priori* theorizing, but conceptualizing on the basis of what has worked on the ground. From this 'how' and from the steps in designing, initiating and multiplying sensitively innovative programmes were set out. These are:

1. Evolving a programme concept and design—including a holistic approach, use of local knowledge and resources, starting the initiative with the poor as subjects and the use of the methodology of PAR.
2. The survey—identifying the concerns of poor women, the intermediary and initiating an innovative programme as a process and not as fragmented 'projects'. The survey itself is to be undertaken in a participatory manner.
3. Training the facilitators and catalysts in group formation, releasing poor women's creativity, using people's knowledge system and local resources.
4. Supporting the establishment of poor women's organizations, setting their own priorities and moving the process from stage to stage.

5. Establishing or re-orienting the government, banking, NGO support systems, including that of sensitive donors. Training and re-training those who are involved in these activities.
6. Analyzing issues in credit, savings and asset building for both economic and social development for sustenance, and taking a holistic approach, even though an 'entry point' may be a partial one.
7. Funding the programme, when required, with a blend of grant and loans, as the case may be, but basing the support on keeping the locally generated surplus on the hands of the poor.
8. Evaluating the process, including establishing cost guidelines and use of the methodology of participatory evaluation to take small corrective actions as the process evolves.
9. Withdrawal of the external facilitation and assistance to enable the internal process to sustain itself.

As has been mentioned, these steps cannot be mechanistically applied and are part of a praxis composed of reflection and action by which poor women bring about the change in their condition. If these steps are mechanistically followed, without involvement of persons who are not identified with and committed to an innovative approach for poverty alleviation, the results will be different and can be manipulated.

These steps elaborated in chapter III have been repeated here so that donors can evolve and internalize a conceptually correct approach. Any donor initiating this process must not only understand the methodology of Participatory Action-Research (PAR) as an innovative approach and the process for enabling the poor women (and other categories of poor) to move essentially through their own efforts out of poverty into sustainable development, but must also understand and internalize the perspective from which the process should be initiated and a minimum set of values that must inform it. Otherwise mere statement of the objective only becomes rhetorical.

The four conceptual issues on which there should be no ambiguity among those initiating a process are worth repeating:

1. Start with the poorest women, so that both the gender and equity issues are addressed simultaneously and homogeneous groups of poor constitute the main actors and

beneficiaries of the process. In such a situation, the rich or richer of the poorer and the real poor can not be grouped together without conceptual or methodological clarity. The focus on the poorest requires several changes in methodology and the process should start with them, if 'seeds' and not bubbles are to be initiated and deeper polarization is not to result. The poor should be identified in a systematic interdisciplinary study and organized into homogeneous action groups.

2. Participation implies that the poor participate as subjects in the whole process and not merely as objects. The question of 'participation' attached to a conventional top-down planning process, where participation equals 'some consultation with a target group' is superficial. Participation requires conscientization. Participation also requires reversal of conventional bureaucratic procedures and of needless controls, and their replacement with new norms that are suitable for self management by groups of poor. Participation and the social mobilization that goes with it should not be confused with 'social marketing', which is manipulating at best. The poor have creativity, knowledge and strength and this is what needs to be brought out for a sustainable process.

3. The process envisaged treats the informal economy as an entity in itself, where the poor women are surviving with their own knowledge system, resource base and culture. The informal economy can be built upon and deepened as an end in itself. There is no need for poor women in every situation to be 'incorporated into the market'. The poor women in the informal sector have a right to access to resources, both local and external, if they are to develop. The process envisaged is one that leads to sustenance and is not one that merely incorporates a few poor or richer among the poor into the market and/or monetized system where real poverty may be alleviated if at all only temporarily. When they have moved out of poverty, the women can decide how to relate to the market and other social forces.

4. The need for comprehensiveness and to view the lives of the poor women as they view it, in its totality. Viewing the lives of the poor in a fragmented sectoral fashion separates artificially the survival, social and economic components which

are inter-related. There can be an 'entry point' but the process envisaged must be comprehensive.

The suggestion here is that without commitment to a minimum, set of values, a comprehensive process, as stated above, and a clear perspective, it will be difficult for a sensitive donor to give the kind of sustained problem solving support that can enable poor women (or any other category of the real poor) to move out of poverty into sustainable development. These values and conceptual issues are often left ambiguous. They are not often discussed and clarified at the highest policy making levels of the organization or at the country level. The resulting ambiguity then leads to a lack of clarity in guidelines, fragmented programmes, with each country office or consultant following their own approach and a process that is beset with so many contradictions as to be self-defeating or only having a marginal impact. The 'seeds' analyzed have indicated a clarity of the perspective and the evaluational framework. An innovative process has been evolved within the available political spaces and even enabled the 'spaces' to be widened. All advocacy, training and educational programmes would need to internalize such a minimal valuation framework and help to further reinforce the process initiated.

As was mentioned earlier, the selection of the intermediary which has the perspective and commitment to the minimum values is critical. When a new programme is to be initiated, if the intermediary has some experience in pursuing an innovative approach, it can speed up the process as was seen in the case of BRAC and the Grameen Bank. The suggestions for Kenya and Mexico are for donors to build on the proven experience of the two NGOs which are innovating. In the cases analyzed in the South Asia, whichever the intermediary, there have been deeply committed persons or teams who have initiated the process, identified with it, protected it and helped to sustain it. These considerations should guide both the selection of the intermediary and the continuous training of their facilitators and catalysts. The argument that all these require a charismatic leader to initiate the process is often carried too far. National leaders can spontaneously emerge or be 'trained'.

A corollary is that the intermediary has to be selected with these considerations in mind and then, in turn, the donor would need to give the intermediary institution whatever support is required and with the flexibility that is required for an evolving process. If the characteristics mentioned are already there, then the leadership in evolving the process can be left to the intermediary and the participatory process. Most donors have a sufficiently broad mandate to do this, as well as respond to the felt needs of the poor women whatever 'entry point' is identified by the women themselves. In the cases analyzed, donor procedures have not stood in the way of it being able to work with any of the three kinds of intermediaries mentioned. Donors must also provide institutional support to the intermediary until it has established itself and then withdrawn. Most donor procedures as currently practiced, seem to create dependence and then suddenly donor support is cut off, destabilizing the fragile process.

Where a new programme for poor women is being initiated it is essential that a sufficient number of donor staff members understand the process and are committed to its perspective and values. This will ensure that a co-ordinating programme can operate with flexibility and the staff can be well enough informed and trained to perform a problem solving catalytic function. This is a difficult and sensitive role to perform. It cannot be done, for instance, by one lone woman programme officer, fighting a lone battle within a country office. The programme officer has to function as a multi-sector co-ordinator focusing the attention of the sector programmes on the innovative initiative. The manner in which the donor office handled the Nepal PCRW and SFDP illustrates this point. In this sense, the donor programme officer becomes a catalyst. Such a role does not necessarily have to be performed by a woman, what is essential is the commitment. It is also very time consuming, in that it goes well beyond bureaucratic sectoral programming, delivery of inputs, funding and conventional evaluating and reporting. There has to be a continuous dialogue with new learning processes for all concerned.

In the Latin American case, the major reviews by donors of their regional programmes for women provided an opportunity to critically evaluate the past activities, identify the new programme package and also to train the staff in advocacy and implementation. The suggestion here is that the sensitization and training for the donor needs to go beyond this. They have to learn from the 'seeds'. This requires that they analyze the experiences even from other regions. The training needs to include concepts and the processes on the ground. This means an exchange of visits and staff between regions. A donor staff member or an expert who is used to programming a campaign or undertaking a sector programme or even one who is a woman with some familiarity with gender issues, is not necessarily the best person to be in charge of a comprehensive programme for poor women. In some cases, as in Nepal, one donor had one staff member programming two inter-related programmes, the SFDP and the PCRW, under the guidance of a senior officer who was able to conceptualize the process. This has permitted the fullest potential of these two approaches for rural poverty alleviation to be brought out. The donor staff member must also be able to spend a great deal of time in the field, identify with the poor and be part of the participatory process. This means use of a great deal more local staff by donors, but local staff with commitment and de-elitized, and de-professionalized in the sense that Robert Chambers has described in 'Putting the Last First'.

The question of training or re-training donor staff in understanding and supporting programmes for poor women cannot be undertaken in a superficial or hurried manner. A critical mass of experienced trainers have to be first assembled and systematic training programmes have to be organized. Once a donor has a critical mass of persons who understand how to design, evaluate, and sensitively initiate these alternative approaches, they will be able to multiply the processes, organize further in-depth training and also help to build the institutions that are capable of sustaining and multiplying the process further. This would also have a 'demonstration' effect on governments and other sensitive donors.

Even when donors have such a critical mass of trained persons, a donor will not be able to function unless there are a large enough number of persons within a country who are able to understand and able to help initiate, evaluate and sustain the process. With the growing recognition that conventional development approaches have failed to reach the poorest, the majority of whom are poor women and the need for participatory development as an alternative approach, there is also a need to build new institutes within countries to bring the lessons of scattered 'seeds' to the center stage, analyze them, retrieve local knowledge systems, and undertake new kinds of learning and training for the large number who need to be involved in a massive poverty alleviation thrust.

In the 1950s when the 'top-down' planning methodology and conventional project analysis were first introduced, several national institutes were established to reinforce the process. Similarly, when the 'Green Revolution' showed a promise of increased growth and a technological breakthrough several new research and training institutions and a co-ordinating global group for agricultural research were established. Today, when it has become increasingly clear that no real poverty alleviation is possible without the participation of all categories of the poor and a sensitive support system, there are few institutions within the poor countries or without for reinforcing the fragile R and D systems, designing new action-research programmes, enabling the poor to participate and to move out of poverty, and evaluating them. If poverty is to be alleviated, with special attention to poor women, then it is imperative that these innovative processes are multiplied and the institutions sustain them to be built or strengthened as the case may be, and properly trained staff is used at all levels.

In capacity building it should be noted that new training and research institutions should also be established within countries and globally. These structures, unlike the formal research institutions, or government departments need to be light structures. In many cases, fragile institutes and NGOs already exist and may only need to be reinforced. These institutions are different from the intermediaries already referred to and would need to have the following objectives:

1. To establish a forum for exchange of experiences in participatory development;
2. To refine the concept and methodology of the participatory action-research approach;
3. To retrieve the knowledge system of the poor and give it scientific validation;
4. To organize policy dialogues with line ministries of government and banks and even the academic community on concepts and methodology;
5. To support training of action-researchers in the experiments initiated or for other organizations willing to experiment;
6. To support the designing and initiation of further experiments in PAR in different locations and provide support to these new experiments;

7. To support exchange of study programmes between action-researchers in PAR experiments;
8. To establish documentation centers in selected locations;
9. To disseminate information on PAR through a journal and in local languages;
10. To help multiply the processes on the basis of lessons learnt.

In fulfilling these objectives these institutes should engage in a detailed recording of all those actions, experiments and discussions which come under the purview of PAR. This can be done in a way that new training and research materials are generated. It will also lead to further conceptualization of the approach and reconceptualization. Through wide dissemination in local languages and new forms of communication like local theatre and audio visual forms the basis for the new learning for all concerned will be provided.

A few specific recommendations made here are intended to strengthen the capacity of those sensitive donors who are planning to systematically support the innovative approach, either through support for designing a programme for poor women *de novo* or by building on an existing one, either a sectoral programme or innovative programme already initiated by the kinds of intermediaries mentioned. The mandate and procedures of most donors who have innovated have proven sufficiently flexible to permit support for these innovations to be undertaken in selected cases and help them to move to scale. Thus donor procedures need not be a constraint. What is required is for the process to be multiplied, if necessary, through further experimentation under different socio-political circumstances.

These suggestions made here have been deliberately enunciated in a non-prescriptive way. When those donors who wish to innovate and review their past women's programmes against the alternative approaches outlined, they can assess what more they can do to have an impact. This self-evaluation itself would be the starting point. From these, the praxis has to evolve, consisting of supporting the first step in initiating an experiment, reflecting upon it, taking the next step and so on. It is essential to ensure that there are persons with commitment to initiate and participate in such a process.

In conclusion, it should be stated that today there is a great deal of clarity and understanding regarding some of past and current conditions that have oppressed, marginalized and locked poor women into a permanent state of poverty. The innovative approaches analyzed have indicated processes by which many of the concerns of poor women can be addressed enabling them to move into sustainable development. There are, however, still a number of issues which need to be understood to overcome some of the structural biases in the system as a whole. For instance, should poor women's struggle only be through autonomous women's groups or as members of a larger community of the poor, along with poor men? How does the autonomous struggle of poor women affect relations within the family as an institution? How much does history tell us of the adaptation of traditional institutions? How are traditional knowledge systems retrieved and upgraded? What is the relationship between these innovative approaches at the micro-level enabling women to move out of poverty into sustainable development, and the larger movements for improvement of the ecology and the democratic process itself? No final answers can yet be attempted to all these basic questions without a deeper probing of the evaluational and historical roots of the role of women in various cultures. While there are many answers even to these complex questions they are also very much a part of the future research agenda and conceptualization exercises that must go on as the process evolves on the ground, and even new problems arise. This is the difference between prescriptive planning and praxis. What is important is that through praxis and the methodology of PAR's innovative processes, that raise the consciousness of poor women, is to establish as many inter-connections as possible between poor women and new forms of accumulation, ecology, culture, work, economic and social needs, and democracy. All concerned need to be involved in a new learning process, and many need to change.

A GLOBAL STRATEGY

What is seen at the micro-level is a social response by the poor themselves to the crisis of poverty. The process has also resulted in new kinds of capacity building for poverty alleviation. Conceptual and methodological issues have been further refined. This then guides the process being multiplied. Donor support in the form of small grants and technical assistance has been provided sensitively, cost-effectively and in a sustained fashion. The conclusion is that sensitive donors have been able to achieve the above results in a few countries. They should now multiply the process in several other countries as well. If the positive experiences in tackling the gender and equity issues that are emerging within South Asian countries are to be multiplied in other regions as well, like minded donors would need to formulate a global strategy towards this end. The support to the positive experience has kept within the donor's mandate and been undertaken by committed staff members with no constraints resulting from the donor procedures.

With governments, donors, the U.N. system itself searching for alternative cost-effective approaches for poverty alleviation and sustainable development, and the gender issues coming to the forefront of development concerns, these donors now have an opportunity, using this experience, to demonstrate how these innovative approaches work and how a sensitive UN and/or donor agency can help to multiply the process. In the same manner that UNICEF and WHO, after the Alma Ata Conference, took a leap forward in advocating cost-effective primary health and child care practices, based on proven technical knowledge (most of it traditional, with some upgrading), a group of like minded donors can now demonstrate the viability of the innovative cost-effective approaches to poverty alleviation based on participation of poor women in development. Other agencies can follow once they are shown the way and build on some of the successful programmes.

The wider global strategy (after Alma Ata) advocated delivering of simple, cost-effective primary health and child care practices to the largest numbers mainly through government programmes. Donors could now, in addition, follow the major concern of women's movement, that is attempting to respond to the concerns of poor women and work with the creative energy released by the women's movement. Through various new intermediaries and the methodology of participation of poor women as subjects in the process, these donors can have a wider impact.

Even donors pursuing narrower sectoral programmes can broaden their perspective and approach to include the participatory approach for poverty alleviation. These two approaches are not mutually exclusive and, as has been demonstrated, can be mutually reinforcing. The second leg would go beyond the economic or social sectoral approach. The sectoral and the technical thrusts cannot be an end in themselves. They are 'entry points'. The process of which they are a part must go beyond to address other aspects of poverty alleviation and move to sustainable development, if these sectoral approaches themselves are to be meaningful.

To be able to move on 'two legs', it is necessary that donors need to support a great deal of capacity building at the micro-level. A great deal of emphasis has been placed on training and new institution building in this book. Further, micro-macro conceptualization and experimentation on the basis of emerging new concepts should also be a part of the global strategy.

In conclusion, in formulating the second leg of such global strategies it is essential that a critical mass of persons committed to this alternative process of poor women's participatory development should be networked and encouraged to undertake the further conceptualization based on the experience on the ground. The conceptualization should not result in a mish-mash of concepts ending with consensus at the lowest common denominator or again be based on opinion theorizing. There should be a network of those who have sufficient experience, have internalized the approach and methodology and can critically review the processes of work. This kind of conceptualization from practice can guide the further experimentation and multiplication process. To enable poor women, who constitute more than 50 per cent of the poor, to move out of poverty into sustainable development would, in effect, be to win more than half the battle.

NOTES

1. See P. Wignaraja (1988); also P. Wignaraja and Akmal Hussain eds.; 'The Challenge in South Asia: Development, Democracy and Regional Co-operation,' Sage Publications, New Delhi, 1989.
2. Both the donor and the cases have been selected merely to illustrate the lessons and reinforce the underlying concepts and methodology.
3. Jowshan A. Rahman (1985).
4. See 'JORIMON of Beltoil Village and Others: In Search of Future' (ed.) Muhammed Yunus, Grameen Bank, Dhaka, 1982.
5. Chandni Joshi (1988).
   UNICEF Report on 'A Mid-Term Evaluation of the Production Credit for Rural Women Project,' (prepared by Mary Church and S.L. Singh) UNICEF, Nepal, 1985.

Collaboration Between
Sensitive Donor Agencies

THE NATURE OF THE COMPULSIONS
FOR COLLABORATION BETWEEN SENSITIVE DONORS

THE global strategy referred to in the previous chapter cannot be embarked upon by a single donor agency working alone. Collaboration between even a few donors is essential, initially even two. What is meant here is not the kind of bureaucratic collaboration as practiced, for instance, in the inter-agency co-ordination committees of the UN system. This is purely an additive approach and hardly touches the conceptual or real issues. This kind of co-ordination and consensus amongst agencies is insufficient and can even lock the agencies back into conventional approaches.

For a donor responding to the gender and equity issues and multiplying the successful processes as suggested, would clearly need to establish much closer collaboration with other sensitive donors within the U.N. system and also with like-minded bi-lateral donors particularly with the international financial institutions like IFAD and the regional banks which may not be rigidly ideological in their approach. This process would need to be at two levels. One would be a strong global advocacy strategy to pursuade these institutions to help bring the experience of poverty alleviation by poor women from the periphery to the center stage as was followed after Alma Ata, and later in relation to the 'Adjustment' problem. The other level is to have a carefully orchestrated negotiating process between the prospective collaborating donor partner or partners as the case may be.

The compulsions for collaboration flows not only from the various directives for greater inter-agency collaboration in the U.N. system but also from the potential for greater cost-effectiveness, pooling of resources and impact that could result from the exchange of 'success' cases between two or more donor agencies. The collaborating partner needs to be selected with great care. The collaborator must demonstrate, through some of its programmes, a greater sensitivity for the felt needs of the poor women and vulnerable groups in a society; accumulate a body of positive and successful experience and should be committed to a meaningful process of collaboration and poverty alleviation.

The failure of much of the ODA and conventional donor approaches to benefit poor women and the newness of this particular challenge is also an added reason for collaboration and poses a further compulsion to these organizations, not only for continuing to re-think the relevance of past approaches, but also for bringing the lessons of their own even small successful experiments from the margins of institutional memory to center stage. Two donors working together can also set an example and have greater impact on the system as a whole. The importance of this demonstration effect must not be minimized in the present climate, where several donors are becoming sensitive to gender and equity issues and are searching for a methodology and new programme designs.

Collaboration, however, between two organizations which have existed and functioned independently, for different periods, with their own cultures, with varying emphasis on economic and social issues, is not easy and cannot be brought about superficially by hastily conducted discussions and/or ad hoc actions. This complex process has to be more systematically undertaken not only with commitment at the top, but also right down the line. The collaborative process has also to be structured in such a way so that the two organizations can, on the one hand, maintain their identity and some of their more essential formal internal procedures, and, on the other, realize the maximum potential from collaboration, not only for the two organizations and the governments of the countries but for their constituencies which are, in the final analysis, the poor women with the double burden and other vulnerable groups.

Such a collaborative process would require clarification of five basic issues (listed below) in a step by step manner. A new kind of dialogue and negotiating process has to be initiated between the collaborating partners, and operational guidelines have to be evolved for initiating the process from programme/project identification, through design and evaluation to eventually sustain, the process, when the donors withdraw.

The *five issues* are:

1. The common mandate in relation to poverty alleviation for vulnerable groups, particularly poor women with the double burden.
2. The approach to programme/project design and evaluation in terms of the mandate and more specifically to address the gender and equity issues with participation of the poor women as subjects in the process.
3. The managing of the total resources available to the programme/project including human resources, knowledge system and natural resources. These have to be dovetailed with financial resources, i.e., savings, loan funds and grants, foreign exchange and local currency, extra budgetary resources and finally resulting in a new accumulation process.
4. The degree of flexibility in the internal procedures of two organizations, willingness to change past approaches and establish new norms.
5. The form of the consultations and negotiating process with the host government.

These are inter-related issues and part of an overall process. They have been separated here only for purposes of highlighting some more detailed aspects of each issue. To the extent that a set of common understandings—to guide the process of collaboration— can be evolved by the partners in relation to the above five issues, not only will it better help sustain a collaborative process but it can have a positive impact on intended beneficiaries. An element of trust and commitment to the common mandate is essential between the collaborating partners, i.e., the two donor organizations and the host government. They must also internalize the concerns of the poor women's groups, if the process is to be sustained in an orderly manner. This implies a non-manipulative process at all stages, open dialogue at all levels, and a willingness to analyze in-depth both successes and failures of past approaches to enable poor women to move out of poverty into sustainable development. It also implies willingness to change procedures which are not essential or relevant. What is called for is a new kind of dialogue initially between the donors themselves, followed by discussions with the host government and the beneficiaries.

In order purely to illustrate how this new dialogue and negotiating process can lead to successful collaboration between organizations, sometimes where necessary a hypothetical collaborative scenario has been envisaged between a grant giving organization like UNICEF and the other international financial institutions like the International Fund for Agricultural Development (IFAD). Some collaboration has in fact started between these organizations in relation to the cases mentioned in South Asia and could be reinforced.

INTERPRETING THE COMMON MANDATE

IFAD's mandate reads 'Food Production, Poverty Alleviation and Nutritional Improvement.' UNICEF's overall mandate as it now stands starts with 'Child Survival and Welfare, Health and Nutritional Improvement' but has gone on to include 'Household Food Security for Vulnerable Groups' and 'Social Mobilization.' Both have made strong policy statements on the importance of poverty alleviation and women in development. Taken as a whole the mandates of both organizations are compatible and intended to have a positive impact on poor women.

In practice, in their project designs the two organizations often focus their projects in relation to one or another element within their overall mandate. However, there are exceptions. For instance, IFAD may formulate a project with food production as the main objective with a number of subsidiary objectives relating to vulnerable groups. Such a project may not always automatically result in poverty alleviation nor benefit poor women or result in nutritional improvement for them. Similarly, UNICEF's subprogramme on immunization or household food security is only one aspect of social development and is no more than an 'entry' point for its larger mandate. In attempting collaboration both organizations would not only need to clarify their mandates but also aspects of it before entering into collaboration. There should be no ambiguity. UNICEF would need to be clearer on what it means by 'household food security'. Both organizations would need to further clarify what they mean by 'social mobilization' in relation to participation of the poor themselves in these processes. 'Social mobilization' cannot be confused with 'social marketing,' nor real 'participation of poor women' with some casual dialogue with NGO groups or with villagers. Formation of groups of the poor merely for use in the 'delivery' of inputs is also not social mobilization with real participation. A real praxis has to be initiated.

Thus, collaboration would need to be based on an acceptance of the end objectives clearly specified within the larger mandate and an agreed understanding of the process. Mere agreement on a single element or an aspect of the package is not sufficient. Further, the separation of 'economic' or 'social' is not only arbitrary when it comes to gender and equity issues but, as has been seen, is also irrational and leads to too many contradictions. The fragmented approach is also a major contributing factor to the failure of past approaches. Poverty alleviation implies starting with the poor and understanding the totality of their lives, where economic and non-economic considerations are inseparable. Thus donor interventions must be seen as initiating or supporting a process whereby development takes place in both economic and non-economic terms together with real participation of the poor, and in a mutually reinforcing framework. The examples analyzed show that sometimes poor men and women can be grouped together, but more often separate women's groups are required for initially dealing with the double burden.

Clarification of these aspects is not merely a philosophical debate but a very practical one. Food production, poverty alleviation and nutritional improvement are compatible objectives in an alternative development paradigm (with participation and social mobilization) but not with the perspectives and methodology of the conventional growth model and the 'delivery of inputs' methodology that goes with most donor approaches. This does not mean that growth is excluded from the alternative process. The alternative process if properly designed can result in growth and new forms of accumulation, savings and asset creation, as well as human and social development.

The point to be emphasized here is that before an intervention the collaborating donors themselves need to have a well articulated overview and comprehensive conceptual policy framework for poverty alleviation with a commitment to the methodology.

They should not rush in with small fragmented joint projects or
superficial consultations as is usually the case. The suggested
approach would also prevent donor interventions taking a fragmented approach and compounding host government's shortcomings.

THE APPROACH TO PROGRAMME/PROJECT
DESIGN AND EVALUATION

Once the common mandate is clarified in conceptual terms,
related to the overall development strategy in the host country and
translated into policy instructions, thereafter mission members,
staff and consultants of the collaborating donors will have to be
briefed in-depth on the concept and methodology, otherwise
fragmentation and distortions could result. The application of the
mandate cannot remain free and ambiguous, where individual
officials of the organizations and consultants used in identifying,
preparing and evaluating the results are allowed to apply their
personal interpretations of the objectives, the methodology or the
process.

The second major issue for clarification thus relates to methodology. Donors have different approaches to project design and
evaluation and a discussion of some fundamental aspects of
methodology is essential. As has been stated, official development
assistance is as yet very poorly equipped methodologically to deal
with the permanent poverty crisis and participatory poverty alleviation at the micro-level of development. Hence, most donors fall
back on conventional project designing and the narrow social cost-
benefit approaches which are part of prescriptive planning. It is
clear that many programmes and projects based on conventional
project development and cost benefit analysis that are planned and
'delivered' from the top and/or from outside have not benefited
the poor and the vulnerable groups and are not able to address the
double burden of poor women. As has been indicated, many
integrated rural development projects and credit schemes have
further marginalized these groups and also led to the waste of
investment and the non-repayment of loans.

Some donors, however, have some innovative experiences
based on a different approach to their credit and have gone quite
far in selected cases like the Grameen Bank project in Bangladesh,

the Small Farmer Development Programme, and the Production Credit for Rural Women programme in Nepal. There are some others and the above are mentioned only illustratively. One or two donors have gone further along the 'process-approach' in designing and evaluating its interventions in these cases and have an advantage in that it is a grant giving agency. These have to be identified, and collaboration can begin with their joining forces.

Thus the next step in initiating collaboration is for the two organizations to analyze their 'successes' and 'failures' in relation to the specification of the poverty alleviating methodology adopted so that past mistakes are not repeated and the innovative methodologies to project development and evaluation based on these alternative approaches, which have worked in selected cases within the two organizations, are analyzed in-depth, conceptualized and given greater legitimacy. These new kinds of projects/programmes and their underlying processes can, then, become the rule rather than the exception.

To do this, it has to be recognized that good theory and practice go hand in hand. The theory has to be abstracted from the reality and follow practice. The further practical methodology has then to flow from this theory and be refined. *A priori* theorizing, which ignores the necessary relationship between theory and practice, is predominantly speculative. As has been mentioned before, this would also require training/sensitization of the staff of the two organizations and consultants if they are not completely familiar with the methodology of these innovative approaches for project designing and evaluation. The application of the methodology has to go beyond the rhetoric or lip service to concepts such as 'target' group and 'participation' and be methodologically correct, whether for poverty alleviation in general or specifically in relation to the double burden of poor women.

To the extent that the donors are more sensitive to the issues surrounding poverty alleviation and more committed to this constituency, it is necessary that as part of an on-going collaborative process they jointly provide the intellectual underpinnings for the new practice and methodology of participatory poverty alleviation—in the same manner as the OECD, UNIDO and World Bank provided the rationale and legitimacy for the conventional project approach and theories of cost benefit analysis. The intellectual underpinnings and operational guidelines for the alternative methodology would logically and naturally flow from the innovative experiments in both organizations and agreement on the nature of the common mandate.

Before evolving the intellectual underpinnings and operational guidelines it is necessary to have an in-depth discussion on why the conventional project approach does not alleviate poverty and what are the alternatives based on their own institutional memory. It is not realistic anymore to talk of poverty alleviation and benefits to the vulnerable groups particularly poor women, and uncritically follow past approaches and methodologies. More so, when donors have some relevant experience, though still at the margins of their operations, from which a clear unmystified approach to poverty alleviation which can give benefits in economic as well as social terms, can be articulated and followed as part of this collaborative exercise.

The 'process' approach, if internalized by both organizations, can save them a great deal of time and cost. Looking at the programming and project cycle of most international financial institutions and their attempt through external missions of short duration that try to identify, prepare, sometimes review, appraise and evaluate a project from the outside, based mainly on quantitative aspects of the project, it is clear that much of this can be avoided and telescoped if a process approach is adopted. Some donors use the country programming approach: that takes more of the process approach and spends more time in evaluating and correcting its projects along the way, consulting with those who have local experience on an on-going and continuous basis, and solving problems on the spot as they arise. This is possible where the donor has a country presence, not necessarily staffed by expatriates. In fact many donors are using local nationals in their country offices, but these have to be carefully identified for their commitment.

An advantage of collaboration would be for both organizations to work together in formulating an integrated macro-economic and social overview and then to initiate/support or design meaningful micro-level interventions in a country.

In the case of identification of a programme for a credit fund for poor women in India, IFAD consultants and UNICEF worked closely in evolving a programme at the pre-identification stage, using national experts and those actually involved locally to establish alternative banks and credit societies for poor women. This kind of joint identification of a programme can be beneficial to all concerned. The experience with the collaboration with the Grameen Bank in Bangladesh and the SFDP and PCRW in Nepal were fed into the discussions so that one did not need to 're-invent the wheel' to take some lessons from the institutional memory of the two organizations and adapt it to suit the Indian conditions. All this represents learning from experience and can ensure a cost effective process of project design right from the identification stage, through to collaboration.

A further point one would like to repeat in this section is on the question of consultants. If poverty alleviation is the common objective and the emerging new methodology is to be used, then the manner in which consultants are recruited by donors and participants in designing programmes and projects needs to be re-examined. Consultants coming from different backgrounds and experiences, not to mention ideological orientations can be quickly meshed into a team. Their experience and expertise to undertake a collaborative task needs to be checked carefully. From the other side of the coin, the conclusion is also inescapable that there is a growing body of expertise within countries, both national and international which needs to be mobilized with care and used with greater precision in designing and evaluating these new style process oriented participatory poverty alleviating programmes. This in-country expertise needs to be tapped more fully in poverty alleviating work.

MANAGING THE TOTAL RESOURCES

The third issue in collaboration that needs discussion relates to the management of the total resources available to both organizations and government for a particular programme.

Resources for poverty alleviation and for poor women have to be looked at in terms of locally available natural resources, human resources, as well as finance. These categories cannot be arbitrarily separated, as in conventional economics. Further, human resources is not only managerial capacity or technical capability but also people's creative potential and their own knowledge system in using natural resources and protecting the environment. When it comes to finance, the first source of resources are often expropriated by others, which is why the poor continue to be poor.

The banking system within a country also mobilizes savings in rural areas and transfers them to urban centers. Mere injection of external resources into a poverty situation of this kind is not the answer. External financial resources can only supplement local resources and human creativity. Donors have yet to understand these relationships fully.

Second, when using external financial resources they can come in the form of loan funds and/or grants, and can have different loans/grant blends for a comprehensive package. If the comprehensive package is fragmented and different donors try to pick up different fragmented sectoral projects, the viability of the total programme becomes diffused.

Third, financial resources can also be looked at in terms of foreign exchange and local currency components, and the latter includes the host country's component and the local counterpart funds generated by the people's savings itself. These are often more important for poverty alleviation.

For poverty alleviation the human factor becomes critical, where the poor become the subjects of development and not merely the objects. It is their creativity which becomes the major asset. In Third World countries, people, not capital and imported technology, are the greatest asset. When looking at the resource issue for poverty alleviation, people, particularly the poor themselves and their knowledge system and its relationship to local resources, have to be the starting point. In this respect the contribution of poor women to development has assumed a significance that cannot be ignored, as shown in the experiments analyzed. External resources, imported technology and the like are supplementary and need to be brought in only at the right time and in the right manner. Once the creative initiative of the poor is released through participation, it becomes not only a powerful starting point for the process of poverty alleviation but also the key element for sustaining the process, through generating local savings, knowledge and wasted resources. Releasing the creative energies of the poor as has been said, sometimes is spontaneous but invariably requires an external catalyst, group formation and an action-reflection praxis through which a set of inter-related activities emerge. These activities are generally based on local surpluses which are drained out of the rural areas. Once the vicious cycle of de-humanizing poverty is broken, the poor themselves, through greater awareness and better organization, are able to keep rural surpluses in rural areas and to use local resources more rationally, and also to assert their right to the external inputs provided through the 'delivery' system. Poor women as savers, producers and as protectors of the family play a key role in this kind of localized development and community activity. But they have to be organized first, as part of initiating a total process.

These issues can again be illustrated in the PCRW and SFDP project in Nepal and the Grameen Bank. The essence of the programmes, to repeat, was to release the creative energy of the poor women, empower them, and generate a more co-ordinated participatory development, thereby alleviating poverty in a vulnerable group. The women development officers (WDO) in Nepal initiate the process, form groups and through a new kind of dialogue with them and the poor women's group decide what their priorities are—it may be social or economic—in the first instance. Credit may emerge as a priority in due course. As a spiral of economic and social activities are generated by the process, they become mutually reinforcing. No donor should impose a priority. In the meantime, a parallel process of re-orienting the bureaucracy and making the delivery process also more flexible can be initiated, keeping in mind that this is an entirely separate process and must not be confused with the kind of participation that results from a release of the creative energies of the poor themselves. In these countries it has been demonstrated that there can be a non-confrontational meeting point between the poor and the bureaucrats and considerable impact in terms of economic and social benefits, which are measurable in qualitative terms rather than always superficially quantified, can result. All this is part and parcel of alleviating the double burden borne by poor women. Donors have contributed to institution building for human resource mobilization.

Where the human potential is carefully mobilized the results are very different from conventional capital intensive development. As indicated earlier, the human potential also includes the knowledge system which people have. This cannot be dismissed purely as 'traditional' knowledge or 'romantic'. Much of the people's knowledge is very scientific and can be validated and used in the participatory poverty alleviation process in a natural and non-alienating way. It can also be related to the natural resource endowments such as forests, water and sun. People 'knew' how to get food, fodder, fuel and medicinal herbs and also renew the forests and maintain the ecological system. Some of this knowledge is half-forgotten or diffused and has to be retrieved as part of the process. Donors also need to help strengthen the fragile R and D systems that are being built around this knowledge base. Collaboration helps this process and can help to reinforce the fragile R and D systems and communication processes.

The lessons here are that poverty alleviation has to start with human creativity and the people's knowledge system and not just with finance and technical inputs. Institutions have to be built for this purpose. At some point in the process credit and other external inputs may become critical. At this point the delivery of small inputs not only goes a long way but a mobilized, conscientized group also is less likely to waste resources and will repay loans, and utilize the inputs more effectively because of the existing motivation and commitment. The process is also less alienating and more environmentally sound. Once there is a recognition of this people, nature, knowledge system mix and its potential, then this can be supplemented by the right quantity and quality of donor funding with the proper timing of support. Donor funding cannot force the pace of expansion or multiplication.

Adequate donor funding must also be applied to institution building such as training of catalysts and group formation and also to sensitizing external interventions. Much of this may not initially require large injections of foreign exchange or the traditional equipment technical assistance packages in the first instance. Some of the funding, in the initial stages, needs to be in grant terms for institution building aspects including training/sensitization. Loan components must be introduced only gradually. This also has implications for the 'blend' in the total funding package, which also has to be a part of collaboration.

Collaborating partners can work out new kinds of 'blend' financing i.e., loan/grant, local currency/foreign exchange, etc. with a great deal of flexibility as the two organizations together could have access to both kinds of funds. In the case of natural calamity or other unforeseen threats to the survival of poor women, the local bank or credit institution supported by a donor may need to give a follow-up loan to help the poor women to recover and re-establish themselves. This kind of repeat loan is part of the larger credit giving and taking process even in conventional project lending and loans to governments. This may also have to be in grant form from a donor. This issue has come up very clearly in the attempt to set up a support fund for poor women in India. This is where the question of new norms for credit programmes for poor women becomes essential. An international financial institution working by itself may not be able to cope with this type of situation.

This then goes back to how donors could identify poverty alleviating programmes differently, design them differently, use a different approach to the use of available human resources, with finance as a supplementary input and with new norms. As a corollary, immediately the question arises again: are the usual consultants able to do this? Are the conventional financial analysts able to understand the process-approach that starts with the people? Even when the process-approach is applied, can it be reinforced by further training of all the actors in the process.

When one analyzes in-depth the success stories based on new approaches which have been undertaken separately, it is possible to see how on the basis of the accumulated experiences it should be possible to come up with another approach to project design, financing and evaluation which are more generally applicable to poverty alleviation. The procedures for management of resources should be relevant to this approach. This would help to manage the total resources of both organizations without needless contradictions and get more impact out of less outlay. This analysis would also help answer the supplementary questions relating to who should be trained, who are the trainers and what should be the content of training.

This issue again is not a philosophical one but a very practical one for collaborating organizations, which are short of funds and want to make maximum impact with small inputs of resources and also to establish their own specificity and identity in the field of poverty alleviation. But it requires attention to detail, institution building, participatory evaluation, flexible financial procedures, and training. All this is not entirely new but, instead of building forcefully on the innovative experiments already on the ground, there is still too much tendency to follow old approaches to project development and resource management uncritically. Where changes are undertaken, these are done very tentatively and often with only marginal adaptations of conventional approaches. There is a great deal of training going on within donor organizations, but the content of the training may need to be looked at more carefully. Collaboration, properly undertaken, can reinforce innovation.

FLEXIBILITY IN THE INTERNAL PROCEDURES OF THE TWO ORGANIZATIONS

It is suggested for discussion that there is greater flexibility in the procedures of most donor organizations than is generally admitted. The procedural issues are often 'mystified'. Outdated concepts of project development and analysis, and needless financial controls and evaluation methods prevent proper justification for a new style poverty alleviating project or a programme in the first instance, and then its evaluation, which has to be undertaken in human terms and in both quantitative (where possible and relevant) and in qualitative terms. The alternative process seeks to strengthen the host government's/recipients' capacity to prepare and implement the projects and programmes. Participatory evaluation also ensures continuous correctives in the field by the poor themselves. Many of the old procedures were based essentially on distrust. The new approach can reduce the need for the cumbrous, time-consuming and bureaucratic procedures which add little to efficiency or sustainability of the poverty alleviating programme/project. A distinction would need to be made by a sensitive donor as to what are the essential internal procedures that are required for meaningful monitoring and which can be eliminated and streamlined. The simplification would not only reduce the current systems' overload with the donor organizations, but would also be more cost-effective. It will at the same time make collaboration easier.

The consultative process between donors is often very superficially carried out (courtesy calls instead of in-depth working sessions on procedural issues). Meetings, when help, cannot be polite or too hurried. Commitment by individual officials of collaborating organizations is essential. Where two organizations are properly linked—starting with a clear understanding that collaboration is a must—there is enough flexibility. It is, however, necessary to work out conceptual and practical difficulties with care as poverty alleviation is a new and complex field which involves an educational process. Procedural difficulties can often be used as an alibi for either overcaution or unwillingness to change on the part of the donor staff.

The normal visiting mission method composed of members who have not been properly trained or briefed on the need for collaboration, results in their doing the usual rounds of U.N. institutions, picking brains of local officials and local experts and then going away and writing their report. Persons familiar with local conditions and long experience with poverty alleviation complain that even when they have raised serious issues, they have had little impact on the recommendations of these missions. As has been said, the lack of experienced consultants and the often use of different ones for each mission creates discontinuity. These are not purely technocratic issues that can be understood by narrow specialists.

The collaboration when established, needs to be further pursued with the same rigour in the subsequent stages of the negotiations. Experience has shown that many of the so-called procedural difficulties can be ironed out through in-depth consultation and commitment to collaboration by the staff of collaborating institutions. Time is of essence.

It is recommended that where collaboration is being experimented with, it starts right at the identification stage with a joint identification mission. It would require a great deal of consultation on (a) the common mandate, (b) the design and preparation and (c) evaluation processes and methodology. It cannot stop with joint identification. If this sequence is followed, with the kind of training/sensitization mentioned, many of the so-called 'procedural' difficulties fall into lesser significance. Of course, there is a need, as has been stated, also for simplification and streamlining of the needless procedures and on the one hand, the introduction of a more flexible response by the two donor organizations, and on the other, for working on essential procedural details. There would also need to be joint consultation on the terms of reference of the mission, mission members, etc.

Having agreed on the above, one alternative would be for the two organizations to initially implement the project/programme separately. They could come together again for joint evaluation periodically. Ideally, however, the organizations should also work together in the implementation stage. Implementation means back-stopping the host government or host institution. The extent of back-stopping required would of course depend on the strength of the host country's institutions.

A further point that needs to be discussed in-depth is the time table used by the two organizations and the steps and internal approval procedures for developing their programmes/projects, to see how to simplify and streamline/dovetail them as the collaborative process evolves. Some of these procedures have become overly sanctified and bureaucratized within the organizations. Parkinson's Law and the Peter Principle then take-over. If poverty alleviation is the real objective then simpler procedures and a flexible response is required. There is evidence that the two organizations in practice are capable of a great deal of flexibility. The question to be addressed is whether the procedures do in effect reflect the flexibility in practice or are some of them anachronisms that can be dispensed with. This is where the donors and governments can learn from the experience of some NGOs. In working with NGOs or committed host government institutions careful selection is an essential pre-requisite for poverty alleviation. The selection, however, would need to be on the basis of experience and commitment rather than on purely political grounds.

If there is a more structured collaboration with a willingness to experiment with new approaches and methodologies for poverty alleviation with the right kind of staff on both sides, the timetables from identification to respective final approval by the donor can be dovetailed and even shortened with minimum difficulties.

THE NEGOTIATING PROCESS WITH THE HOST GOVERNMENT

Just as conventional development paradigms and the approaches to project development that go with it cannot respond to the needs of vulnerable groups particularly poor women, so there is need also to change the consultation and negotiating process by a new kind of dialogue with the host government, if the collaboration is to be effective and poor women are to benefit.

The rhetoric of most host governments are for poverty alleviation and for a positive response to women's concerns—not necessarily only poor women. But they are also locked into the same difficulties as donors, i.e., conventional development approaches based not on the reality of the permanent poverty trap, but on *a priori* theorizing; single discipline analysis; fragmented sectoral orientation; overly bureaucratic delivery processes; lack of co-ordination and, of course, the local politics and other distortions not to mention the lack of understanding of the double burden poor women face.

This compounds the difficulties of introducing sensitive donor approaches for poverty alleviation. However, to the extent that there is 'political' space and sensitive bureaucrats who are willing to experiment and protect the process, sensitive donors can work through them, beginning with a new kind of dialogue that involves the more sensitive among the bureaucrats, to get their support in eliciting programme/project profiles that are more responsive to the needs of the poor women and vulnerable groups, build new counterpart institutions where necessary, transform traditional projects through ensuring real participation of the poor women and other vulnerable groups.

The merit of this method of project identification and preparation and the process it generates is that it uses local experiences and knowledge and speeds up the process. The process involves organizations of the vulnerable groups right from the outset.

This method of evolving a process also has great merit in that it is not only sensitively undertaken with participation of trusted intermediaries of the poor women and vulnerable groups, but they are also brought into dialogue with government officials in an open and frank discussion. At the end, there is full not fragmented information, and a workable concensus achieved on the government's side to which donors could respond. The educational value of this process and the institutional building aspects should also not be ignored. In the follow-up and implementation phase there will naturally be better co-ordination among all concerned, as a result of this process. Any problem that comes up in the implementation stage can be overcome through the political and bureaucratic commitment generated. Over a period of time a country develops a capacity for generating a process of poverty alleviation.

This kind of consultation in the host government, cutting across sectoral ministries has to go on till after the initial negotiations, until all the procedural details are ironed out. When speaking of the host country the role of local NGOs and organizations of the poor women must also be involved at all relevant stages. Building this local capacity should also be a major objective of collaboration and in due course this will permit donors to withdraw, leaving a sustainable process.

The conclusion is inescapable. With poverty perpetuating itself and having gone beyond crisis proportions, this concern must be brought to center stage of global action. With governments, donors, and UN systems itself searching for alternative cost-effective approaches for poverty alleviation and sustainable development, some of the forward looking global organizations, using their even experience, can now demonstrate how these innovative approaches work and how a sensitive donor can help to multiply the successful processes. In the same manner that UNICEF and WHO took a leap forward in advocating cost-effective primary health and child care practices, based on proven technology (most of it traditional with some upgrading and being given modern scientific validation), sensitive and forward looking donors can now demonstrate the validity of the innovative cost-effective approaches for poverty alleviation based on participation of poor women in development, using primarily local knowledge and local resources. Other donors can follow once they are shown the way and provide sensitively the flexible support system required. The operative word is 'sensitively'. Donors also have to change.*

---

   * In a forthcoming publication** under the auspices of the UNU South Asian Perspectives Project, the relevant knowledge system for participatory development is further elaborated: *'The discussion of the knowledge system starts at a philosophical level where the dominant paradigm of positivist knowledge influenced development action and legitimised one type of social action and delegitimised another. Praxis and PAR were located outside this knowledge system. Therefore, it was necessary to demystify both the nature of this knowledge and the premises and method of this knowledge transfer, before proceeding to the concept of cognitive knowledge and to the many stocks of knowledge and technology that can be drawn on for sustainable development. The discussion then goes on to elaborate on the relationship between knowledge, action and power on which PAR is premised. This then helps to bridge the gap between real knowledge and wisdom, and development action and social change. Praxis and PAR have to be premised on the alternative knowledge system that is also available, where the knowledge system provides greater technological choice, the power to bring about a change in the condition of the knower and generates the new social process.'*

   ** Wignaraja Ponna, Akmal Hussain, Harsh Sethi and Ganeshan Wignaraja, *Participatory Development: Learning from South Asia*, Oxford University Press, Karachi and Oxford, forthcoming.

Select Bibliography

This selected list consists of published books on the general questions of gender and equity and case studies of innovative approaches by poor women. It also includes a number of other unpublished studies or papers on the critique of the conventional development models in relation to the double burden poor women face, as well as, those which help to understand the more positive experiments and responses by poor women to their marginalization.

ACHARYA, MEENA and BENNET, LYN 'The Rural Women of Nepal: An Aggregate Analysis and Summary of Eight Village Studies,' Center for Economic Development and Administration, Kathmandu, 1981.

ADEYOKUNNU, TOMILAYO, 'Women and Rural Development in Africa,' 45–46, UNESCO, *Women on the Move: Contemporary Changes in Family and Society*, UNESCO, Paris, 1984.

AFSHAR, H., *Women, Work and Ideology in the Third World*, Tavistock, London, 1985.

AGARWAL, B., 'Agricultural Modernization and Third World Women,' ILO, Geneva, May 1981.

——, 'Women, Poverty and Agricultural Growth in India,' *The Journal of Peasant Studies*, 13:4, July 1986.

AHMAD, Z., 'Advancement of Rural Women: The Emerging Networks,' *Ceres*, FAO, Rome, Mar.–Apr. 1986.

——, 'Rural Women: Their Conditions of Work and Struggle to Organize,' ILO, Geneva, November 1984.

AHMED, I., 'Technology, Production Linkages and Women's Employment in South Asia,' *International Labour Review*, ILO, Geneva, Jan–Feb. 1987.

ANANT, S., S.V.R. RAO and K. KAPOOR, *Women at Work in India: A Bibliography*, Institute of Social Studies and Sage Publications, New Delhi, 1986.

ARIZPE, LOURDES, 'Women in the Informal Labor Sector: The Case of Mexico City,' in The Wellelsely Editorial Committee, *Women and National Development: The Complexities of Change*, The University of Chicago Press, Chicago, 1976, pp. 25–37.

ARIZPE, L., and J. ARANDA, 'The Comparative Advantages of Women's Disadvantages: Women Workers in the Strawberry Export Agri-Business in Mexico,' *Signs: Journal of Women in Culture and Society*, 7:2, Winter 1981.

ARMSTRONG, A. and W. NCUBE, *Women and Law in Southern Africa*, Zimbabwe Publishing, Harare, 1987.

ARUNACHALAM, JAYA 'Credit Needs of Women Workers in the Informal Sector, Case Study of WWF, 1987.

AZAD, NANDINI 'Empowering Women Workers: the WWF Experiment in Indian Cities,' The Offsetters, New Delhi, 1986.

BAHUGUNA, SUNDERLAL, 'Protecting Their Life: Sources of Community Women's Non-Violent Power in the Chipko Movement,' *Manushi*, July–August, 1980.

BAKTEERI, QURUTUL-AIN, 'An Integrated Strategy for Development of Squatter Settlements: the Case Study of Karachi,' (PhD thesis submitted to the University of Technology, Loughborough, U.K., 1984).

BANERJEE, N. and D. JAIN, (eds.) *Tyranny of the Household*, Shakti Books, New Delhi, 1985.

BANGLADESH LAWS, STATUTES, etc., 'Grameen Bank Ordinance, 1983,' *Bangladesh Gazette, Extraordinary*, Dacca, 1983.

BARROSO, C. and M. SCHMINK, 'Women's Programs for the Andean Region and the Southern Cone: Assessment and Recommendations,' Ford Foundation, New York, March 1984.

BENERIA, L. and G. SEN, 'Accumulation, Reproduction, and Women's Role in Economic Development: Boserup Revisited,' *Signs* 7:2, 1981, pp. 279–298.

BHASIN, KAMALA, 'Women and Technological Change in Agriculture: The Asian and African Experience,' paper presented at the workshop on women, technology and forms of production held at MIDS, 1984.

BHASIN, KAMALA, 'Towards Empowerment,' Report of the South Asian Workshop for Women Development Workers, FFHC/AD, FAO, New Delhi, 1985.

BHASIN, KAMALA, and NIGHAT SAUD KHAN, 'Grappling with Each Other: Action and Theory,' FFHC/AD, FAO, New Delhi, 1988.

BIFANI, P., 'Women and Development in Africa: A Tentative Approach through Scenario Building,' *Journal of Eastern African Research and Development*, Nairobi, 1985.

BLEIE, T. and R. LUND (eds.), *Gender Relations: The Missing Link in the Development Puzzle—A Selected and Annotated Bibliographic Guide to Theoretical Efforts and South Asian Experiences*, The Christian Michelsen Institute, No. 184, DERAP Publications, Norway, 1985.

BOSERUP, E., *Women's Role in Economic Development*, St. Martin's Press, New York, 1974.

BOULDING, ELISE, 'Integration, into What? Reflections on Development Planning for Women,' Chapter 2 in Dauber, Roslyn and Melinda L. Cain (eds.), *Women and Technological Change in Developing Countries*, Westview Press, Boulder, CO, 1981.

BURNAD, F., 'Rural Development and Women's Liberation: Caste, Class and Gender in a Grassroots Organization in Tamil Nadu, South India,' Adult Education and Development, Bonn, 1986.

BUVINIC, M., 'Projects for Women in the Third World: Explaining Their Misbehaviour,' International Centre for Research on Women, Washington D.C., April 1984.

BUVINIC, M., 'Women's Issues in Third World Poverty: A Policy Analysis,' in Buvinic, Mayra and Margaret A. Lycette, *Women and Poverty in the Third World*, The Johns Hopkins University Press, Baltimore, 1982, pp. 14–34.

CATER, N., *Sudan: the Roots of Famine*, Oxfam, Oxford, 1986.

CHAKRABORTY, S., 'Rural Women's Claim to Priority: A Policy Debate: Selected Documents from International and Indian Archives, 1975–1985,' Centre for Women's Development Studies, New Delhi, 1985.

CHAMBERS, ROBERT, *Rural Development: Putting the Last First*, Longman, Harlow, 1983.

CHAMBERS, R., 'Working Women's Forum: A Counter Culture by Poor Women,' UNICEF Regional Office for South Central Asia, New Delhi, 1985.

CHEN, MARTHA ALTER 'A Quiet Revolution: Women in Transition in Rural Bangladesh,' Bangladesh Rural Action Committee Prokashana, Dhaka, 1986.

CHEN, M., 'Poverty, Gender and Work in Bangladesh', *Economic and Political Weekly*, Bombay, Feb. 1986.

CHEN, M., 'Working Women's Forum: Organizing for Credit and Change,' *Seeds*, New York, 1983.

CHIMEDZA, R., 'Savings Clubs: the Mobilization of Rural Finances in Zimbabwe,' Preliminary Draft, ILO, Geneva, 1984.

Committee on the Status of Women in India, (1974), 'Towards Equality: Report of the Committee on the Status of Women in India,' Dept. of Social Welfare, Ministry of Education and Social Welfare, Government of India, 1974.

CORNIA, ANDREA, RICHARD JOLLY and FRANCIS STEWART *Adjustment with a Human Face*, Oxford University Press, Oxford, 1987.

CREEVEY, LUCY E., (ed.), *Women Farmers in Africa: Rural Development in Mali and the Sahel*, Syracuse University Press, Syracuse, 1986.

CROLL, ELISABETH J., 'Rural Production and Reproduction: Socialist Development Experiences,' in Eleanor Leacock, and Helen Saffa, *Women's Work, Development and the Division of Labor by Gender*, Bergen and Garvey, South Hadley, MA: 1986, pp. 224–253.

CURTIN, LESLIE B., *Status of Women: A Comparative Analysis of Twenty Developing Countries*, Population Reference Bureau, Washington D.C., 1982.

DANFORTH, SANDRA 'Women, Development and Public Policy: A Selected Bibliography,' in A. Kathleen Staudt, and Jane S. Jaquette, (eds.) *Women in Developing Countries: A Policy Focus*, The Haworth, New York, 1983, pp. 107–124.

DASGUPTA, S. and A.S. MAITI, 'Rural Energy Crisis, Poverty and Women's Role in Five Indian Villages: Technical Co-operation Report,' People's Institute for Development and Training, New Delhi, Geneva, 1986.

DEERE, C.D., 'Rural Women and State Policy: The Latin American Agrarian Reform Experience,' *Women in International Development*, Michigan State University, East Lansing, 1985; *World Development*, Oxford, Sep. 1985.

DE SILVA, G.V.S., NIRANJAN MEHTA, ANISUR RAHMAN and PONNA WIGNARAJA 'Bhoomi-Sena: a Struggle for People's Power,' *Development Dialogue*, No. 2, Uppsala, 1979.

Development Dialogue, 'Another Development with Women', 1:2, 1982.

DIETRICH, GABRIEL, *Women's Movement and Religion*, Breakthrough, Bangalore, 1988.

DIXON, RUTH B., 'Mobilizing Women for Rural Employment in South Asia: Issues of Class, Caste and Patronage,' *Economic Development and Cultural Change*, 30:2, January 1982, 353–390.

EGGER, P., 'Banking for the Rural Poor: Lessons from some Innovative Saving and Credit Schemes,' *International Labour Review*, ILO, Geneva, Jul–Aug. 1986.

EPSTEIN, T.S. and R.A. WATTS, (eds.), *Women in Development Series*, (Vol. 1, Nelson, N. *Why has Development Neglected Rural Women*, Vol. 2. Searle-Chatterjee, M. *Reversible Sex Roles: The Special Case of Benares Sweepers*. Epstein, T.S. and Watts, R.A. *The Endless Day: Some Case Material on Asian Rural Women*).

EVERETT, J. and M. SAVARA, 'Bank Loans to the Poor in Bombay: Do Women Benefit,' *Signs*, Chicago, 1984.

FAO, 'Forward Looking Strategies: Women in Agriculture and Rural Development: Mandates and Proposals of FAO for the 1985 World Conference to Review and Appraise the Achievements of the United Nations Decade for Women,' Rome, 1984.

FALS-BARDA, ORLANDO (eds.), *The Challenge of Social Change*, Sage Publications, London, 1985.

FUGELSANG, ANDREAS, and DALE CHANDLER, 'Participation as Process—What We Can Learn from the Grameen Bank,' NORAD, Oslo, 1986.

GALAN, B.N. and A.A. GERMANI, 'Latin and Central America: Slow Change for a Woman's Lot,' *Ceres*, FAO, Rome, 1987.

GHAI, DHARAM, 'An Evaluation of the Impact of the Grameen Bank,' IFAD, Rome, March 1984.

GRAN, GUY, 'Capacity Building for Effective Social Change,' an Annotated Guide to Global Development, Economic and Social Development Programme, University of Pittsburgh, Pittsburgh, 1987.

GRIFFIN, KEITH, *Alternative Strategies for Economic Development*, Macmillan Press, London, 1988.

GUPTE, MANISHA and ANITA BORKER, 'Women's Work, Fertility and Access to Health Care—Socio Economic Study of Two Villages in Pune District,' Foundation for Research in Community Health, Bombay, for Task Force on Health, National Commission Self-Employed Women (and women in the informal sector), 1987.

HAQUE, WAHIDUL, NIRANJAN MEHTA, ANISUR RAHMAN, PONNA WIGNARAJA, 'Towards a Theory of Rural Development,' *Development Dialogue* No. 2, Uppasala, 1977.

HARRISS, BARBARA and ELIZABETH WATSON, 'The Sex Ratio in South Asia,' in Janet Henshall Momsen and Janet Townsend, (eds.), *Geography of Gender in the Third World*, State University of New York Press, Hutchinson, NY, 1987, 85–115.

HEYZER, N., 'Towards a Framework of Analysis,' *IDS Bulletin*, 12:3, July 1981 (Special Issue on Women and the Informal Sector).

HEYZER, NOELEEN (ed.), *Women Farmers and Rural Change in Asia: Towards Equal Access and Participation*, Asian and Pacific Dev. Center, Kuala Lumpur, 1987.

HIMMERLSTRAND, K. and N. BICKHAM, 'Peripheral Centre: Swedish Assistance to Africa in Relation to Stockholm,' Swedish International Development Authority, Office of Women in Development, Stockholm, 1985.

HIRWAY, INDIRA, 'Impact of Anti-Poverty Programmes on Women.' Gandhi Labour Institute, NCSEW, 1987.

HOKSBERGEN, ROLAND, 'Approaches to Evaluation of Development Interventions,' *World Development* 14:2, Oxford, 1987.

HOWELL, MARTHA C., *Women, Production and Patriarchy in Late Medieval Cities*, University of Chicago Press, Chicago, 1987.

IFAD Study on 'Rural Women's Access to Credit: An Overview,' Rome, 1987.

ILO/DANIDA, Report on 'Rural Development and Women: Lessons from the Field,' Geneva, 1985.

ILO Jobs and Skills Programme for Africa, 'Women's Employment Patterns, Discrimination and Promotion of Equality in Africa: The Case of Tanzania,' Addis Ababa, 1986.

JAHAN, ROUNAQ and HANNA PAPANEK, (eds.), *Women and Development: Perspectives from South and Southeast Asia*, The Bangladesh Institute of Law and International Affairs, Dacca, 1979.

JAIN, DEVAKI, 'The Situation of Women in the Handloom and the Construction Sectors,' Ministry of Labour, Government of India, 1984.

JAIN, DEVAKI and CHAND MALANI, 'Report on a Time Allocation Study—Its Methodological Implications,' Institute of Social Studies Trust, 1982.

JAIN, S., 'Women and People's Ecological Movement—A Case Study of Women's Role in the Chipko Movement in Uttar Pradesh, *Economic and Political Weekly*, October 13, 1984.

JAIN, S. 'Women's Development Programme—A Review,' Institute of Development Studies, Jaipur, December 1986.

JHABVALA, RENANA, 'Neither a Complete Success, Nor a Total Failure— Report of a SEWA Campaign to Organize Beedi Workers,' *Manushi*, No. 22, New Delhi, 1984.

JIGGINS, J., 'Women and Seasonality: Coping with Crisis and Calamity,' *IDS Bulletin*, Brighton, Jul., 1986.

JOSHI, CHANDNI, 'Empowering and Releasing the Creativity of Rural Women for Participatory Development,' paper prepared for the United Nations University South Asian Perspectives Project, Kathmandu, October 1988. (unpublished).

JUMANI, USHA, 'Dealing with Poverty in India: the Experience of SEWA and the SEWA Bank,' Paper for the NABARD Workshop on Poverty Control Through Self Help, Pune, 1985; (unpublished).

JUMANI, USHA, 'Analysis of Licensing Policy for the Use of the National Resources of Land, Forest and Its Effect on Women Labour Force,' Self Employed Women's Association, NCSEW, 1987.

KALPAGAM, U., 'Organizing Women in Informal Sector—Policies and Practice,' MIDS (Madras Institute of Development Studies) Off print 14.

KALPAGAM, U., 'Solidarity, Strength and Success: Working Women's Forum (India) Points the Way,' National Union of Working Women, Working Women's Forum, Mylapore, 1985.

KATONA-APTE, J., 'Women and Food Aid: A Developmental Perspective,' *Food Policy*, Guildford, Aug., 1986.

KELKAR, G., 'Impact of Household Contract System on Women in Rural China,' *Economic and Political Weekly*, Bombay, Apr. 1985.

KHAN, S., *Fifty Percent: Women in Development and Policy in Bangladesh*, University Press Limited, Dhaka, 1988.

KISHWAR, MADHU, 'Gandhi on Women,' *Economic and Political Weekly*, No. 40, New Delhi, Oct. 4, 1985, pp. 1695–96.

KISHWAR, MADHU, 'Zameen Kenkar? Jute Onkar': The Story of Women's Participation in the Bodh-Gaya Struggle,' (Based on an interview with Manimala of Chhatra Yuva Sangharsha Vahini) Manushi, New Delhi, 1983.

LE COMTE, BERNARD, 'Project Aid: Limitations and Alternatives,' OECD Development Center, Paris, 1986.

MAAS, M., 'Women's Groups in Kiambu, Kenya: It is always a good thing to have land,' African Studies Centre, Leiden, 1986.

MARSH, D.K.V. and R.P. DAHAL, 'Evaluation of the Small Farmer Development Programme in the Khardep Area,' Agricultural Development Bank, Kathmandu, 1984.

MAZUMDAR, V., K. SHARMA, and S. ACHARYA, 'Country Review and Analysis on the Role and Participation of Women in Agriculture and Rural Development in India,' Indian Council of Social Science Research, New Delhi, 1979.

MHATRE, S., S. BRAHME, and G. KELKAR, 'Bank Credit to Women: A Study of Khanavals or Working Class Lunch Suppliers,' National Institute of Bank Management, Bombay, 1980.

MIES, M., 'Lace, Class and Capital Accumulation—the Dynamics of the Sexual Division of Labour in a Household Industry,' Institute of Social Studies, The Hague, 1980.

MIES, M., *Indian Women in Subsistence and Agricultural Labour*, Women, Work and Development Series (12), ILO Press, Geneva, 1986.

MIES, M., 'The Dynamics of the Sexual Division of Labour and Integration of Rural Women into the World Market,' in Lourdes, Beneria, (ed.) *Women and Development: The Sexual Division of Labour in Rural Societies*, Praeger Scientific, New York, 1–28.

MITTER, SWASTI, *Common Fate, Common Bond: Women in Global Economy*, Pluto Press, London, 1986.

MITRA, ASHOK, 'Participation of Women in Socio-Economic Development in Women and Development,' UNESCO, 1981, p. 51.

MUKHOPADHYAY, M., 'The Impact of Modernization on Women's Occupation: A Case Study of the Rice Husking Industry of Bengal,' *Indian Economic and Social History Review* XX:1, January–March, 1983, pp. 27–46.

MULWA, FRANCIS W., 'Participation at the Grass-roots in Rural Development: Case Study of the Development Education Programme of the Catholic Diocess of Machakos in Kenya,' Paper for SID Workshop on Participatory Grassroots Development in Africa, Dar-es-Salaam, 1986.

MUMTAZ, KHAWAR and SHAHEED, FAUDA (eds.), *Two Steps Forward: One Step Back?* Zed Press, 1987.

MUNTEMBA, S., 'Women as Food Producers and Suppliers in the Twentieth Century: The Case of Zambia,' *Development Dialogue*, 1982.

MUZAALE, P.J. and D.K. LEONARD, 'Kenya's Experience with Women's Groups in Agricultural Extension: Strategies for Accelerating Improvements in Food Production and Nutritional Awareness in Africa, *Agricultural Administration*, Barking, 1985.

NASH, JUNE and MARIA PATRICIA FERNANDEZ-KELLY, *Women, Men and the International Division of Labour*, State University of New York Press, Albany, NY, 1983.

NOVOGRATZ, JACQUELINE, Study on 'Women's Activities in Nairobi and Kisumu: Approaches to Income Generation,' UNICEF, Nairobi, 1987.

OKEYA, A.P., 'Definitions of Women and Development: An African Perspective,' in *Women and National Development: The Complexities of Change*, University of Chicago Press, Chicago, 1977.

OKEYA, A.P., 'Toward Strategies for Strengthening the Position of Women in Food Production: An Overview and Proposals on Africa,' U.N. International Research and Training Institute for the Advancement of Women, Santo Domingo, 1985.

OMVEDT, G., 'Women in Popular Movements: India and Thailand during the Decade of Women,' U.N. Research Institute for Social Development, Geneva, 1986.

OMVEDT, GAIL, 'Women in Rural Revolt in India: Programme in Comparative Culture,' University of California, Occasional Paper, January 1978.

OUEDRAGO, LEDEA B., 'Les Groupements pre-cooperatifs au Yatenga,' Centre de Recherches Co-operatives, Paris, 1977.

OVERHOLT, CATHERINE, MARY B. ANDERSON, KATHLEEN CLAUD and JAMES AUSTIN, (eds.), *Gender Roles in Development Projects*, Kumarian Press, 1985.

PALMER, I., 'Integration of Women in Agrarian Reform and Rural Development in Asia and the Far East,' FAO, Rome, 1978.

PALMER, INGRID, *The Impact of Agrarian Reform on Women: Cases for Planners*, Kumarian Press, West Hartford, CT, 1985.

PAMLER, I., M.E. BURFISHER, N R. HORENSTEIN, and K. STAUDT, *Women's Roles and Gender Differences in Development: Cases for Planners*, Kumarian Press, West Hartford, 1985.

PANINI, M.N., 'Women Workers in the Unorganised Sector: A Study of the Effects of Industrialisation in India,' Centre for Study of Social Systems, JNU, NCSEW, 1988.

PHONGPIACHIT, P., *From Peasant Girls to Bangkok Masseuses*, ILO, Geneva, 1982.

PDP Report on 'Support to the Informal Economy as an Instrument of Education and Organization,' Mexico, 1985.

PONNIAH, GOWRIE, 'Hindu Ideology and the Role of Women,' Paper prepared for the United Nations University, S.Asian Perspectives Project, Colombo, 1986 (based on M.A. thesis at Sussex University, U.K.).

PRATES, S., 'Women's Labour and Family Survival Strategies Under the Stabilization Models in Latin America,' Expert Group Meeting on Policies for Social Integration, CSDHA/UN, Vienna, September 1981.

QUASIM, M.A., S.R. SAHA, and B. SAHA, 'Study of the Impact of Grameen Bank Project Operation on Landless Women,' Bangladesh Institute of Bank Management, Dhaka, 1981.

RACELIS, MARY, 'Transforming the African Crisis into People-Based Development,' Paper for Conference on Training for Social Development Methods, Association for Social Work Education in Africa, Addis Ababa, 1985.

RAHMAN, A., 'Dual Role of Tradition in Social Mobilization: The Grameen Bank and Rural Poor Women in Bangladesh,' Bangladesh Institute of Development Studies, Dhaka, 1987.

RAHMAN, JOWSHAN A., 'Grameen Bank: Development From the Bottom,' UNICEF, 1985.

RAHMAN, R.I., 'Impact of Grameen Bank on the Situation of Poor Rural Women,' Grameen Bank Evaluation Project, Bangladesh Institute of Development Studies, Dhaka, 1986.

RAJULA DEVI, A.K., 'Women in the Informal Sector,' _Kurukshetra_, New Delhi, Dec. 1985.

Report of the Institute of Development Study on 'Women's Development Programme of the Government of Rajasthan: A Review,' (prepared by Sharada Jain, Mumta Jaitly, Kavita Srivastava, Nirmala Nair and Kanchan Mathur) Institute of Development Studies, University of Rajasthan, Jaipur, 1986.

Report of the UNU-UNDP Interaction programme for Senior Action-Researchers in South Asia, in collaboration with PIDA Sri Lanka and SETU-LOKAYAN India 'Re-focussing Praxis,' (prepared by Harsh Sethi), The United Nations University Asian Perspectives Project South Asia, Colombo, 1987.

RIDDELL, ROGER C., 'Foreign Aid Reconsidered,' James Currey, (in association with ODI) London, 1987.

ROHINI, P.H., S.V. SUJATA, and C. Neelam, _My life is one long struggle—women's work, organisation and struggle_, Pratishabd Publishers, 1983.

Sanday, Peggy Reeves, _Female Power and Male Dominance: On the Origins of Sexual Inequality_, Cambridge University Press, Cambridge, 1981.

SCHNEIDER, HARTMUT, 'Small Farmers' Associations and Agricultural Productivity: Cases from Africa,' OECD Development Center Papers, Paris, 1988.

SCHUMACHER, I., J. SEBSTAD, and M. BUVINIC, 'Limits to Productivity: Improving Women's Access to Technology and Credit,' International Center for Research on Women, Washington, 1980.

SEBSTADS, JENNIFER, 'Struggle and Development: A Case Study of SEWA,' (to be published by ZED Press) 1988.

SEIDMAN, A., 'Impact of Aid on Women's Projects: A Pilot Participatory Research Project,' _Afhad Journal_, Omdurman, Dec. 1986.

SEN, AMARTYA, _Resources, Values and Development_, Harvard University Press, Cambridge, MA, 1984.

SEN, S.K., 'The Working Women in West Bengal: A Study of Popular Movements and Women's Organizations,' paper prepared for the African and Asian Interregional ILO Workshop on Strategies for Improving Employment Conditions of Rural Women, Tanzania, August 1984.

SHARMA, K.N., 'Bondages of Nepalese Women,' _Community Development Journal_, Newcastle, Jan. 1986.

SHIVA, V., H.C. SHARATCHANDRA, and J. BANDOPADHAYAYA, _Social and Ecological Impact of Social Forestry in Kolar,_ Indian Institute of Management, Bangalore, 1981.

SIDA Evaluation Report 'Mobilising Rural Women in Kenya,' Stockholm, 1987.

STAUDT, K., 'Uncaptured or Unmotivated? Women and the Food Crisis in Africa,' _Rural Sociology_, Knoxville, 1987.

THOMAS, G.M., 'Tamang Women: Ten Years of Change: Small Farmers Development Programme, Tupuche, Nepal,' Agricultural Development Bank, Kathmandu, 1983.

TILLAKARATNE, S. 'The Animator in Participatory Rural Development: Some Experiences from Sri Lanka,'- ILO Working Paper (WEP 10/WP. 37), Geneva, 1985.

TRAVERSO, C.A and E.V. IGLESIAS, _Basis for a Latin American Response to the International Economic Crisis_, SELA-ECLA, May 1983.

TRIPATHY, G.C., N.D. VASUDEO, R.D. MUJUMDAR, and P.G. DEOTALE, 'Study of

Some Health Problems of Beedi Workers', *Indian Journal of Occupational Health*, 29:4, October–December 1986.

U.N. DEPARTMENT OF INTERNATIONAL ECONOMIC AND SOCIAL AFFAIRS, *World Survey on the Role of Women in Development*, New York, 1986.

U.N. ECONOMIC COMMISSION FOR AFRICA, 'Review and Appraisal of the Achievements of the U.N. Decade for Women, 1976–1985, E/ECA/RCIWD/OAU/4, August 1984.

U.N. ECONOMIC COMMISSION FOR LATIN AMERICA AND THE CARIBBEAN, 'Report of the Group of Experts on Operational Strategies for the Advancement of Women Up to the Year 2000,' LC/G. 1322, September 1984.

UNICEF REPORT entitled 'Income Generation Project for Independent Workers of South Eastern Zone of Cartagena,' Bogota, 1987.

UNICEF REPORT on 'A Mid-Term Evaluation of the Production Credit for Rural Women Project,' (prepared by Mary Church and S.L. Singh) UNICEF, Kathmandu, 1985.

UNICEF STUDY on 'The Invisible Adjustment: Poor Women and the Economic Crisis,' Regional Programme on Women in Development, UNICEF Regional Office for the Americas and the Carribean, Bogota, 1987.

U.N. SECRETARIAT, World Conference of the United Nations Decade for Women Documents, A/CONF. 94/1–30, New York, 1980.

UPADHAYA, SHREE KRISHNA, 'Small Farmer Development Projects: Nepal's Experience in Improving Small Farmers Access to Credit,' paper for Workshop on Improving Small Farmer Access to Credit, Bali, 1986 and also 'Small Farmer Community Irrigation Programme', Agricultural Bank of Nepal, Kathmandu, 1987.

USAID STUDY on 'Women in Development: AID's Experience 1973–1985,' Washington, D.C., USA, 1987.

WALLACE, BEN J., et al, *The Invisible Resource: Women and Work in Rural Bangladesh,* Boulder, CO: Westview Press.

WEEKES-VAGLIANI, WINIFRED, *Women in Development: At the Right Time for the Right Reasons*, Paris: OECD, 1980.

WIGNARAJA, P., 'Women, Poverty and Access to Credit: Innovative Approaches,' UNICEF Staff Working Paper No. 1, UNICEF Programme Division, New York, 1988.

WIGNARAJA, P. and HUSSAIN, AKMAL, (ed.), *The Challenge in South Asia: Development Democracy and Regional Co-operation*, Sage Publications, New Delhi, 1989.

WIGNARAJA, P., A. HUSSAIN, H. SETHI, and G. WIGNARAJA, *Participatory Development: Learning from South Asia*, Oxford University Press, Karachi and Oxford (forthcoming).

WILSON, F., 'Women and Agricultural Change in Latin America: Some Concepts Guiding Research,' *World Development*, Oxford, Sep. 1985.

WOMEN FOR ECONOMIC JUSTICE, 'When the Rich Get Richer and the Poor Get Poorer, What happens to Women and Children?' Economic Literacy Paper 1, Boston, 1984.

WOODFORD-BERGER, P., 'Monitoring Women: The Use of Checklists in Rural Assistance Programmes Against the Background of Ten Case Studies,' paper submitted to the OECD/DAC/WID Meeting, Paris, January 1983.

YUNUS, M., 'Grameen Bank as I See It,' ILO, Geneva, 1986.

YUNUS, M., 'Grameen Bank: Bank Credit for Rural Poor,' *Social Development Newsletter*, Bangkok, Dec. 1984–Mar. 1985.

YUNUS, M. 'Jorimon of Beltoil Village and Others: In Search of a Future, Grameen Bank, Dhaka, 1984.

YOUSSEF, NADIA HAGGAG, *Women and Work in Developing Societies*, Greenwood Press, Westport, CT, 1976.

YOUSSEF, N. AND HETLER, C., 'Rural Households Headed by Women: A Priority Concern for Development,' WEP Research Working Papers, ILO, Geneva, March 1984.

Index